ɔn

ı:

SELF-ASSERTION FOR WOMEN

A GUIDE TO BECOMING ANDROGYNOUS*

Pamela E. Butler

*fully human

Do you have difficulty saying "No"?

Can you decide what you want and take steps towards getting it?

Are you able to assert yourself without fear of being labeled "pushy" or "aggressive"?

Can you express anger without feeling guilty?

> Dr. Pamela Butler demonstrates specific skills for overcoming traditional feminine dilemmas."
> Dr. Sandra Bem
> Stanford University

Pam is a woman who cares about women. In **Self-Assertion for Women: A Guide to Becoming Androgynous,** she shows you how to assert yourself without being aggressive, how to become "equalized" without being defeminized, and how to express yourself fully and openly without fearing ridicule or guilt.

self-assertion for women:

a guide to becoming androgynous

Pamela Butler

Canfield Press San Francisco

A Department of Harper & Row, Publishers, Inc.

New York   Hagerstown   London

Designer: Judith McCarty
Cover and illustrations: Doris Harrison

Composition by Chapman's Phototypesetting; printed and bound by George Banta Company.

Harper & Row, Publishers, Inc.
10 East 53rd Street
New York NY 10022

Library of Congress Cataloging in Publication Data

Butler, Pamela
    Self-assertion for women.

    Bibliography
    1. Women—Psychology.   2. Assertiveness (Psychology)
3. Androgyny.   I. Title.
HQ1206.B85   301.41'2   76-44230

Paperbound: ISBN 0-06-381217-7
Casebound: ISBN 0-06-381218-5

 76 77 78 79 80   10 9 8 7 6 5 4 3 2 1

contents

foreword

Assertive training is not new. It did not arise from a major social revolution, and it does not represent the latest fad in humanistic psychology. Indeed, the original formulation of assertive training procedures can be traced to the work of Andrew Salter and Joseph Wolpe more than twenty-five years ago. Based on systematic scientific inquiry, assertive training reflects the principles of behavior as applied to human needs, specifically the needs to express oneself fully, openly, and without fear of ridicule or guilt.

Books on assertive training are not new either. Numerous pamphlets, professional reports, and publications on the subject are currently available. However, Dr. Butler provides a unique contribution to assertiveness for women. Raised in the deep South with the prevailing mores of the times, Dr. Butler was brought up to be "polite," "ladylike," "passive," and "compliant," even at the expense of her true feelings. This touches on a crucial element of Dr. Butler's work, namely, accepting one's own feelings as valid and legitimate, irrespective of what others may think. Dr. Butler proceeds to show how a woman can overcome social and personal constraints to emerge as a whole individual. Although Dr. Butler addresses herself to women, there is a message here for men too. Men and women must be free to express all feelings and emotions in order to overcome society's rigid sex-role prescriptions.

The effectiveness of Dr. Butler's style and the confidence she exudes are based on hard experience; Dr. Butler has lived through the metamorphosis from stereotyped femininity to androgyny. I personally had the opportunity to observe this transcendence. The extent to which her life has been enriched by the simple approach adopted in her book is best illustrated by comments she often receives from members of the groups she conducts on assertive training: "powerful and gentle"; "feminine and competent"; "compassionate, sensitive, and strong." Giving women the option to control the influences in their lives, Dr. Butler's approach allows for more direct communication between men and women and removes the "burden of dependence" from both.

Dr. Butler's treatment of androgyny makes it clear that this is *not* a process of defeminization but one of equalization. Dr. Butler demonstrates that self-assertion and the positive aspects of femininity are not mutually exclusive.

Dr. Alan Salamy
Staff Psychologist
University of California
San Francisco

thanks

I want first to acknowledge the many women—clients, trainees, and students—who were willing to share with me their own personal experiences in learning to be assertive. Without them, truly, this book could not have been written.

I also want to thank Doris Harrison, who struggled long and hard with me to put the concepts of assertiveness into pictorial form.

Many discussions with my friend Mary Hidalgo helped me formulate a clearer perspective on many feminine dilemmas.

Carol Inglis was a dedicated typist and a very real support during the writing of this book.

My colleague and friend Portia Shapiro allowed me to share with the reader her technique of influence analysis.

Jacqueline Pourciau made many valuable suggestions during the preparation of the manuscript, and Sandra Bem provided important feedback about the book as a whole.

Shirley Luthman was a terrific model for me of female assertiveness.

John Harrison was kind enough to interview me and write the biographical material on the jacket.

David Fisher, my colleague, was always available for discussion and feedback.

More indirectly, but of no less importance, my mother Chlora Butler, and my father, Henry Butler, always encouraged me to develop my abilities and never instilled in me the view that a woman should be less concerned with fulfilling her potential than a man.

Finally, my husband Alan encouraged me in asserting my own feelings and ideas and supported me in more ways than I can name.

SELF-ASSERTION FOR WOMEN

A GUIDE TO BECOMING ANDROGYNOUS*

*fully human

To Alan

The man behind this androgynous woman

What are little girls made of, made of?
What are little girls made of?
Sugar and spice and everything nice.
That's what little girls are made of.

What are little boys made of, made of?
What are little boys made of?
Snails and shells and puppy dog tails.
That's what little boys are made of.

Mother Goose Nursery Rhyme

the stereo-
typic feminine
woman

1

Kay is a graduate student in mathematics. She is twenty-six years old, bright, petite, well liked. She is unmarried and lives alone in an attractive apartment in San Francisco. Today, sometime about 10:00, Kay is expecting a visit from her former roommate Carol, who married the summer before. At 7:00 A.M., Kay is awakened by a phone call from Carol. Carol and her new husband Dave have arrived earlier than they had expected. They ask if Kay will pick them up at the airline depot in the city. Kay agrees and suggests that because it is so early, they have breakfast together before returning to her apartment.

Feeling mildly annoyed that she was not told of the change in plans the night before, Kay gets up, dresses, and drives across town to the terminal. When she gets there, she finds no Carol and no Dave. After waiting several minutes, Kay goes to the message desk. Carol has left a note saying that Dave ran into a business acquaintance and that she and Dave have gone with him for a bite to eat. They will be back shortly. Forty-five minutes later, Carol and Dave arrive, greeting Kay as if nothing has happened. Kay is glad to see Carol; they are close friends and have not seen each other since the previous summer. Kay is also angry. She resents the hour's wait. After a moment of debate, Kay decides not to reveal her negative feelings at the moment. She tells herself that she will bring up the issue later when the time is right. But during the two days of Carol's visit the right time never seems to come up.

Joan M., age forty, is a successful attorney who runs her own legal practice and supervises a large office staff. Joan is also married and the mother of two teenage daughters. Joan prides herself on her efficiency in doing two jobs well. She has always been a hard worker. She is also a self-starter, a self-motivated woman who returned to school at the age of thirty to obtain her law degree.

Between her profession and her family, Joan has little time for herself. At home, her one day off, Sunday, is regularly interrupted with phone calls by clients and friends who want to ask "just one legal question." Most of these telephone conversations last for only ten or fifteen minutes. However, Joan often finds herself ruminating about the legal issues involved long after the caller has hung up.

Joan's own time is limited also because her work load is exceptionally heavy. Along with paying clients, Joan sees a large number of people who simply cannot manage her fees. Joan finds it difficult to bring up the issue of money. By the time she does mention her fee, she has become too involved with her client and her or his problem to refuse further contact.

2

Nancy, age thirty-five, is a secretary in an accounting firm. She makes a good salary and in general enjoys her job. Nancy does research and background work in addition to her general secretarial duties. In fact, Nancy performs many of the same functions as the accountants in the firm. Still, Nancy is paid as a secretary. Her work earns her none of the financial and personal benefits that come to the male accountants. Nancy has thought about returning to school; she has thought about taking classes at night to earn her own degree. Her employers urge her to do so. They have a place waiting for her as an accountant in the firm. Yet, somehow Nancy never manages to meet the application deadline.

Wanda, age twenty-three, a college undergraduate, considers her main problem to be shyness. Wanda has several classes with a man whom she would very much like to meet. Yet she finds herself sitting as far away from him as possible and turning away rather than smiling at him on those occasions when he looks at her. Wanda knows she is sending him discouraging messages, but she is unable to allow her interest to show. She fears that he will think she is "pushy" or "too bold."

Illustrated here are four major problems women face in asserting themselves. Each of the women in the previous examples is inhibited in expressing who she is as a unique individual. Kay, the graduate student who was stood up by her roommate, is unable to express negative feelings. Joan, the attorney, cannot set limits with other people. She is unable to say "no." Nancy, the secretary, has problems in self-initiation. Wanda finds it difficult to express positive feelings in a female-male relationship. I chose these examples from a pool of many others precisely because each highlights a particular dilemma for women. Self-assertion in each of these situations goes against the tenets of the stereotypic feminine role.

SELF-ASSERTION VERSUS TRADITIONAL FEMININITY

The woman in our society who conforms to the traditional feminine role is basically a nonassertive woman. She is a woman who is affectionate, cheerful, childlike, compassionate, flatterable, gentle, gullible, loyal, sensitive to others, soft-spoken, sympathetic, understanding, warm, and yielding. Her role is to nurture and convey positive feelings to other people. She does not use harsh language; she is eager to soothe hurt feelings; she loves children. The traditional feminine woman is not aggressive, ambitious, analytical, assertive, athletic, competitive, dominant, forceful, independent, individualistic, self-reliant, self-sufficient, or strong. She does not act like a leader, defend her own beliefs, or make decisions easily. She is not willing to take a stand or take a risk. These latter qualities, at least, are considered significantly less important for her than for a man.

"Not so!" you are saying? Well, this list is not drawn from some outdated textbook. This description of the ideal woman is in fact quite contemporary. It was taken from a 1974 article published by Dr. Sandra Bem, who at the time of her research was an assistant professor of psychology at Stanford University. This list was formulated from the responses of one-hundred Stanford undergraduates, both women and men, who rated each characteristic in terms of its desirability for a woman and for a man.

An equally severe assessment of appropriate feminine behavior has been made by seventy-nine mental health professionals. Broverman and her associates found that psychologists, psychiatrists, and social workers considered the emotionally well-adjusted woman to be more submissive, more emotional, more easily influenced, more excitable in minor crises, less independent, less competitive, less adventurous, and less objective than the well-adjusted man.

Unfortunately, this narrow assessment of what a woman should and should not be is almost totally incompatible with free self-assertion. The woman who learns that it is undesirable to act like a leader or be ambitious, compe-

4

titive, independent, forceful, or willing to take a stand will undoubtedly have difficulty expressing herself. The woman who tries to be submissive, childlike, gullible, shy, and yielding will find important areas of self-assertion "off limits" to her.

If this rigid view of femininity stopped with the one-hundred undergraduate students or the seventy-nine clinicians, there would be no problem. But stereotypic femininity is alive and flourishing in America. In this society, women are caught in a role that, according to Suzanne Keller, a sociology professor at Princeton University, includes the following tenets:

1. A concentration on marriage, home, and children as the primary focus of feminine concern
2. A reliance on a male provider for sustenance and status
3. An expectation that women will emphasize nurturing and life-preserving activities
4. An injunction that women live through and for others rather than for themselves
5. A stress on beauty, personal adornment, and eroticism
6. A ban on the expression of direct assertion, aggression, and power strivings

American women are pressured, constantly and continually, to mold themselves to fit this rigid sex role. The "push" toward traditional femininity, for example, is clearly present in two recent bestsellers: *The Total Woman,* by Mirabel Morgan, and *Fascinating Womanhood,* by Helen B. Anderlin, a book that has sold more than a million copies. The message of both books is clear: a woman should stifle any behaviors not fitting the requirements of the feminine role. Anderlin makes no bones about it. She instructs her female readers, "You must first dispense with any air of strength and ability, of competence and fearlessness, and acquire instead an attitude of frail dependence upon men to take care of you." The reward—protection by a man— is held out to the woman who "guards against having unyielding opinions," the woman who remains childlike and submissive.

THE NONASSERTIVE WOMAN

Many women have accepted this limiting and limited view. For example, at least fifty percent of the 750 female undergraduates at Stanford whom Bem tested described themselves as operating according to a rigid sex-role definition. This percentage is probably higher with women in the general population. Stanford undergraduates, who are predominantly young, academically astute, and financially well-to-do, do not constitute a representative sample.

The acceptance of traditional femininity clearly interferes with female assertiveness. Women in our society are significantly less assertive than men, an observation I confirmed in a study comparing women and men on the Wolpe-Lazarus assertive inventory. Moreover, the traditional feminine role allows self-assertion in some areas and not in others. For example, there are clearcut female-male differences when assertion is conceptualized as a term encompassing free self-expression in at least four areas: positive feelings, negative feelings, limit setting, and self-initiation.

My research demonstrated that in only one area—the expression of positive feelings—were women freer than men to assert themselves. Alternatively, women were less able than men to express negative feelings (particularly anger and resentment) and to set limits (prevent other people from intruding on them). Women and men tended to have equal difficulty in initiating for themselves activities and contacts that they wanted to pursue. However, even in this area there was a distinction between the sexes: women indicated more freedom to express their *feelings*. Men were more comfortable asserting their *opinions*.

The assertive pattern of the women in my study was entirely consistent with what would be expected from adherence to the feminine sex role. According to the tenets of stereotypic femininity, women are expected to concentrate upon nurturing and life-preserving activities and to live through and for others rather than for themselves. Although these two expectations have no inhibiting effect on the expression of positive feelings, both have a dramatic impact on the expression of negative feelings, on setting limits, and on initiation for one's self.

For example, how can a woman express anger, an emotion deriving from the frustration of her own needs, when her role is to nurture other people? How does a woman say "no" to another person's request when she has been taught to live *for* that other person? How can she initiate an action that derives from her own sense of what she wants to accomplish when she has been instructed to receive her satisfactions *through* the accomplishments of someone else? Why does she need to look at her own talents and potentials when another tenet of her sex role instructs her to rely on a male provider for sustenance and status? By adding, for good measure, a ban on the expression of direct assertion, aggression, and power striving, society closes off three major areas of self-assertion for women.

By allowing free self-expression in only one important area, stereotypic femininity has created a woman who is not completely whole. Like the woman in Figure 1.1, the traditional feminine woman is not allowed to express who she is as a complete human being. She is not permitted to assert those desirable human qualities such as forcefulness, self-reliance, and ambition that society has earmarked for men alone.

Let us explore each area of self-assertion in more detail. In examining the four areas, you may observe that you have been confining yourself to outmoded concepts of

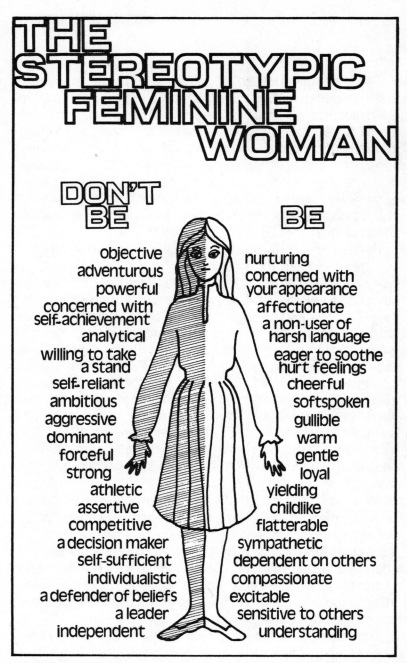

THE STEREOTYPIC FEMININE WOMAN

DON'T BE

objective
adventurous
powerful
concerned with
self-achievement
analytical
willing to take
a stand
self-reliant
ambitious
aggressive
dominant
forceful
strong
athletic
assertive
competitive
a decision maker
self-sufficient
individualistic
a defender of beliefs
a leader
independent

BE

nurturing
concerned with
your appearance
affectionate
a non-user of
harsh language
eager to soothe
hurt feelings
cheerful
softspoken
gullible
warm
gentle
loyal
yielding
childlike
flatterable
sympathetic
dependent on others
compassionate
excitable
sensitive to others
understanding

FIGURE 1.1 The stereotypic feminine woman in our society is taught to express certain desirable characteristics and to inhibit others. In one sense, she is allowed to assert half of who she is as a complete human being.

femininity and masculinity. Furthermore, since problems in self-assertion are unique for each individual as well as determined by sex-role prescriptions, you may find that you have problems in some areas but not in others. Or you may find yourself agreeing with the women in almost every assertive training group who admit, "Everything about assertion is difficult for me. I can't assert myself in any area." Now is the time to begin examining where you tend to hold back in expressing who you are as a unique individual.

POSITIVE FEELINGS

The first area of self-assertion—the expression of positive feelings—involves sharing with other people feelings of warmth, appreciation, and affection. The assertion of positive feelings may range from thanking a stranger for a small favor to letting those people close to you know that you love them.

In the assertive group, when I introduce positive feelings as the first area of self-assertion, many women are surprised. They have not thought that revealing positive feelings was connected in the least to self-assertion. Assertion has been defined solely in terms of standing up for oneself or preventing other people from taking advantage. Although these abilities involve self-assertion, assertiveness can be more broadly defined as the continuing statement, "This is who I am." And the expression of positive feelings is an important part of this self-definition.

As we have noted, women are generally freer than men to assert their positive feelings. It is in this area that the stereotypic feminine role has encouraged women to express themselves. Even books instructing women to follow rigid sex-role prescriptions do not prohibit the assertion of positive feelings. For example, in *The Total Woman*, Morgan encourages women to learn the four *A*'s in relating to their husbands: Accept him, Admire him, Appreciate him, and Adapt to him. Much of Morgan's advice to women involves increasing their expression of positive feelings toward their husbands.

Although women are generally less inhibited than men in expressing their positive feelings, asserting feelings of warmth, affection, and love does occasionally become associated with anxiety. Because of individual conditioning experiences, some women learn to hold back their assertion of positive feelings for fear of being thought forward, insincere, or pushy. One woman, for whom showing warm feelings had always been a problem, shared that she felt "predatory" when she made friendly overtures to other people. Other women fear that they will be rejected if they begin to express positive feelings. Also, although this is generally less true for women than for men, a woman may never have learned *how* to convey her positive feelings to other people. Within her family of origin, love and affection may not have been expressed openly. She may never have had anyone to model after in expressing feelings of tenderness and warmth.

The finding that women express positive feelings easily has, moreover, two broad exceptions. First, in beginning relationships with men, the traditional feminine role dictates that women allow men to take the lead. There is a prohibition against active self-initiation in female-male relationships that affects even the expression of positive feelings. Expressing affection in female-male relationships is only permissible for women under certain conditions.

One condition is that the man has already initiated such expression. I recently received a letter from Karen, a young teacher who had taken one of my assertive training workshops. One of Karen's new assertive accomplishments involved expressing positive feelings in a female-male relationship. Karen wrote, "I told a friend tonight whom I really like that I thought he was neat and that I really enjoyed him. And he said, 'You know, that's the first time you've ever said anything like that to me.' And that really felt good. I love it!" Karen's new freedom to express positive feelings in a female-male relationship is a good example of a woman overriding her sex-role training to express herself freely as a complete human being.

The second exception to a woman's general ease in expressing positive feelings occurs when she talks about herself. Few women feel comfortable in describing their own positive attributes and accomplishments. Many women find it difficult even to accept compliments. For example, when Amy is told, "I like your dress," she responds with self-disparagement, "It's about worn out," rather than accept the positive feedback from someone else. The traditional feminine sex-role encourages modesty and self-effacement. With rules against power strivings and instructions that a woman live through others, this role deemphasizes the development and expression of positive feelings about one's self.

Before leaving our discussion of positive feelings, I would like to mention one final issue. In becoming more assertive in nontraditional areas, it is important that a woman does not reject aspects of the feminine role, such as the ability to be warm, tender, and gentle, which *have* permitted her to assert "who she is" as a unique human being. As Keller notes, "Qualities stressed for the female role, such as nurturance, warmth, and sympathy, are intrinsically pleasant both to exercise and acquire." The traditional viewpoint, nourished by psychological theory and sex-role research, assumes that a person either abides by the stereotypic feminine role *or* adopts the stereotypic masculine role. According to this view, a woman can be either sensitive to other people *or* assertive; she can be understanding *or* forceful; she can be warm *or* willing to take a stand. Nothing could be further from the truth. A woman can acquire the capacity to be forceful without losing the ability to be nurturing. In becoming more assertive a woman need not take on the stereotypic masculine role—a role that is as rigid and confining as that of stereotypic femininity.

NEGATIVE FEELINGS

The second area of self-assertion is the expression of negative feelings. The assertion of negative feelings runs the gamut from "I feel uncomfortable" to "I am annoyed," "I am upset," "I feel irritated," "I resent," "I am angry," to "I am furious." In other words, the whole range of negative feelings from discomfort to fury can be expressed assertively.

Expressing negative feelings is difficult for many women. The stereotypic feminine role teaches women to suppress any "bad," that is, negative, feelings. It has not been by chance that a foregone conclusion of any psychological experiment concerning the expression of anger or aggression is that women will express less direct aggression, either verbally or physically, than men. This is true even though women have been shown (by such investigators as I. Sarason) to be equally as hostile as men in their attitudes toward other people.

Kindra, a prelaw student in one of my classes, summed up her own learned inhibition against expressing anger in this way: "My past life had a repressing effect on my behavior. I was scolded strongly by relatives for showing anger. I got the impression that anger was very wrong, and to let even a bit slip out was shocking behavior. I had models for expressing anger, but it was expressed in an aggressive, explosive manner. I concluded that anger was terrible and only nasty people let it out. Since I was still loaded up with my own anger, I assumed I was nasty, and I decided to hide it."

Kindra's learning experiences are probably very similar to those of most women. We are taught that anger is bad. We are taught to keep our negative feelings hidden. Unfortunately, negative feelings do not just go away. And until negative feelings are expressed, there is little room available for the experience of positive feelings. As I usually tell the couples I counsel, "Until you express the negative feelings that you have accumulated, it is unlikely that you will know if there are enough positive feelings to keep you together." Negative feelings, unexpressed, stop all other intimate contact.

SETTING LIMITS

The third area of self-assertion is known as limit setting. By setting limits, we let another person know "This is where I draw the line." Setting limits involves saying no to the external demands of other people when these demands go against our own internal needs. Common areas of limit setting concern time, privacy, energy, and money. The example of limit setting that I typically share with assertive classes is this: If I go to bed at 11:00, and a friend frequently telephones me at 11:30, then my time/privacy limits are being intruded upon. I can set my limits by stating at a low level, "I'd prefer that you call me before 11:00. I generally go to bed by that time." If I make this assertion, the issue will be settled immediately. But if I don't set my limits with my friend, I may find myself—for some "unknown" reason—developing a dislike for her or him, or on the occasion of my twenty-sixth interruption from a sound sleep, I may find myself aggressively attacking, "Don't you think anyone goes to sleep at night?" In other words, if I don't express my limits, I or my friend, or both of us for that matter, will eventually suffer the consequences.

There is a second important function of limit setting. By the limits that I set, I teach other people how to treat me. Another example will illustrate what I mean. Many women fear making a comment or voicing an opinion in front of a group. The fear behind their lack of assertion is often expressed in questions like, "What if someone were to say that my opinion is stupid?" or "What if someone were to laugh· at me?" Such aggressive responses from other people occur only rarely. But if such a comment did occur, and a woman was free to assert her limits, the attacking person would quickly learn to stop her or his aggressive remarks. If I made a comment in a group and someone said to me, "Pam, that is the most stupid comment I have ever heard," I would reply by setting my limits: "I don't mind your disagreeing with my comment, but I don't like my observations labeled as stupid, and I don't want that to happen again." By my response, I would be teaching the other person how I expect to be treated.

Because of the examples I give in introducing the concept, some women feel that limit setting is essentially identical to expressing negative feelings. This is not the case. In fact, if a woman is free to set her limits, she will actually find herself bypassing many negative emotions. For example, a person I like very much may ask me to go to a movie I would enjoy seeing. My feelings toward the person and the situation are positive. However, it may be that I need to be alone tonight. Maybe I am not feeling well; maybe I had a difficult day; maybe I want to begin a new painting. Whatever the reason, I may not want to go. If I assert my limit and say something like "I'd love to go another time, but tonight I really need to be by myself," I will continue to have positive feelings toward the friend who invited me. But if I ignore my limit and go to the movie, my negative feelings will quickly begin to surface. And my friend will know it. As a member of one group shared, "If I agree to accommodate my friends, against my wishes, I feel resentful. This leads to shutting down my positive caring feelings for them, and I end up communicating to them. through subtle gestures, just the attitudes of uncooperativeness and unfriendliness that I was trying to avoid in the first place by not setting my limits."

SELF-INITIATION

Whereas through limit setting we say *"no,"* through self-initiation we say *"yes."* By self-initiation, a woman expresses what she *does* want to do. She initiates those actions and expressions that do fit her as a person. This area of self-assertion involves taking risks to enhance one's own life. No one forces a woman to go back to school, to meet new people, to ask for a raise or a promotion. Yet the failure to take such actions decreases the probability that she will achieve her full potential as a human being. There are two situations where women are particularly hindered in self-initiation: (1) when the initiation involves the expression of competence and authority and (2) when it involves taking the lead in a female-male relationship.

A study by K. Hall provides a detailed look at the first type of situation. Hall studied the behavior of women in female-male problem-solving groups. She found that within these groups women acted in a manner which corresponded closely to the permissions and prohibitions of the feminine role. Specifically, women asserted themselves less than men. Whereas men contributed fifty-six percent of all verbalizations in the group, women contributed forty-four percent.

There was an even more important contrast between women and men with respect to speech content. Men tended to assert opinions or provide information directly related to the problem at hand, that is, express their competence and ability. In contrast, women tended to praise the suggestions of other people. Hall also found that however generous women were in their support of the ideas of other group members, they were less likely than men to support and defend their own beliefs. Although a man supported his own idea seventy-five percent of the time, a woman supported her own idea only forty percent of the time. Not surprisingly, men influenced the groups more. Of the nineteen, four-person groups in Hall's study, a man proved to be the most influential member in fourteen groups.

The social programming against self-initiation is equally evident in the second type of situation: female-male relationships. As a young woman in one group revealed, "With first dates, I'm afraid to be assertive for fear of being thought too bold." Another woman's anxiety in this area was uncovered by her question, "How soon *after* you know a man should you start being assertive?" The lack of assertive self-initiation, beginning on a couple's first date, frequently sets up an unequal relationship between a woman and a man that lasts throughout their married life. Many women allow themselves to be placed in a passive position where a man controls the relationship. A woman in this situation waits for a phone call, waits to be asked out on a date, allows a man to initiate sexual contact, and yokes her expression of affection to his. It is not surprising that so many women feel extremely vulnerable in romantic relationships. The feminine role allows them very little direct control.

Joyce, a professional woman who attended one of my assertive training workshops, is one of a growing body of women who no longer accept this passive position. One of Joyce's assertive statements in a group rehearsal beautifully illustrates self-initiation in a female-male relationship. The assertion "I don't want to be coy with you. I like you and I want to feel free to write you and call you, just as I want you to feel free to write and call me" is one that initiates an equal female-male relationship.

In reviewing the four areas of self-assertion, we can see that the woman who is nonassertive in any area is not fully in touch with her potential or her power as a unique human being. This was the case with Kay, Joan, Nancy, and Wanda, the women in the opening examples. These women, at the beginning of assertive training, were limited by some aspect of the feminine sex-role stereotype. They were not yet free to express those feelings that ran counter to the traditional femininity—feelings of anger and resentment, feelings of concern for and nurturance of their own self, and feelings of power and strength. In short, these women had not yet accepted their own psychological androgyny (a term deriving from the Greek *andro* for man and *gyny* for woman). They had not yet accepted their masculine as well as their feminine characteristics. They had not yet learned *how* to be assertive.

sugar and spice: is everything nice?

2

A large number of women in their attitudes and by their behavior conform to the traditional feminine role. Noting this, we might ask ourselves, "Has stereotypic femininity served women well?" "Have qualities of nonassertion, passivity, and submissiveness helped women?" "Do women gain more benefits or face more risks by conforming to their prescribed sex role?" "Is it indeed desirable to strive for childlike dependence on a man, as some women suggest?"

Before answering these questions, let us put the current situation of women in proper perspective by examining the reality of women's lives. In other words, let us look at how women fare throughout the feminine life cycle, not just young women, but middle-aged and older women. Surprisingly, one of the most striking realities of this life cycle is that in contrast to stereotypic notions, many women do not have a male provider to support them. Today in our country there is a growing trend toward female-headed families. For example, in 1973 almost ten percent of white families and thirty-five percent of black families were headed by women. Fourteen percent of American children under eighteen were reared by their mothers alone.

Furthermore, the majority of women rely on a male provider in only one segment of their lives. Robert Butler, a noted advocate for the aged and author of *Why Survive: Being Old In America,* suggests that because women live close to eight years longer than men and marry men about three years older than they are, the typical woman is destined to living alone for the last ten years of her life. Statistics agree. At the present time, one out of every six women living in the United States is a widow. Many other women find themselves alone because of divorce. In the March 1974 census, thirty-seven percent of American women over forty were listed as having no husband. The core message of these figures is that many women will live alone, rear their children alone, and at least at some

20

point in their lives be totally responsible for their own welfare.

The woman who does not rely on a male provider faces a situation where she earns less than a man for doing identical work. In 1973, almost forty-four percent of women in the United States were employed. However, the majority of these women were clustered in low-status jobs and earned only sixty-six percent of the wages that men earned. Widows and single women over sixty-five have less money than any group in our society. Their average income is well below the poverty level. As Butler noted,

> Because of the inequities of employment opportunities and inequities in the Social Security system, the woman's economic status is much less promising than the man's. The amount of poverty among women is really quite extraordinary. And when coupled with loneliness and isolation, the effects can be devastating.

Women who are married or secure in a female-male relationship do not escape the impact of stereotyped femininity. Within the marital relationship, the lives of women (and men) are significantly shaped by the traditional feminine role. A woman's status in society, the area of the country she lives in, her economic well being, the division of labor and the decision-making power in her household, and what she does with her talents and her time are all intimately tied to the feminine role. Iris Fodor, a leading behavior therapist, has noted that married women have been found to be more depressed and less satisfied with their lives than single women and that agoraphobia (fear of leaving home), the most common phobia in women, typically develops in *married* women five years after their marriage.

In my own opinion, any woman pays a high price for adhering to the stereotypic feminine role. This is true for the married woman as well as for the woman alone. One of the major costs of stereotypic femininity is a reduced ability to be assertive. Conformity to a rigid feminine role robs a woman of the freedom to assert herself by controlling the external influences in her life, by expressing anger, and by experiencing herself as a competent, problem-solving human being. The nonassertive position of stereotyped femininity frequently has three additional untoward consequences: emotional distress, powerlessness, and depression.

EMOTIONAL DISTRESS

Saturday is my day to do all of my household chores, errands, watching the kids' soccer games, etc., since I work full time during the week. Last Saturday, as I got ready to leave the house for a quick trip to the market in between the jobs I had scheduled for myself, my husband asked me to stop at the hardware store and pick up an electrical item for a remodeling project he was doing. As he talked, he added another and then another item to the list. The more things he wanted, the angrier I got. All I could think was:

1. He had been to the hardware store the day before. Why hadn't he gotten the items himself?
2. I knew the store would be crowded and service slow.
3. I already had more to do that day than I would complete.
4. Usually the items he asked for required decisions to be made, that, not knowing to what use they would be put, I could not make.

However, I swallowed my resentment and went to the store where my worst fears were realized. They didn't have the exact item, so it required two phone calls home to see if a substitute would be okay. By the time I did my errands, the shopping trip had taken almost three hours out of my day, my stomach was churning, the tendons in my neck were tight, and a headache was well on its way. I was angry at the crowds, at my husband, and at myself for not expressing my unwillingness to add his chores to my already full day.

So wrote Eleanor, surgical nurse, wife, and mother of three, in outlining a nonassertive experience that she had had, and its consequences.

In her description, Eleanor clearly described what is by far the most obvious cost of nonassertion: emotional distress. When she failed to set her limits and say "no" to her husband's request, Eleanor immediately began to pay for her nonassertion. She spent the day with an upset stomach, a headache, and an abundance of hostile feelings.

Most of us have experienced emotional distress similar to that described by Eleanor. The human organism is finely tuned to send out distress signals whenever we are in danger or whenever we are being intruded upon. Eleanor felt the signals. She was exquisitely aware of her growing annoyance as her husband added items to her list. Yet she ignored her internal message. Unusual behavior? Not particularly. Very early, women learn to ignore the internal messages from their bodies. Women learn to follow instead a learned set of "shoulds" and "oughts" that are handed down from parent to child, from teacher to student. We have already alluded to one of the important shoulds of the feminine role: a woman *should* be other-oriented. A woman *should* do what her husband or her children want, regardless of how it interferes with her own needs and plans. To say "no," to deviate from the sex-role stereotype, is a difficult and stressful task.

POWERLESSNESS

In front of me sits Barbara, twenty-seven year old mother of two. Barbara is holding, with trembling hands, a cup of coffee I have offered her and is looking at me anxiously from her chair. I ask her what brings her in to see me, and Barbara begins to cry softly. She stares at her hands and begins to tell me about her husband Bob. It seems that Bob is a successful young executive in one of the many banks that dot San Francisco's Montgomery Street financial district. Bob's job in San Francisco is new. Several months ago Bob was given the opportunity to transfer from a small community near Boston where he managed a branch office to San Francisco. The move did not entail any higher salary, but his chances of promotion were much greater.

Without any real discussion, Barbara had accepted Bob's decision to move. She ignored her feelings of uncertainty and anxiety, and mechanically packed up the family's belongings (Bob had gone on ahead) and moved herself and her children to San Francisco. A few weeks later, Barbara and Bob bought a house. Barbara explained that she herself had wanted to take an apartment in San Francisco so she could be near theaters and museums and city life. But Bob felt that they could live more economically in one of the outlying suburbs, where schools are good and children have yards to play in.

Bob was ecstatically happy with his job. He had the bustle of the city, lunches and cocktails with clients, and a job where he was sure he could advance. Barbara, as she was now telling me, felt miserable. She resented Bob's enthusiasm. She was beginning to withdraw from him, sexually and emotionally.

"I've been here three months," Barbara was saying, "and I haven't met anyone that I like. I went to some women's meetings when I first got here, and I used to ride my bicycle around the block every day, but I haven't met any adults whom I have anything in common with. I go around feeling like a child all the time. I'm a grown woman, and I have two children of my own, but I feel like a child," Barbara repeated, as if trying to grasp the contradiction in her statement. "I'm alone most of the day and lately, a lot of that time, I just sit around and cry."

"I don't want you to think that I've always been such a nobody," Barbara insisted. "When we were back in Boston, I was always doing something. Several women and I had gotten together a small gift card company. You see, I'm an artist," Barbara said, as she looked directly at me for the first time, "and the company was well on its way to becoming something. I had increased my income from almost nothing to an average of about $400 each month and the business had just begun to expand. I've thought about doing something like that here," Barbara continued, looking again at her hands, "but even taking a class seems like too much effort. I've lost all confidence in myself. I just don't feel like trying anymore."

As a practicing behavior therapist, I see many women like Barbara, women who find themselves in situations that they feel powerless to change. Some women feel trapped by an unsatisfactory marriage; other women leave a bad marriage, only to find themselves powerless to alter an intolerable work situation or even to find a job. I see other women who feel powerless to get what they need from a female-male relationship and women who feel powerless to say "no" to the unreasonable demands of family, friends, and relatives. These women, in describing feelings of helplessness and lack of control over their own lives, are usually speaking about an inability to influence other people. They are speaking of an inability to make a satisfying environment for themselves, an environment where they can truly develop as a unique individual.

Phyllis Chesler, author of *Women and Madness,* has commented that the modern female condition is one of powerlessness. The traits that women typically possess (compassion, sensitivity, docility) are not those which are rewarded by our society. In fact, a woman who permits herself to be only compassionate, sensitive, and docile is likely to be victimized. A woman who develops only feminine qualities learns to tolerate toxic situations through stoic acceptance and silent martyrdom rather than take steps to change them.

The experience of powerlessness is ubiquitous. A close friend of mine went to a luncheon that was attended by ten or eleven other women. The next day my friend related to me at least four examples of self-victimization which various women had revealed during the luncheon. For instance, Alice takes an older woman in her neighborhood grocery shopping each week. This is a small favor that she is happy to perform. However, when she brings the older woman home, Alice keeps the car motor running. She hopes that if she does not shut off the motor, the older woman will be aware that she does not want to stay and talk. One day Alice sat in her car for an hour with the car motor running, talking to her neighbor, unable to say, "I have to go now."

Alice clearly fits Chesler's description of the powerless woman. By permitting herself to be only compassionate, she ends up a victim of her own good deeds. Had she also the capacity to be assertive, she would be able to consider her own needs as well as those of her older friend. Under these circumstances, she might even feel comfortable visiting on occasion with her neighbor.

Let us return to Barbara's situation for a moment. Three months before my first meeting with her, Barbara was by her own description happy, active, and satisfied with her life. She was in an environment that was encouraging her growth as an artist, a businesswoman, and a person. Yet without a whimper, not to mention a fight, Barbara gave up her interests and moved to San Francisco. She failed to express any of her negative feelings about leaving a very satisfying set of surroundings. In fact, the idea that she could legitimately object to moving was completely alien to Barbara. Once in San Francisco, Barbara dutifully agreed to buy a house in the suburbs, again going against her own desires. She did not fight for a compromise solution, one that would have increased her chance of meeting some of her own needs.

In talking to Barbara, I observed that both the intolerable situation in which she found herself and her feelings of powerlessness to change her situation were a direct result of her lack of self-assertion and her rigid conformity to the traditional feminine role. I found that in dealing with

Bob, Barbara habitually allowed him to make the decisions. Barbara operated from a passive position, trying never to do anything that might displease or "make waves." She was afraid of Bob's anger, and she was afraid of her own.

I had the impression from Barbara's description of events that Bob's decision to move came more from not knowing her feelings than from ignoring or overriding them. Had Barbara asserted herself, in all likelihood she would not have been sitting in my office crying. She would not have been resenting Bob, and she would not have been neglecting her development as an artist. But Barbara felt powerless. She saw little possibility of controlling her environment. Like most women caught in the confines of stereotypic femininity, Barbara *underestimated* the influence she actually had.

DEPRESSION

When intense enough, the experience of being powerless or helpless can lead to a more debilitating form of emotional distress: depression. Barbara began her move to California under a great deal of emotional stress. Her negative feelings intensified when she and Bob bought a home in the suburbs, and she found that she had no effective means of integrating her own needs with those of her husband and her children. As Barbara began to experience that she had no control over her own life, and this experience became progressively more intense, her emotional distress changed in form. Barbara became depressed.

Depression is no stranger to women. Statistics indicate that women are depressed more frequently than men. M. Roth has reported that as many as eight percent of the women in this country suffer from depression, as compared to four percent of the men. Of course, the higher incidence of depression reported for women may simply reflect a greater freedom on the part of women to seek therapeutic assistance. However, this seems unlikely to be the cause of the female-male difference when we consider that there are two important environmental conditions thought to cause depression, and these conditions affect women more than men. One condition is the experience of lacking power and control over one's own life, that is, helplessness. The other condition is the experience of not receiving sufficient reward or satisfaction from one's surroundings, that is, low positive reinforcement and non-recognition. Helplessness, lack of reinforcement, and nonrecognition are all intimately related to the traditional feminine role.

Depression: the consequence of helplessness

We noted that feelings of powerlessness can lead to the development of depression. According to Martin Seligman, author of *Learned Helplessness,* when a woman experiences that she has no effect on her environment, she often develops a general feeling that what she does does not matter. If these feelings persist, depression is the usual result. For example, if a woman finds that regardless of her efforts to advance in her career, her advancement is stopped by superiors who discriminate against women, she will ultimately feel that nothing she does will lead to a promotion. She may feel depressed. If this woman has had other experiences in her past, where she has attempted to resolve a problem to no avail, and these experiences have been numerous and/or intense, she may develop a more general pessimism as to the effectiveness of her actions. If this general feeling of powerlessness develops, she will almost certainly become depressed. Rather than moving to a new company that does not have discriminatory practices, she will resign herself to her lot and stop trying.

According to Seligman, it is not so much what happens to a woman as it is her inability or her perceived inability to control what happens to her that leads to depression. And as we have seen, the traditional feminine role encourages women to surrender control of their lives to someone else. One of the most tragic plights in today's society is that of the widowed or divorced woman who has spent her life as a homemaker and suddenly finds that she has no means of supporting herself. More than a million women under sixty, widowed or divorced, find themselves in this predicament. In their role as homemaker, these women surrendered their care to their husbands—often not knowing what care he provided, not knowing about insurance, wills, or investments. When their husbands died or when they divorced, they found themselves without any adequate means of support and without the skills needed for self-support. These women realistically find themselves powerless to control their own lives.

Many women actually begin their marriage by relinquishing their own power base. These women neglect their own education to support their husbands through school, expecting that in return they will be taken care of. Instead, they find that their trust in marriage was ill founded, and that by living for and through their husbands they are left with no job, no training, no money, and very little control over what happens to them. These women are frequently depressed.

The view that depression results from a lack of control or perceived lack of control over one's own life also explains why many women who are considered by society's standards to be "successful" frequently become depressed. Aaron Beck noted in an article about depression in women that little girls are rewarded not for their achievement in mastering problem situations but for their beauty and appeal to men. Many little girls grow up accepting stereotypic femininity's emphasis on beauty, personal adornment, and eroticism. When they become women who "have everything," they find themselves miserable. They have married the man of their dreams; they have a house in the suburbs, two cars in the garage, a swimming pool, yet they are miserable. Their "American dream" was not earned by their own efforts.

Although these "successful" women may have a great deal of material reward, status, and recognition, their reinforcement comes from the provisions and accomplishments of other people, their husbands, and their children. These women have relied on what Anne Steinmann has called "gratification by proxy." A woman's reward is her husband's promotion. Her feeling of achievement comes from her son's going to law school. Her recognition relates to being Mr. J.'s wife. The particular vulnerability to depression which these women share comes from the fact that their position has little direct connection to their own action and is only to a very limited extent under their own control.

In her book *Widow,* Lynn Caine warns women about the consequence of basing their feelings of accomplishment on the achievements of someone else.

A widow feels empty and incomplete because, like most women, she gained her identity through marriage, and when her husband died, there she was. A widow. Empty. Without her husband to validate her existence. Without an identity of her own. It is sad that the progression of grief is so much more difficult for widows than for widowers. But there is a reason for it. Men do not think of themselves as primarily husbands and fathers. They have been encouraged to develop their full potential as unique human beings. So when a man becomes a widower, it is truly a heartbreaking blow, but it does not spell an end to his whole way of life. He still has his identity, one that has developed through work, through play, through living.

Depression: the lack of positive reinforcement

A second view, that of Peter Lewinsohn, says that depression results from a lack of positive reinforcement in a person's life. Again we can see that the feminine role is relevant. Because of the traditional focus on marriage, home, and children, women do not typically have as many external rewards as men. Although men typically obtain satisfactions from both their jobs and their homes, many women have only their home. Once children begin to move away, a major source of gratification for the traditional woman is reduced or eliminated. The "empty nest" syndrome— the feelings of uselessness and depression that hit a woman when her children move out of the home—is a frequent and common female experience. As for those women who do work, they are often in low status and poorly paid positions from which little reward is forthcoming. Only seventeen percent of the women in the nation's work force are in the presumably more rewarding professional positions, and most of these women are teachers and nurses.

One very personal account of the difference between women and men in the amount of gratification and satisfaction in their lives was given by Marilyn Alexander in her article "The Way We Were." Alexander writes,

I had loved my husband dearly. But there was a time in my marriage when I was truly unhappy and thought divorce might be the only way out. I had stayed home and raised the children. I had felt resentment as I served my husband's breakfast day after day, year after year like some kind of downstairs maid, as he read the paper and went out into the world. He was getting out of the goddamned house while I was stuck there like those other wives with cold Pablum on my shoulder. . . . There was no hope of having an adult conversation. . . . My future really seemed hopeless. He was achieving, developing, thriving. I wasn't. (An excerpt from

Alexander ultimately became deeply depressed and sought professional help. Her "rebirth" came in developing her own interests, in caring for her own needs as well as those of the family, and in learning to assert her feelings— in short, in disentangling herself from the major tenets of the stereotypic feminine role.

Depression: the consequences of nonrecognition

In speaking of the narrow range of gratification that has traditionally been available to women, I would like to mention another reward-limiting factor women in our society face. Women are frequently treated as "nonpersons." Their actions are not recognized, not to mention rewarded, because society has rigid and limited expectations for women.· Social custom alone takes away a woman's existence as a full, complete human being. An example of this that comes to mind is one which was told to me by Ken, a man whom I met when I conducted an assertive training course for a group of professional therapists. Ken and a woman friend, Marie, went to an exclusive restaurant for dinner, the kind of restaurant that had prices on the man's menu but not on the woman's. When Marie ordered for herself, the waiter looked somewhat askance. He seemed even more upset when Marie made the wine selection. Marie was the expert on wine, so it seemed quite natural to her and Ken that she should order for them. However, when the waiter returned with the wine, he poured it for Ken's sampling and approval. Social custom had relegated Marie to the position of a nonperson— a decorative appendage to Ken. Marie's expertise was ignored.

Another woman, Jan, a consultant from a state agency, shared a striking example with me of a professional woman receiving nonperson status. Jan joined a group of local consultants in one community for a discussion of a mutual problem. Fifteen minutes after the meeting began, someone asked, "Where is the man from the state?" It was assumed that any state consultant would be male. After all, consultants, along with college professors, doctors, and attorneys, are "hes." Nurses, elementary school teachers, and secretaries are "shes." *Hes* receive recognition; *shes* do not.

Nonrecognition means nonreinforcement, and as we have seen, nonreinforcement frequently means depression. Yet it is typical for the feminine woman not to expect or demand recognition for her own accomplishments. In *Zelda,* Nancy Milford describes Zelda Fitzgerald, who began her marriage to F. Scott Fitzgerald in many ways the stereotypic feminine woman. Zelda is the "southern belle" par excellence. Yet Zelda is also a talented writer, who as her life progresses finds that she needs and wants recognition. But Zelda's needs are not in accord with the traditional feminine role. For example, in her own creative writing, Zelda comes up against her husband's assumption that her life is his literary property. Her ideas and portions of her letters are used in his books as *his* creations. Even some of her short stories have F. Scott Fitzgerald as coauthor. His name is first, her name comes second.

The depression and emotional disturbance that haunt Zelda for most of her married life may or may not relate to her struggle to gain recognition. However, Chesler suggests that the confines of the feminine sex role made illness one of the few possible options for a creative talent such as Zelda. Zelda's conflict is replayed today by women who submit to earning less then men for identical work and who do the same job as a man without the same status position. It is replayed by women who funnel their ideas and suggestions through the mouths of their male colleagues.

ACTIVE, ASSERTIVE, ANDROGYNOUS

Stereotypic femininity with its injunction against self-assertion is intimately connected to the feelings of help-lessness and the lack of reward and recognition that women experience. The rigid strictures of the traditional feminine role undoubtedly contribute to the high incidence of female depression.

Many women feel that an overhauling of the stereotypic feminine role is overdue. Many women want to function as complete people. They want not to be confined by society's idea of what women are *supposed* to be. They want to reown those desirable human qualities that society has reserved for one sex alone. They want a new view of femininity.

This new woman is an active woman; she is an assertive woman. She is an androgynous woman. She is a woman who embraces what Steinmann terms a "self-achieving" orientation, fulfilling herself directly by realizing her own potential. She is a woman who is ambitious as well as understanding, adventurous as well as gentle, willing to take a stand as well as to yield. She is a woman who acknowledges, develops, and uses her own power. She is a woman who moves away from what Carolyn Heilbrun terms "sexual polarization and the prison of gender toward a world in which individual roles and modes of personal behavior can be freely chosen."

A woman reowns those qualities that have been pro-hibited by traditional femininity by freely asserting her feelings and opinions. Sometimes, self-assertion involves behavior that is contrary to the stereotypic feminine role. Sometimes, self-assertion involves actions that have here-tofore been considered the masculine perogative. Sometimes, self-assertion involves a woman getting in touch with her own power, her own anger, and her own need for achievement and recognition.

Carol Hing, an elementary school teacher, described to me an experience that punctuates how a woman can reown her own power by asserting herself and by refusing to conform to the traditional feminine role. I'll let Carol describe the experience to you.

> When guys ask me for my number, I usually give "it" to them. "It" means power—the power to make me wait for them to call. Well, no more. I've learned to ask for their number as well so that at least we share the power of the telephone call.
>
> One night in a bar, I met a real neat guy I will call Tom. I really wanted to see Tom again, so we exchanged phone numbers. Well, as it turned out, with classes, other dates, and other commitments, I was busy every night for one-and-a-half weeks straight. Having not been home to hear the phone ring, I began to get anxious. Did he call? Did he lose my number? Does he want to get together again?
>
> Well, I decided to be assertive and call Tom first. (Note: this was something new. I have never called a guy *before* he called me, and I rarely call guys unless we have been dating for awhile.) Nervous? Yes. I even had my girlfriend over to give me reassurance. But I had to know. Was he really interested in me or did he just pass me a line in the bar that night?
>
> Guess what. Tom wasn't home that night either. And he wasn't home the next night. Another week went by and something from within told me to be assertive and call him at work. He surely must be there. Ring-Ring-Ring. "Hello, may I speak to Tom, please?" "Robin! Hi Robin. Ummm—is this Robin?" "No, this isn't. Is Tom in?" "No, he's at Captain Cook's. I thought you were Robin because Tom left a message here for her. Call Captain Cook's, okay?" (Captain Cook's is a local hustle bar. The time was 4:00 P.M.) "Okay. Bye."
>
> Well, I found out. Tom is in my terms a playboy—probably dating Robin and others. I'm glad I found out too. I stopped worrying about him and was glad I made the call. No, Tom never called me, and I'm not upset about it. In fact, I'm glad because right now I don't need another swinger in my life. For real.

By taking an active, assertive position in her interaction with Tom, Carol was able to resolve her question "Did

Tom want to get together?" By not limiting her behavior to what is expected of the stereotypic feminine woman, she retained the power to respond to her feelings of concern and to do what she needed to maintain her own sense of comfort and well being. The philosophy and the techniques of self-assertion to be presented in the following chapters can serve as a guide for any woman who wants to express her individuality as a unique human being, unconstrained by society's expectations of what a woman should or should not be.

taking the
first step

There are at least five major reasons why a woman does not assert herself: (1) she may be unaware that she has the option of behaving in an assertive manner; (2) she may be afraid to assert herself; (3) she may talk herself out of expressing her legitimate feelings; (4) she may not know what to say; or (5) she may not know how to say it. Table 3.1 sets forth these obstacles.

Many women fall into the first category. They are not aware that they are nonassertive or that they have an alternative way of responding to their environment. As we have seen, many women learn very early in their lives to operate through a filter of shoulds and should nots that does not permit them to trust in or rely upon their own feelings. Women learn to shape their actions and behaviors to conform with the traditional feminine role, even when that role is not advantageous to them.

This lack of awareness was highlighted for me in a recent workshop. Lena, a chemist, shared with the group that for several years she had had a standing Monday morning appointment with her boss. However, she had met with him only one out of every two times because he would habitually cancel their meetings without notice. Lena related to us that upon hearing of the cancellation, she would go quietly back to her office, thinking to herself, "Of course, it's right that anything else is more important than me." Only in the few months before attending the workshop had she even become aware enough of what she was doing to herself to consider alternatives. Without such awareness there is little chance that a woman will become more assertive.

Other women tell me that the awareness is already there. Their feelings tell them loudly and clearly that they are being intruded upon, that they are not acting in ways which would enhance their lives, that they are allowing hostility to build up. But in spite of their awareness, they do not assert themselves. Their assertion is blocked for a second

TABLE 3.1   Obstacles to Self-Assertion

1.	Lack of awareness	Are you aware that you have the option of responding in an assertive manner?
2.	Anxiety	Are you afraid to express yourself even when you know what you want to say?
3.	Negative self-talk	Do you inhibit your self-assertion by what you tell yourself?
4.	Verbal deficit	Is it difficult to find the words to express yourself verbally?
5.	Behavioral deficit	Are you hindered by a nonassertive manner?

reason. The thoughts of asserting their limits, of voicing their anger, of reaching out to take hold of what they want is fraught with anxiety. In this chapter we will focus on these first two obstacles to self-assertion.

BECOMING AWARE

The first step in becoming more assertive is to increase your awareness of those situations where you do not express your feelings and opinions easily. This involves looking at both the specific areas of assertive expression you find difficult (the assertive analysis) and the specific people in your life with whom you are unable to communicate effectively (the influence analysis).

The assertive analysis

In Chapter 1 we discussed four areas in which women typically have problems in being assertive. Now that you are familiar with these areas, you are ready to begin your own assertive analysis. The first step in this analysis is to ask yourself where you have most difficulty in being assertive. Is it in expressing positive feelings, expressing negative feelings, setting limits, or self-initiation? Rank these four areas in terms of their difficulty to you.

Least difficult 1. _____

                2. _____

                3. _____

Most difficult 4. _____

Having arranged the areas from least to most difficult, you can now look at each one in detail. Your ability to express positive feelings, negative feelings and so on may differ depending upon whom you are asserting yourself with. For example, with women you may find it easy to express affection. With men, asserting positive feelings may be more difficult.

Table 3.2 presents a checklist of people with whom women frequently have problems in being assertive. Ask yourself how you respond with each person or group of people. For example, the first item questions your ability to be assertive with strangers. Are you able to compliment a stranger? (Positive feelings). If a stranger is annoying you, can you express your annoyance? (Negative feelings). Are you able to refuse a request from a stranger who asks you to volunteer your time for a project? (Setting limits). At a party, are you able to approach a stranger to talk? (Self-initiation). Rank each area of assertion with a stranger on a scale from one (least difficult) to four (most difficult).

As you go down the list, ask yourself similar questions about people in authority, members of the opposite sex, and so on. Within each of these categories rank the assertion in terms of its difficulty to you. After you complete the list, add up the total difficulty score for positive feelings, negative feelings, limit setting, and self-initiation. Which area has the highest difficulty score? Which has the lowest? Does your checklist assessment agree with your initial overall ranking? Does it give you any new ideas about your difficulty in self-assertion?

TABLE 3.2

Category	Positive feelings	Negative feelings	Setting limits	Self-initiation
1. Strangers	————	————	————	————
2. People in authority	————	————	————	————
3. Members of the opposite sex	————	————	————	————
4. People older than I	————	————	————	————
5. People I want to like me	————	————	————	————
6. People close to me	————	————	————	————
7. People I supervise	————	————	————	————
8. My partner, my husband	————	————	————	————
9. My father	————	————	————	————
10. My mother	————	————	————	————
11. Teenagers	————	————	————	————
12. My children	————	————	————	————
13. Others	————	————	————	————
Difficulty factor	————	————	————	————

Diane, a student in one of my classes, agreed to share her reactions to her own personal assertive analysis with you. Diane writes:

> In first viewing my assertive analysis, I recognized a number of nonassertive behavior patterns. A frequently recurring problem for me is that I do not express my negative feelings. I assume instead that the other person knows that I am upset. Then, I expect the person to do something about the problem. For example, I was angry at Jim, an intimate friend, because he wouldn't help me with my car. I became very silent and withdrawn for an entire day. I was waiting for him to ask me what was the matter so we could talk. If I had been direct in expressing my negative feelings, I would have saved a day of hard feelings. Although I have been responding in this manner throughout my life, I now recognize that it is a result of being nonassertive. As a result, I am already making progress in changing this pattern of mine by being spontaneous and direct in minor situations with Jim.
>
> The problem area that will be most challenging for me is setting limits. This has been a problem for me with almost everyone I know. It is especially noticeable in my career as a teacher. I may verbally set a limit for a classroom, but then I don't carry it through. I therefore haven't set a limit at all. I am learning, slowly, to do this more effectively in my classes, and it has brought rewarding results. I have not yet been able, however, to set limits effectively in my personal relationship with Jim. Last Sunday I proposed to Jim that we do not drink alcohol on Sundays. Although we did not discuss it, he did not disagree. Sunday night we went out to dinner, and Jim ordered wine. I did not speak up and restate my limits so we had wine with dinner, and he continued drinking after dinner.
>
> I am less concerned about the two other areas of assertiveness. As with most women, I am able to express positive feelings. I am also very independent in many ways, and the area of self-initiation does not create conflicts for me. I pretty much do what I want to. When I don't, it is most often a result of one of the problem areas mentioned above.

Influence analysis

The second analysis is somewhat more complex. This analysis examines the people in your life who are influencing you right now and how you deal with them. Influence analysis is a procedure my friend and colleague Portia Shapiro developed as a tool for increasing a woman's self-awareness about her own behavior. In assertive training classes, Portia takes each group through an influence analysis, similar to the one presented here. To begin your influence analysis, ask yourself the following four questions concerning you and the people around you.

1. Who influences you? Write down the names of at least five people in your life who affect you in some way. List in particular the people who have an important effect on your day-to-day existence. For example, your boss may frequently demand that you work overtime; your husband may give you encouragement to return to school; or your children may want you to be at home when they are. Each of these people exerts a major influence on you. List them in the following spaces:

    (a) _____
    (b) _____
    (c) _____
    (d) _____
    (e) _____

    A woman who is nonassertive, a woman who is unable to set limits or say "no," frequently finds that she has little personal space left to her because of the influences in her life. Figure 3.1 illustrates a woman caught in such an environment. How much space is available for this woman? What do you think she is experiencing as other people cut more and more into her world? How much space is left for you in terms of your influence environment?

2. What type of influence do you face? Now that you have identified the important people in your life, consider the manner in which each person affects you. Influences generally fall into two categories: positive/supports and negative/constraints. Often an individual affects

43

FIGURE 3.1 Examine your influence environment. How many external influences surround you? Are they supportive or constraining? Do they prevent you from being yourself?

you in both a positive and a negative way. For example, your parents may offer to stay with your children while you attend an out-of-town conference. Your parents are supporting you in this situation. So is your husband when he encourages you to seek a promotion at your job. Conversely, these same people may make demands on you that constrain what you would prefer to do. Your parents may expect you to come home for major holidays, although you have other things you would like to do, or your husband may demand that you spend time entertaining his clients when you need time for yourself.

Table 3.3 describes one woman's major influences. Note both the constraints and the supports in her current life situation. Now list again each person who influences you, this time specifying the type of influence this person provides. As you document the kinds of influences in your own life, consider whether you have surrounded yourself with a supportive or a toxic environment.

	Who	*Positive (Support)*	*Negative (Constraint)*
(a)	_____	_____	_____
(b)	_____	_____	_____
(c)	_____	_____	_____
(d)	_____	_____	_____
(e)	_____	_____	_____

3. How do you respond to the influences? At this point you have identified the significant people in your life and the ways in which they affect you. Consider now how you respond to these people. What do you say or do when you are faced with constraints from another person? Do you passively comply, blow up in anger, or withdraw as a way of handling the negative influences in your life? Also consider how you respond to

TABLE 3.3   Influence Content

Who	Positive (Supports)	Negative (Constraints)
Intimate partner	Provides emotional intimacy, intellectual stimulation	Has numerous housekeeping expectations
	Offers praise, encouragement	Sets time schedule to accommodate his needs, not mine.
		Provides too little sexual intimacy
Boss	Backs up decisions	Makes excessive time demands
	Rewards work	
	Provides training	Sets unrealistic work schedule
	Serves as role model	Assigns servant-type tasks (doing personal errands)
		Has unspoken work expectations
Parents	Provide understanding	Give me love on a conditional basis (I will love you if. . . .)
	Offer financial assistance	Make time demands
Friend	Provides opportunities for intimate conversation	Expects me to be always available as a problem solver
	Goes places with me	Borrows money, personal articles
Myself	Enjoy my company	Criticize my own mistakes severely
	Recognize my abilities	Push myself too hard

positive influences. What is your reaction when someone offers you needed assistance? Do you accept or
refuse? How do you respond to a compliment? Do you
minimize it? Do you allow yourself to experience the
good feelings that a compliment can bring? Table 3.4
lists many possible reactions to both positive and negative influences. List your reactions to the constraining
and supportive people in your own life. In subsequent
chapters we will discuss how to determine whether
your responses are passive, assertive, or aggressive.

	Who	Kind of Influence	Response
(a)	_____	_____	_____
(b)	_____	_____	_____
(c)	_____	_____	_____
(d)	_____	_____	_____
(e)	_____	_____	_____

Responding to these first three questions should provide you with a fairly clear and comprehensive picture
of your behavior with the people who influence you
the most. However, in its present form the information
you have yielded about yourself, although rich, is still
somewhat fragmented. Look at all the information: the
people who influence you, the content of the influence,
and how you respond. Do you see any patterns emerg-
ing? This brings us to the final question.

4. Is there a pattern to your behavior? For some women,
    trouble dealing with authority figures, whether it is their
    fathers, bosses, or older friends, may emerge as a pat-
    tern. For some women a pattern of withdrawal may sur-
    face as the principal form of relating to other people.
    Other women may find themselves always accommo-
    dating, putting their own needs aside because of some-
    one else's needs. What pattern do you find as you
    examine your own behavior? Are you conforming to

TABLE 3.4   Reaction Possibilities

Express anger	Tune out the situation
Confront the other person	Remain silent
Cry	Acquiesce to demand
Shout	Explain my behavior
Avoid responding	Delay responding
Withdraw	Ignore the situation
Become depressed	Escape by overeating, sleeping, drinking, or taking drugs
Explode	Talk about what I would like to have said later to friends
Say inside my head all the words not expressed in the encounter	Use sarcasm
Make indirect comments	Refuse to take the other person seriously
Minimize my own worth	Apologize excessively

---

the traditional feminine role? Do you typically respond by nurturing or taking care of other people? Do you find yourself being passive because you confuse self-assertion with aggressive or masculine behavior?

After asking herself the various questions and completing the four steps involved in the influence analysis, Katha summarized her own pattern in this way:

The most influential person in my life is the man I live with. His is a very positive influence, providing love, affection, encouragement, honesty, support (emotional and financial) and a measure of respect. He demands time and attention, flexibility, compliance and the willingness to play a "supporting role." I respond to his influence in many positive ways and feel I'm enjoying much growth in the process. On the negative side, I feel that I'm too dependent on him. I'm afraid of losing him and make very few plans that might conflict with time I could spend with him. I also feel jealous more often that I would like.

Because I both work for and live with Bill, my world of influence is smaller than most. However, I do have several women friends in my life. On the positive side, I enjoy their ability to listen and frequently to give valuable feedback. I usually feel encouraged by their interest in me. When I listed the negative aspects of my relationship with each of them individually the word "competitive" was on almost every list! What seems to be happening is that I am aware of feeling put down, left out, or ignored, while my friends receives attention or dominates the situation. I tend to withdraw my trust and affection, leaving myself resentful and angry, rather than "rise to the occasion", by testing the reality of the situation and/or joining in the (not always so frightening) competition.

Even though I talk with her on the phone less than once a week, my mother is a strong influence on me and the patterns of our relationship continue to be important in my life. My mother has throughout my life offered financial support and expressed affection verbally. I usually feel that she enjoys talking with me. However, I experience her as persistently and subtly undercutting me, taking the position of being superior and more competent at all times and conveying the expectation that I will fail while seeming to encourage me. Always I felt that she dealt with me only as a set of needs and problems.

The pattern that I see most clearly is my expecting to lose and to be rejected. This seems to be a part of my response to eveyone in my life, both intimates and strangers. It is combined with a tendency to withdraw from conflict and difficulty, rather than risk failure or loss. I have in fact spent a lot of energy avoiding difficulty and have enjoyed few feelings of successful achievement or satisfying self-expression in the process.

My goal is to increase both the quantity and quality of my risk-taking behavior in many areas of my life. Right now, one of the most difficult times for me is when I'm with Bill and another woman, in a three-way conversation. I withdraw, get uncomfortable and nervously wait for someone or something else to change the situation. In the future, I want to hold my own in initiating conversation when talking with Bill and another woman.

By now you may have discovered through your assertive analysis the areas in which you have difficulty expressing yourself. In your influence analysis you have become aware of negative external influences in your life. The awareness you have gained is the first step toward changing your behavior. The next step involves the development of specific goals and objectives. These goals must be set up in such a manner that you can confront effectively the major barrier which prevents most women from responding assertively: anxiety.

WORKING TO DECREASE ANXIETY

When we get right down to it, most women are reluctant to enter new assertive territory (areas where they are now nonassertive) because of the emotion connected with self-assertion. For example, when a woman who has been afraid to speak up in class decides, "Today's the day. I'm going to answer a question," she will immediately find that her stomach begins to knot up, her hands perspire, her face flushes, and her throat gets dry. The moment that she decides, "Actually, today isn't the day. Tomorrow's the day," all these physiological signals will subside. In other words, when a woman asserts herself in new areas, she will encounter anxiety. When she decides not to assert herself, but to conform instead to her old patterns, the anxiety will disappear. This all sounds rather dismal. After all, no one enjoys anxiety. If assertiveness is so unpleasant, why even try to change?

Fortunately, anxiety is not a permanent companion of self-assertion. When a woman begins to assert herself and finds that the negative consequences she has always expected do not materialize, her anxiety will be reduced. When she finds that the roof does not fall in, the floor does not swallow her up, and people do not run away from her screaming, she begins to relax. With repetition, her anxiety is eliminated. A good example of this anxiety reduction is found in public speaking courses. The first time a woman makes a speech, she typically experiences intense anxiety. By her fourth attempt, she may begin to realize that the audience is not a group of hired assassins. By her tenth speech, she may even begin to enjoy herself.

Joseph Wolpe was the first behaviorist to describe the underlying mechanism by which anxiety responses, initially evoked by assertive behavior, come to be reduced and eliminated. In his book *Psychotherapy by Reciprocal Inhibition,* Wolpe explains that the emotions (anger, feelings of mastery, and so on) which accompany self-assertion are incompatible with anxiety. Since two opposing emotional states cannot exist simultaneously, the feelings engendered by self-assertion gradually come to replace anxiety. Thus my anger at someone cutting in front of me in a line substitutes for my anxiety about speaking up. My enjoyment at having someone respond to my request replaces my anxiety about asking.

In his initial work on assertion training, Wolpe recognized that in some situations anxiety is too pronounced to be overcome. For example, Megan might be so frightened of speaking in front of a large group that she experiences no feeling except anxiety. However, there are other situations where the anxiety response accompanying self-assertion would be lower. Megan might find that she is able to speak to an audience of two without feeling panic. In these situations, her anxiety response would be inhibited by her self-assertion. To take into consideration the degree of anxiety evoked by different assertive encounters, each member in my assertive training group constructs what is known as an assertive hierarchy. Wolpe and Arnold Lazarus were the first behavior therapists to use this systematic, graduated approach to the learning of assertive behavior.

A hierarchy is essentially a list of assertive situations arranged in increasing order of difficulty. The hierarchy provides a format for self-assertion. Moving up the items of a hierarchy is somewhat analagous to climbing the rungs of a ladder. Obviously, it would be foolish to jump to the tenth rung of a ladder without first taking steps one through nine. The same reasoning applies to the assertive hierarchy. If a woman attempts to master the tenth item before mastering the first, she is not likely to succeed.

At this point you may want to take a moment to draw up your own assertive hierarchy. Begin by thinking of a situation where you would like to be assertive. Make sure this first situation is relatively easy; that is, it creates only a small amount of anxiety. This will be your first hierarchy item, the first rung of your ladder. To help you decide on your first hierarchy item, look at your pattern of external influences. Of the people listed who influence you in a negative way, which person is easiest to deal with? Look at your assertive analysis. In which *problem* area of self-assertion do you experience the least anxiety? Put these two bits of information together to form your first hierarchy item.

Next, think of a situation where you would like to assert yourself, but the idea of doing so causes great anxiety. Again, in reviewing your assertive analysis and your influence analysis, who is the most difficult person to deal with? What kind of assertive expression to this person would create the most anxiety? This situation will be the top of your hierarchy, the top rung of your ladder. Choose other encounters that are intermediate in terms of the anxiety they cause. Figure 3.2 illustrates one woman's assertive hierarchy. As you can see, her principle difficulty involves setting limits. The first step of her assertive ladder involves saying "no" to a child, her least difficult external influence. The top rung of her ladder involves setting limits with her most difficult influence: her husband.

The structure that a hierarchy provides serves to focus your attention on those situations which you are now able to confront assertively. It also reminds you not to punish yourself for failing to be assertive in those situations that are too high on your list. As you master the lower items on your hierarchy, you may find that the higher items seem less difficult as well. If we go back to our analogy of a ladder, when a person has climbed to rung five, taking a step to the sixth rung is relatively easy. In moving to step six, a person really goes only the distance of one step,

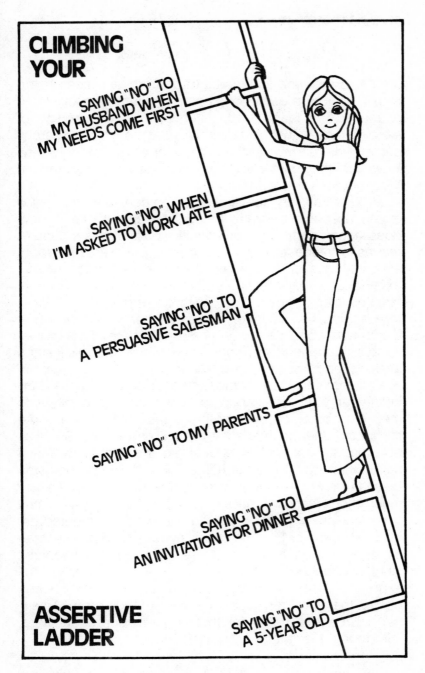

CLIMBING YOUR

SAYING "NO" TO MY HUSBAND WHEN MY NEEDS COME FIRST

SAYING "NO" WHEN I'M ASKED TO WORK LATE

SAYING "NO" TO A PERSUASIVE SALESMAN

SAYING "NO" TO MY PARENTS

SAYING "NO" TO AN INVITATION FOR DINNER

ASSERTIVE LADDER

SAYING "NO" TO A 5-YEAR OLD

FIGURE 3.2   The assertive ladder provides a blueprint for self-assertion. It allows you to overcome your problems one step at a time.

the same distance that it took to go from step one to step two. Table 3.5 presents two sample hierarchies for you to examine. The least difficult items are at the bottom of each hierarchy; the most difficult are at the top. A hierarchy can contain as few as three items or as many as twenty. However, the more situations described, the clearer the blueprint for self-assertion will be.

Although anxiety does not remain a constant companion of the assertive woman, it bears repeating that anxiety does accompany a woman's initial assertive attempts. In the assertiveness workshop, trying out new behaviors almost always leads to a feeling of anxiety. But the internal experience usually is much more intense than its external manifestations. When Nancy was describing her problem in asserting herself, she interrupted her description with a comment about her current emotional state, "This is what always happens to me when I'm nervous. My voice starts shaking, and I have to stop talking."

I immediately gave Nancy my own perception. "I don't hear your voice shaking. You sound clear and direct to me." The other group members gave Nancy the same feedback. She may have felt intense anxiety, but she was not communicating it to the group through her voice. I have found that the same holds true with the woman who blushes or whose hands shake. She notices her anxiety much more than anyone else. Of course, there are times when our anxiety will be picked up, even commented on, by other people. So what? Anxiety is a legitimate human emotion, just as anger, sadness, and joy are. To inhibit self-assertion because of anxiety is to deny oneself full expression as a human being. Gloria Steinem, in a speech before the San Francisco Chapter of "Women in Advertising," made a comment that is very appropriate here: "Stage fright isn't fatal."

TABLE 3.5 Assertive Hierarchies

Hierarchy I

8. Saying to a new male friend, "I'm sorry I can't see you tonight. I have too much schoolwork."
7. Saying to a new male friend, "I really don't feel like cooking tonight. I'd like to go out somewhere nice for dinner."
6. Asking strangers not to smoke in my home.
5. Arguing with department store accountants when I think there's been an error on my bill.
4. Saying to the principal, "I don't agree with your evaluation of me concerning my activity in school events. I feel I can't accept that."
3. Asking unexpected visitors to help with extra housework.
2. Saying "no" to an old friend when he wants me to stay up late with him and go to an activity that doesn't interest me.
1. Limiting the time I spend with women friends when I really want to spend time with my children.

Hierarchy II

9. Accepting criticism without feeling put down. An example is not feeling attacked when someone says, "I don't like the way you did that."
8. Refusing unreasonable requests from family or friends. Saying no without feeling guilty.
7. Expressing negative feelings. Two examples are telling friends I disagree with their opinion and saying, "That makes me angry" or "What you said hurts."
6. Speaking up in a large group (especially of unfamiliar people), making observations, asking questions.
5. Asking not to be interrupted, such as when someone interrupts what I'm saying, learning to say, "I would like to finish my thought before you share yours."
4. Asking for a favor. An example is asking a friend to babysit for me when I have something special to do.
3. Learning not to say, "I'm sorry, but. . . ."
2. Cutting off an inconvenient telephone conversation. Example: a friend who calls with something important to share, but I must go to an important meeting.
1. Expressing positive feelings to the man I am dating; e.g., telling him I love him when he hasn't said he loves me first.

what are you telling yourself?

4

If you are a woman in this society, undoubtedly you have confronted the third obstacle to self-assertion: your own internal dialogue. In fact, in becoming more assertive, opposition from other people is likely to be minor compared to the opposition you give yourself. This opposition comes from what you tell yourself. And, as women, we have learned to talk to ourselves in some extremely negative ways.

The idea that what people tell themselves is influential in how they feel or behave is not a novel one. Cognitive psychologists and psychiatrists such as Albert Ellis and Aaron Beck have based entire systems of psychotherapy on this premise. Basically, as Ellis explains it in his A-B-C framework, a situation or event A does not automatically lead to a specific action C. What determines whether a woman will act or not and the character of her action is what she tells herself at point B.

Since internal self-talk (what we tell ourselves) can have a profound inhibiting effect on self-expression, I usually devote a substantial portion of time during each assertive training workshop to exploring how each woman in the group talks herself out of being assertive. As we go around the circle of members (professional women, students, women raising children, women returning to school), we begin to ferret out some of the self-dialogue (the point B occurrences) that blocks a woman from expressing herself.

I fear that if people really got to know me, I wouldn't measure up.

If I think of something to say, in my mind it's already suspect.

I keep thinking that I might hurt someone's feelings, so I never say anything negative.

I'm afraid that someone will think that I'm not intelligent, so I don't give my opinion.

I have trouble saying what I want or need. Someone may think I'm being too demanding, and they won't like me.

When I talk to my girlfriend, I always end up just listening to her. I guess I tell myself that she wouldn't be interested in what I have to say.

Each of these women, in one way or another, is blocking her own self-assertion by what she is telling herself. One woman is thinking of all the possible dire consequences that might occur if she were to express her feelings. She is catastrophizing, to use a term coined by Ellis. She tells herself, "I wouldn't measure up, *and that would be awful.*" Another woman is denigrating her own impulses toward assertion by labeling them in a negative way. "My desires are *demanding.*" A third woman is setting rigid require- ments for her own self-assertion. She tells herself, "I will express my opinions only *if* I'm sure that other people are interested in what I have to say." Unfortunately, any of these processes (catastrophizing, negative self-labeling, or setting rigid requirements) is sufficient to stop a woman from asserting herself.

As we might assume, the most profound inhibiting effect of self-talk is in nontraditional or androgynous areas. Acting forcefully, taking charge of a situation, or disagreeing with another's opinion are actions that are especially vulnerable to negative self-talk. For example, a woman supervisor may need to tell her assistant that she is making too many errors. Although as supervisor she is in a position of legit- imate authority, she will label herself *perfectionistic* or *bitchy* for feeling annoyed about the errors in the first place. She will think to herself how awful it will be to lose her assistant's friendship (and she of course knows that the friendship will crumble under her criticism). She will decide that she must wait for just the right time to tell her assistant about the errors to make sure the upset is mini- mized. All these inhibiting processes will tend to increase as a woman moves further from the stereotypic feminine role. Let us look at each process in more detail.

NEGATIVE SELF-LABELING

As we noted, negative self-labeling is putting a pejorative tag on one's own assertive impulses or actions.
Most women venturing into androgynous areas face a
barrage of negative self-labels they must overcome before
asserting themselves. A woman calls herself *selfish* when
she thinks of going back to school while her children are
young. She is *bitchy* when she suggests that her husband
share the housework. She is *unfeminine* when she defends
her position on environmental protection at a social gathering. She is *impolite* when she tells her friend's child not
to open the dresser drawers. She is *castrating* when she
suggests to a male colleague that she has a different point
of view. Selfish, bitchy, aggressive, unfeminine—these are
the terms women have listed again and again as interfering
with their self-assertion. In Table 4.1 I have accumulated,
with the help of several assertive training workshops, a
more comprehensive list of negative self-labels.

I initially became aware of negative self-labeling during
the first assertive training group I conducted. The group
was participating in an exercise, originally suggested by
Wolpe and Lazarus, that involved using direct assertive
language. As we went around the circle, the first woman
read, "I've been waiting fifteen minutes, why are you late?"
The second stated, "Would you please stop talking during
the movie?" The third suggested, "This steak is rare. I
ordered it well done." When Jane's turn came, she stated,
"This is a line. Would you please go to the back." She
made the statement softly, and her voice had a hesitant,
apologetic quality. This was in fact Jane's usual manner
of speaking. The group, feeling that even if Jane were
heard she would be ignored, urged her to repeat the
statement—this time more forcefully. Jane began again,
"This is a line. Would you please go to the back." Her voice
was firm, and for the first time she sounded like she really

TABLE 4.1   Negative Self-Labels

1.	Nagging	32.	Old
2.	Cold	33.	Bad mother-in-law
3.	Compulsive	34.	Ugly
4.	Dull	35.	Nosy
5.	Uninteresting	36.	Incapable
6.	Aggressive	37.	Competitive
7.	Castrating	38.	Strong
8.	Immature	39.	Adament
9.	Egotistical	40.	Unladylike
10.	Ungrateful	41.	Too much
11.	Irresponsible	42.	Wears the pants
12.	Unfeminine	43.	Overreactive
13.	Harsh	44.	Troublemaker
14.	Bossy	45.	Childish
15.	Parental	46.	Willful
16.	Domineering	47.	Menstrual
17.	Selfish	48.	Menopausal
18.	Wrong	49.	Stuck up
19.	Demanding	50.	Unimportant
20.	Illogical	51.	Too idealistic
21.	Irrational	52.	Petty
22.	Thoughtless	53.	Frigid
23.	Hysterical	54.	Nitpicker
24.	Crazy	55.	Self-centered
25.	Insensitive	56.	Emotional
26.	Pushy	57.	Nice guy
27.	Impolite	58.	Super wife
28.	Bitchy	59.	Perfect
29.	Stupid	60.	Good mother
30.	Dumb	61.	Gracious hostess
31.	Shrill	62.	Infallible

---

meant what she said. The group spontaneously responded with applause. However, the positive reaction of the nine other group members was not enough to stop Jane's own negative self-labeling. She immediately questioned the group, "But didn't I sound like a bitch?"

The self-label *bitch* (as well as the other labels we have mentioned) is a difficult one for a woman to override. And even if a woman by chance does get past such a barrier, she is likely to present herself in an apologetic, submissive manner, exactly as Jane did. I can imagine, but only with some effort, a man labeling himself a *bastard* because he firmly asked someone to go the end of a line. A man would be more likely to be pleased and view himself as someone willing to take a stand. The discrepant way in which women and men label identical behavior can have a profound influence on how women and men act in the same situation. Negative self-labeling is a major factor in tying women to the stereotypic feminine role.

There is a second, though less frequent, kind of self-labeling that can also lead to restricted responding. In going around the circle of members, accumulating negative self-labels, I noticed that invariably a few women would suggest that positive (or seemingly positive) labels also interfered with self-assertion. Trying to live up to labels like "nice guy," "perfect," "super wife," or "good mother" made certain areas of self-expression off limits. One woman specifically illustrated this in describing her problem in setting limits at work. Although she already had more than enough to do, she found it impossible to refuse a request from her supervisor. Her supervisor, a man, saw her as the "perfect secretary," and she did not assert herself because of fear of losing that image. Any such image or any such role is confining if it prevents a woman from responding according to her feelings or needs at the moment.

SETTING RIGID REQUIREMENTS

Many women limit their self-expression in a second way. They set rigid requirements as to when, where, and how they will be assertive. A woman tells herself, "I will be assertive if. . . ." Only when certain rigidly prescribed conditions are met will she permit herself to express her own feelings and opinions.

In one assertive workshop, I asked each woman to share with the group her major requirement for self-assertion and then discuss with the group the requirements inhibiting influence. We went around the circle, and each woman expressed a condition that applied to her. Anne, a bank auditor, began, "I'll assert myself only if the issue is vital, or at least very important." In discussing the effect of this requirement, Anne acknowledged that it eliminated most of her self-expression. After all, how many of her opinions and feelings (or anyone else's for that matter) are *vital*. Anne made the further observation, "I can see how that criterion does cut off most of what I have to say. I can actually count on one hand the number of times I've given my opinion in a professional meeting."

Another woman, Joan, indicated, "I can speak up if I'm doing it for someone else and not for myself." Joan, like many women, is a good fighter for a friend or an acquaintance. Yet when it comes to expressing her own needs, desires, and limits, her self-assertion falls short. After all, as we have seen, society has not fully supported the view that a woman's needs are legitimate. Joan's requirement is in perfect accord with the stereotypic feminine role in that it negates practically all *self*-assertion.

Eleanor, an attorney for a large corporation, added a third condition, "I'll express myself if I can do so without being emotional." This is another requirement having severe consequences. If Eleanor really abides by this condition, she is in effect cutting off all assertion that matters. We are emotional when something really counts. One woman, in a recent workshop, had actually eliminated one-hundred percent of her assertion of negative feelings by two combined and mutually exclusive requirements. She disallowed assertion "When I'm too intense," meaning when she felt angry. Her second requirement ensured that no assertion would occur when her intense feelings had subsided. By then she ran into the blockade, "I'll assert myself if I haven't waited too long."

Other requirements? "I'll express myself if I can remain congenial." "I'll say something if I'm sure I won't be disliked." Or, "If no one else says what I'm thinking, then I'll say it." A more complete list of rigid requirements is shown in Table 4.2. If a woman habitually filters her assertive impulses through conditions such as these, at the very least she eliminates her spontaneity, a basic characteristic of self-assertion. At worst, she cuts off large areas of self-expression that make up who she is as a unique human being.

CATASTROPHIZING

Catastrophizing is the third process that blocks self-assertion. The term catastrophizing, as we have mentioned, originated with Ellis as a way of describing a particular kind of self-talk. One way to catastrophize is to think of something you would like to say or do and then tell yourself all the horrible consequences that could occur if you followed through on your impulse. Lynn tended to do just this whenever she was annoyed with her boyfriend Bob. Her dialogue with herself went, "If I tell Bob I'm angry at him, he probably won't listen. That will make me feel even worse than I do now. If he does listen, that will really be a disaster. He will decide that he doesn't like me anymore. He will tell me all of the things he dislikes about me, and I'll start crying. He may never want to see me again. And I'll never meet anyone else who will like me. My life will be ruined." This catastrophizing may sound farfetched. Yet many intelligent, capable women fail to take action for themselves because they are anticipating that highly improbable negative consequences will occur.

A second form of catastrophizing goes something like this. "If I ask my boss for a raise, I may not get it." (So

---

TABLE 4.2   Setting Rigid Requirements

I'll be assertive
if it is vital.
if someone is not in a bad mood.
if I can not live with the situation as it stands.
if someone else doesn't do it.
if no one else is around to see me.
if I can't get my husband to do it.
if the other person will be assertive back.
if I have all the facts or information.
if I have done everything else perfectly.
if the other person can take it.
if I am feeling good about myself.
if it's what I should feel.
if I am sure about what I feel.
if I am justified.
if I am dealing with a peer.
if I won't hurt anyone's feelings.
if I will still be liked.
if no one will be angry at me.
if my assertion is without flaw.
if I can be unobtrusive.
if I'm perfect.
if it's part of my job.
if it's a matter of principle.
if I know the outcome.
if the time is right.
if I don't antagonize.
if it's *really* going to bug me.
if I can be witty, eloquent, and brilliant.

---

far we have a fairly accurate statement of fact.) But then a woman adds, *"and that would be awful."* This catch phrase repeated often enough can completely stifle self-expression. Assertiveness does involve taking some risks. I may not get the job I apply for. Someone may be busy when I call. My request might not be granted. I may hurt someone's feelings. Yet when a woman can change an anxious question such as "What if someone thinks I'm a woman's libber?'', implying *"that would be awful,"* to "So what, if someone thinks I'm a woman's libber?", she has taken a major step toward self-assertion. Table 4.3 lists several common catastrophic self-statements. The first three statements are slight modifications of Ellis' list of irrational ideas that cause disturbances.

SELF-PUNISHMENT

There is a final form of negative self-talk that occurs *after* a woman has asserted herself: self-criticism or self-punishment. Subjectively, the experience of self-punishment is somewhat like having a scolding, critical person following you around, watching your every move, a person who is never pleased and never satisfied. In one assertive workshop, we saw a vivid demonstration of self-punishment when Charlotte, a self-employed writer, described her habit of, as she called it, "getting down on herself." "When I do something wrong, I tell myself, 'You idiot, you never learn. How can you make the same mistake over and over again!'" As she talked, Charlotte began to hit her knee with a pencil. When I called Charlotte's attention to what she was doing, she was surprised. She had not been aware of her silent spanking. In a two-minute nutshell, Charlotte had given the group a clear example of self-punishment. She had beat herself figuratively over the head and literally over the knee.

Unfortunately, our culture seems to promote strong habits of self-criticism along with correspondingly weak habits of self-reward. As Michael Mahoney and Carl Thoreson note in their book *Self-Control: Power to the Person,* positive self-evaluation is discouraged by society as "bragging," whereas stoic self-denial or stringent self-criticism is admired.

The cost of self-criticism is high. A major characteristic of clinical depression, which we have seen affects women more than men, is excessive self-disparagement. De-

---

TABLE 4.3   Catastrophic Self-Talk

It would be awful
if every person in the world doesn't like and approve of me.
if I ever make a mistake.
if I can't find a perfect solution.
if someone doesn't want to see me again.
if I am wrong.
if my opinion is challenged.
if someone gets angry at me.
if I am disapproved of.
if I get angry.
if I get emotional.
if I lose my job.
if my relationship doesn't work out.
if I am criticized.
if I can't think of anything to say.
if I am rejected.
if I blush or if my voice is shaky.
if everyone doesn't consider me to be a nice person.
if I am accused of being unfeminine.
if someone doesn't listen to me.
if someone knows more than I do.

---

pressed people devalue themselves. For example, Beck and his colleagues have found that depressed adults evaluate their performance in a significantly harsher manner than nondepressed adults, even though their achievement is actually identical.

Although a woman may not become severely depressed every time she talks to herself in a negative way, the effects of self-punishment usually can be felt immediately. D. C. Rimm and S. Litvak performed a simple experiment that vividly demonstrated how self-punishment can influence a person's emotional state. These investigators had one group of students read critical sentences, and a second group of students read neutral statements to themselves. As the students were reading, physiological measures were taken. Only the group reading critical statements became emotionally aroused, reacting negatively to the criticisms, even though they were supplied by someone else. If simply reading a critical sentence can cause such reactions, imagine the effect of a woman's own self-disparagement on her feeling state.

Estella, a social worker, attended one of my two-day assertive workshops for professional women. After completing the first full day of the workshop, Estella decided to try out what she had learned and assert herself on the way home. She stopped at a grocery store to get change, a fairly simple assertive action, but something she had always been reluctant to do. She handed the clerk a $5 bill, and he gave her back five ones. Although she actually wanted some quarters, Estella decided not to ask for them. She told herself that the line behind her was getting too long and that she had already taken too much time. Notice that no one else had said a word. Estella herself stopped her second assertive attempt. When she returned to the group the next morning, she was feeling annoyed with herself. She had no positive feelings about her assertion the night before.

What had occurred was fairly clear. Estella had asserted herself once in a situation that was difficult for her. She had been unable to follow through with a second assertion. Although there were two separate actions, all of Estella's focus was on the second failure. She barely acknowledged her first success. This pattern is one which many women share. They overemphasize self-punishment and completely forget about self-reward.

It is not difficult to see from this example how habitual self-criticism can have a detrimental effect upon future self-expression. If a woman punishes herself every time a new attempt at self-assertion overhits or underhits the mark, she will soon give up. Self-assertion just will not be worth the pain and contempt that inevitably follows self-criticism. A new behavior must be rewarded if it is to occur again.

Unfortunately, many people learn to set exceedingly stringent standards for themselves at a very early age. For example, young children under certain conditions will refuse to give themselves available candy because they feel their performance on a task has not been good enough. Albert Bandura and his colleagues have done numerous studies in this area. They have found that the children who adopt the most austere standards for rewarding themselves are those who are exposed to an adult model who has an excessively high criterion of self-reinforcement. Children are particularly influenced by an adult model who is both demanding and nonnurturing. Many parents provide such a model of rigid self-denial to their children. Anything less than perfection is devalued, and a mistake is seen as a catastrophe. Without doubt, a rigid self-punishment structure can significantly retard the learning of self-assertion.

FROM SELF-CRITICISM TO
SELF-SUPPORT

Let us assume that you talk to yourself in a negative way. Have you been able to identify any specific incidents where you have talked yourself out of expressing your feelings by setting rigid requirements, by catastrophizing, or by negative (or positive) self-labeling? Have there been times when you have criticized yourself so much after an assertive attempt that you have felt reluctant to try again?

If you have answered yes to any of these questions, you may want to take a moment to write down the specific self-labels that block your self-assertion. What requirements cut off your ability to express yourself? What catastrophies frighten you so that you do not speak up? Write them down. Many women find that one pejorative label, one unrealistic image, one requirement, or one catastrophe

69

stifles totally appropriate and legitimate self-assertion. Which label, requirement, and catastrophe do you find yourself using most often?

Negative self-label   _____

Positive self-label   _____

Rigid requirement   _____

Catastrophe   _____

In examining your negative self-talk, you might also want to consider whether or not you are in the habit of rewarding yourself. In other words, when your self-assertion is anything less than eloquent, witty, and brilliant, do you fail to give yourself proper credit? Do you follow your assertive attempts with criticism rather than reward? If there is a punishing self-statement you habitually use, write it down also.

Self-criticism   _____

Becoming aware of how you interfere with your own self-assertion is the first step in changing how you talk to yourself. The second step involves keeping an accurate record of just how often your negative self-talk occurs. This involves self-monitoring, the systematic observation of your own behavior. Social scientists have found that self-monitoring by itself sometimes leads to change in the behavior that is being recorded. However, the main purpose of self-observation is to increase your awareness of the specific factors that influence your assertion.

This is how we began with Meg, a graduate student in nursing. When she first started therapy, Meg was depressed and constantly anxious. She was also, as she reluctantly admitted, very lonely. She had no real friends, women or men. Meg lived in a rooming house with seven other students, but she tended to avoid them as much as possible by staying in her room. When she did encounter someone, she would review the conversation they had had time and time again. Most of Meg's rehashing involved finding fault with something she had said or done. Although Meg knew that any minor situation could lead to her punishing herself for hours, she had never actually counted the frequency of her critical self-statements. She decided to do so by keeping a running record of the number of times each day she criticized herself. She kept the record by using a small portable hand counter. To Meg's genuine surprise, she found that she punished herself well over one-hundred times each day. The constant barrage of aversive stimulation was clearly affecting her life.

At this level of awareness, Meg was ready to take a third step in changing how she talked to herself. She interrupted her self-critical tirade with the firm statement "Stop." This "thought-stopping" procedure was pioneered by Wolpe, a leading behavior therapist cited previously. Meg found that by shouting "stop" (either silently or out loud), she could at least temporarily interrupt the familiar negative phrases. However, Meg found that unless she concentrated on or became involved in something else, her negative thoughts came back. As Meg explained, "It's like not knowing how to talk to myself, except in the old critical ways. Even when I stop punishing myself, there's a vacuum left and nothing new to fill it up."

The development of something new takes genuine effort and concentration. Only in recent years has the psychological importance of positive or supportive self-talk been carefully examined by behavioral psychologists. Donald Meichenbaum and Roy Cameron have spent much time looking at how people can learn to modify what they tell themselves. They have found that supportive self-talk, like any other skill, must be practiced before it has any influence in changing maladaptive habits or feelings. Many people also find that before they can change their negative self-dialogue, they have to observe someone

FIGURE 4.1 Notice how negative self-labels, rigid requirements, and catastrophies block her spontaneous ideas.

else demonstrating alternatives to self-criticism. Without a model of self-support, many people can think of nothing positive to say to themselves.

This was essentially the problem Meg faced. She had no repertoire of supportive self-talk from which to draw. To overcome this obstacle, I put together a list of positive self-sentences I had accumulated from working with various assertive training groups. These sentences are presented in Table 4.4. Several of the statements are modifications of Ellis' basic irrational assumptions; one statement comes directly from the title of Thomas Harris' book *I'm Okay, You're Okay*. I asked Meg to practice making these positive comments to herself each day. You too might want to try out these statements. Add some of your own if you wish. These supportive self-statements are useful at three points: when preparing for self-assertion, when engaging in an assertive dialogue, and when assessing the assertive experience.

I suggested to Meg that in order not to forget to practice the statements, she might want to use an external cue as a signal to verbally support herself. Women who smoke can use "lighting up a cigarette" as a signal to say something positive to themselves. However, Meg decided that her own internal feeling of anxiety was clear enough to serve as a "warning" to begin talking to herself in a different way. Whenever she became aware of any self-punishment or negative feelings, she told herself to stop. Then Meg supported herself. This involved something as simple as acknowledging that she did not have to be perfect or that she was not in this world to live up to other people's expectations. Meg sometimes went further and made contact with the environment. She called a friend or took a walk. She allowed herself to check out any negative perceptions with someone else. That is, if Meg thought someone was angry at her, she asked them if her inference was correct. By not requiring herself to be a mind reader,

---

TABLE 4.4   Positive Self-Statements

Preparing for self-assertion
No negative statements. I'm just going to express my feelings.
My purpose here is not to be liked and approved of by everyone.
It isn't awful to make a mistake.
I'll express my feelings. If I'm honest and direct, then I've been assertive.
I'm not going to apologize for where I am now.
Stop catastrophizing. I'm doing them a favor by letting them know what
   I feel.

Handling an assertive encounter
I'll go at my own rate. I can back up if I'm feeling overwhelmed.
I have a perfect right to express my feelings.
Everyone doesn't have to agree with me for me to be okay.
It's okay to feel nervous. That's part of entering new territory.
There is no perfect way of saying this.
I can't *not* think of something to say if I just express my feelings.
If my mind goes blank, it's okay to say "My mind has just gone blank."

Giving yourself credit
I'm really glad that I was honest.
I'm really pleased. That was hard for me to say.
I'm still feeling a little shaky, but I did it. I deserve a lot of credit.
I was terrific.
Hey, the roof didn't fall in. I'm getting better every time.
They didn't respond as I would have liked, but that's not important. The
   important thing is that I asserted myself.

Meg was able to find out where she stood in relationship to another person. She no longer spent her time wondering about another person's feelings.

By our last meeting Meg had developed a romantic relationship with a fellow student. She was no longer chronically anxious or depressed. As a parting comment, I cautioned Meg that there would always be situations where she would not assert herself in the way she desired. Her reply actually surprised me. "That really isn't a problem anymore. Whenever I don't assert myself now, I say 'So what. Now I'm not assertive in this area. I will be in the future. Some people who are very assertive have other problems that I don't have. Not asserting myself isn't a crime.'" Self-support had obviously become a habit with Meg.

Having examined how women are inhibited by lack of awareness, anxiety, and negative self-talk, we can now turn to the fourth obstacle to self-assertion: not knowing what to say.

the verbal message: what you say

5

One morning, as I was going out to run some errands, my husband called me over to the side of the house. He told me that he wanted to dig out the weeds and crabgrass, and he wondered what he should do with a couple of bushes.

At that point, I wanted to tell him that I didn't want him to do anything with them until we had had time to settle on a landscaping plan. But I was concerned that I would hurt his feelings and cause him to stop working if I said anything, so I told him it didn't matter to me where he put the bushes.

When I returned, he had denuded the entire area and put the bushes into another flower bed. They looked terrible where they were, but I smiled bravely and unenthusiastically said, "They look fine, honey." A few minutes later, my husband dug up a plant that I had planted a few days earlier and replanted it in a slightly different place.

I decided it was time for me to assert myself, but I was annoyed at the previous incidents. Rather than being assertive, I said, "Don't do that! You'll ruin the plant!" in a louder voice than was necessary. Charlie was a little sharp himself when he replied that the plant would not have lived where I had planted it.

That did it! I burst into tears and ran into the house. Charlie, when we discussed my crying, could not understand why I was so upset, and I was unhappy with my behavior. However, at the time, I was not able to pinpoint the reason for that unhappiness or to see how my behavior could have differed.

This nonassertive experience was detailed by Elizabeth as part of a class assignment. Had Elizabeth been assertive in her interaction with Charlie, her verbal message would have differed in, at least, three basic ways. In being assertive, she would have expressed herself *directly, honestly,* and *spontaneously,* attributes of self-assertion outlined by Herbert Fensterheim. In other words, Elizabeth would have listened to her feelings and said in the beginning, "Charlie, I'd prefer that you don't do anything with the bushes until we settle on a landscaping plan." By doing this, in all probability she would have avoided the subsequent misunderstanding, the outburst, and the tears.

Direct, honest, and spontaneous self-assertion, however, goes against the teachings of the traditional feminine role. Women learn at an early age to suppress their true feelings instead of asserting them. Patricia described such a situation when she wrote, "As a child and young woman, I was taught by my family that one should never be obvious. Courtesy, deference, self-control, and subtlety were the appropriate behaviors. Motive should never be clear to others; women should be devious and indirect." Patricia's experience is not an unfamiliar one to women. The disguise of one's true feelings, especially negative ones, is a hall-mark of stereotypic femininity. To change this pattern, to learn how to respond assertively, many women need to become intimately acquainted with assertive verbal com-munication, with exactly what directness, honesty, and spontaneity involve.

DIRECTNESS

Directness, first of all, means stating exactly what you feel or what you think. If you are direct, you are not subtle, sneaky, or manipulative. You have no use for feminine wiles or hints. Instead, if you are direct, you let another person know out loud your feelings, needs, and limits. You voice your feelings verbally, rather than through your actions. If you are angry, everyone in the room may know it because you are slamming doors, shuffling papers, or refusing to look at anyone. However, until you have directly stated, "I am angry with you" to the person toward whom your anger is directed, you cannot claim to have been assertive. In groups I conduct, woman after woman says, "But surely my friend (husband, son, daughter) knew that I was hurt (annoyed, disappointed)." Perhaps they did, but unless you have expressed these feelings directly you cannot be *sure.* Of even more importance, they may not know *why* you are upset with them.

The opposite of directness is sneakiness. Nonassertive people are often "sneaky." They try to get what they want in subtle and indirect ways. Powerless and oppressed people (such as women) almost always learn to operate in an indirect manner. For many women this has meant getting what they want through cunning and the use of feminine wiles rather than by direct self-assertion. This process is beautifully illustrated in Ibsen's 1879 play *A Doll's House.* In the beginning of the play, Nora portrays the stereotypic feminine woman. Her lack of directness is spotlighted in one early scene when she sneaks a piece of candy in her own home, as if she were a naughty child. However, as the play progresses, the role through which Nora interacts with Torvald, her husband, gradually changes. After Nora confronts a life and death crisis, she begins to shift from plaything to adult woman. Her change is accompanied by an increase in direct communication.

NORA: Sit down here, Torvald—you and I have much to say to each other.

TORVALD: You alarm me, Nora, and I don't understand you.

NORA: No, that's just it—you don't understand me and I've never understood you either before tonight. No, you mustn't interrupt me. You must simply listen to what I say. Torvald, this is a settling of accounts.

As Nora talks further, she described her former lack of self-assertion.

NORA: When I was at home with Papa, he told me his opinion about everything, and so I had the same opinion. And if I differed from him, I concealed the fact because he wouldn't have liked it. He called me his doll-child, and he played with me just as I used to play with my dolls. And when I came to live in your house—

TORVALD: What sort of an expression is that to use about our marriage!

NORA (undisturbed):   I mean that I was simply transferred out of Papa's hands into yours. You arranged everything according to your own tastes, and so I got the same tastes as you . . . or else I pretended to. I am really not quite sure which . . . I think . . . sometimes the one and sometimes the other."

Nora's directness effects a shift in Torvald's reactions. As Nora threatens to leave, he chides, "You're out of your mind. I won't allow it—I forbid it." Nora stands firm to her decision, his chide changes to the appeal, "Nora—can I never be more than a stranger to you?"

The direct self-assertion Nora models does not occur automatically. Even when a woman is aware that she operates indirectly, she may find herself unable to change. Awareness alone does not lead to change for most women. For change to occur, awareness must be accompanied by practice. New methods must replace those learned in childhood. Joyce, for example, returned home after the first day of assertive training promising herself that she would directly express her feelings. She had someone specifically in mind, her friend Jenny. Jenny habitually called Joyce every night around 7:00. Joyce would answer the phone, interrupt her dinner, and talk for ten minutes or more before she returned to a cold plate.

This time the phone range at 7:00, but Joyce did not answer. Instead she completed her dinner. She felt mildly anxious about the unanswered telephone. What if it were her mother calling long distance rather than Jenny? What if there were some emergency? But she steeled herself against her anxiety and finished eating. At 8:00 the telephone rang again. This time Joyce did answer. Jenny demanded, "Where were you?"

Joyce replied, "So what else is new?", and after a brief pause Jenny and Joyce conversed as usual.

Joyce had intended to assert herself, but she had not yet acquired the skill of expressing herself directly. Not answering the telephone, Joyce's first indirect action, simply delayéd her necessary assertion. Joyce's indirectness served only to increase her anxiety because she knew Jenny would call again. In addition, by making herself unavailable for an emergency or a long distance call, Joyce was potentially hurting herself.

When she did answer the telephone, Joyce's response "So what else is new" was another indirect way of letting

Jenny know that she did not want to be called at dinner. In fact, it was so indirect that when Joyce shared her experience with the assertive group, no one deciphered the message she had wanted to convey. As for Jenny, who knows how she interpreted Joyce's comment? Jenny may have decided that Joyce was angry about something that happened two weeks previously. Jenny may stop calling at all. Or she may ignore the comment and continue to call at dinnertime. Joyce's indirect expression was little better than no response at all.

Had Joyce expressed herself *directly,* the interchange might have gone something like this:

SCENE (7:00):   Joyce has just sat down to dinner. The telephone rings.

JOYCE: Hello.

JENNY: Hi, what's happening?

JOYCE: Hi, Jenny, I'm just setting down to dinner. Why don't I call you back in about an hour. (Setting limits)

JENNY (surprised, taken aback):   Okay.

Scene (One hour later. Joyce has finished dinner. She calls Jenny back)

JOYCE: Hi Jenny.

JENNY: What kept you so long?

JOYCE: I just finished dinner. But that brings up something I would like to talk to you about. (Self-initiation) I usually have dinner between 7:00 and 8:00, and I would prefer that we talk after I have finished. Otherwise, I have to interrupt my dinner. (Setting limits)

JENNY (critically):   Well, you never told me that before.

JOYCE: That's right. But I would feel more comfortable talking after 8:00. (Reaffirming her limit)

JENNY: Okay.

Recognizing that direct self-assertion takes practice, the assertive training group participates in a number of exercises that permit and encourage assertive expression. One such exercise emphasizes the use of direct assertive language. You may wish to see how comfortable you feel with an assertive verbal message by following the instructions I give to group members. As the beginning step, write down five direct statements that you would like to be able to assert. Make your statements relevant to problem situations that you confronted yesterday, last week, or last year, or to situations that you are anticipating in the future. For example, if you are unable to express negative feelings, you might choose to write statements that express anger, resentment, or annoyance. If you have difficulty setting limits, give the message "no" in several of your sentences. Try to direct your statements to those people who influence you in a negative way.

The instructions for this exercise sound easy. Yet you may find that expressing your feelings without disguise is not such a simple matter. We learn not to be direct for a purpose. That purpose may be to decrease our vulnerability to the reactions of other people, to avoid criticism, or even to keep ourselves in the dark about our own feelings.

I have accumulated a large number of direct statements, written by women who have taken my assertive training course. Table 5.1 groups these statements according to the four principle areas of self assertion: positive feelings, negative feelings, limit setting, and self-initiation. You may wish to try out some of these assertions along with those of your own. Say the statements aloud, preferably to someone else. Practice them several times until the language becomes familiar. The directness of the statements may seem strange at first. If your reaction is "I could never say that," look further to see what internal prohibitions you have learned against assertive language. Examine any negative self labels, "impolite," "abrupt," or any catastrophies, "I will hurt someone's feelings," that are getting in your way.

The major value of direct verbal assertion is that it decreases the probability our message will be misunderstood. As we will see later in more detail, any message

---

TABLE 5.1   Direct Assertive Statements

Positive feelings

I really like the way you did that.

You look attractive tonight.

I wanted you to know how much I enjoyed the meeting.

Thank you for appreciating me and being concerned about me as a human being, not just an employee.

I really enjoy being with you.

I think that Linda deserves a promotion. Her work is outstanding and goes far beyond her present position.

I like the way you handled matters at work.

You are really witty.

I love you.

Self-initiation

I need your comfort and understanding right now.

I'd like to go out somewhere for dinner.

Will you help me take these groceries out to the car?

I want to have some experience as a buyer. I'm confident that I can do a good job if I get the chance.

I'd like to know you better.

I don't want to be coy with you. I like you and would like to feel free to call you or write you.

Let's split the check

I would like to be able to tell you my feelings. Would you be willing to listen?

I want more information about this prescription.

What is your fee?

I would like to bring up something that's bothering me. I feel some people are doing more work than others.

I'm starting to do something positive with the rest of my life and I'm starting right now.

Limit setting

I understand that you would like to read this book, but I have a no lend policy.

I'd rather not answer that.

That is not one of my priorities.

I was in line first.

I'd like to pay my own way.

TABLE 5.1   Direct Assertive Statements *(cont'd.)*

Ethnic jokes bother me. I don't want to hear them.
I don't want to hear critical things about other people.
I would like to be alone tonight.
I don't doubt your concern, but I want to make my own decision.
I don't feel like making love tonight.
That's not my responsibility. Please find someone else to take care of it.
Thanks, but I don't need any help.
I don't think that this is part of my job description.
I wish that you wouldn't make commitments for me.
I'd rather talk a little later. Right now, I need to collect my thoughts.
I would appreciate your not smoking.
I would like to think further about that before deciding what to do.

Negative feelings
I resent your not showing up on time.
I don't agree with you.
I want you to stop that. I don't like what you're doing.
The project that you just completed for me is not what I had hoped for.
I feel put down by comments like that.
I am annoyed that you want me to make an exception for you.
I was disappointed that we had a change in plans.
I am not satisfied with the work done on my car. I would like you to correct it without charge.
I don't like you taking my lab book off my desk without asking.
I feel that I'm doing all the reaching out to you.
I am unhappy that you give your secretary instructions through me.
I am furious that you did not call me.

---

can be misinterpreted at several points. The message I *intend* to convey may be different from the one I *send,* which may be different from the one you *receive.* Because of this potential for misunderstanding, it is very important that I send to you the clearest message possible. It is important that I send you a message devoid of subtleties, manipulation, or disguise.

In sending you a clear message, I must remember that I am going against the diplomacy of the stereotypic feminine role. Before I am able to be completely direct, I may need to eliminate old habits of unnecessarily apologizing and explaining, of giving only a limited picture, and of talking through another person instead of for myself. We will explore each of these self-obscuring habits in detail.

Excessive apologies and explanations

The amount of time spent apologizing and explaining becomes clear to many women as they compose their assertive statements. In fact, some women find that they preface any direct assertion with an apology. As I was constructing the table of assertive statements from notes of former groups, I came across one woman's list of ten sentences. Each began with the phrase "I'm sorry." One of the statements was particularly striking. "I'm sorry, but I can't commit myself to taking care of your dog two years in advance!" A simpler statement such as "I really don't want to make that kind of commitment so far in advance" would have sufficed. By this illustration, I do not want to create the impression that to be assertive means never to apologize. If an apology is sincere, "I'm sorry" is an assertive statement. However, many times "I'm sorry" is simply tacked on by force of habit as a way of reducing anxiety rather than from a genuine expression of concern.

Similarly, many women tend to offer excessive and unnecessary explanations for their behavior. Mitzi spent at least ten minutes in one group attempting to omit the explanations from a statement she had written. Mitzi's assertion was directed toward her mother, with whom she had always had a difficult time standing her ground. Mitzi had learned as a child to defend her decisions with numerous explanations and justifications, and as she practiced her statement in the group, this habitual pattern was still evident. Mitzi sounded like a little girl, half appealing to and half standing against a powerful adult.

Mitzi wanted to say, "Mother, I want you to know that I let Marilyn have the coat that you gave me several years ago." However, every time she made this statement to another group member, Mitzi was unable to stop with the direct assertion. Instead, she continued, "Mom, you know how much Marilyn needs a coat. She lives in Vermont and the weather there is much more severe than in San Francisco. And besides, I could never quite get the coat to fit. The sleeves just didn't hang right on me, but it fits Marilyn very well." Each time Mitzi practiced, there was another explanation or justification. It took Mitzi five times before she was able to confine herself to her one sentence assertion. Her explanations, the group had pointed out, would not make her mother feel any better about her giving the coat away. They simply put her in an old "one down" position.

I heard from Mitzi several weeks after the group ended. She had called her mother and told her that she could not visit during Christmas. She did not offer any elaborate explanations for her decision but simply conveyed to her mother that she would genuinely like to visit but could not comfortably get away from her work. To Mitzi's surprise, her mother was not upset. Her own fear that Mitzi did not want to see her had been responded to. She needed no further explanation.

Giving the full picture

In telling her mother that she could not visit, Mitzi had avoided the justifications and defensive explanations that made up her childhood pattern. However, she did not go so far in the opposite direction that she neglected to offer her mother legitimate information. Had Mitzi said only, "I'm not visiting you this Christmas" without expressing her desire to see her mother, her mother might have responded very differently. There is a fine line between defensive justification and giving the full picture. Mitzi successfully distinguished between the two.

In contrast, Josie, a college senior majoring in elementary education, fell into the trap of withholding needed information. Josie was going to graduate in a few months and was spending her last semester student teaching. Josie liked children, but at the end of an eight-hour day she discovered that she just wanted to be around adults. In her spare time, Josie took a course in Chinese cooking one night a week. When a college friend, Martha, asked her if she would like to try out her new culinary skills, Josie readily agreed. Martha would buy the ingredients, and Josie would prepare the meal. It sounded like fun. They made plans to get together on Saturday, along with Martha's husband and Josie's boyfriend.

About the middle of the week, Martha called Josie to say that another couple would be in town and that she had invited them to join the Chinese dinner. Martha casually mentioned that the couple had a five-year-old daughter and a two-year-old son.

As Josie explained, "Chinese cooking takes a tremendous amount of time. Everything has to be chopped. Adding two other adults (not to mention the two children) about doubles the preparation time. After working hard all week, I couldn't see myself standing in front of a kitchen counter all Saturday afternoon, chopping vegetables. I didn't particularly want to spend my Saturday around children either. Feeling really overwhelmed, I called Martha back on the phone and told her that I wanted to cancel our dinner arrangements. When she asked why, I said 'Well, I just don't like to be around children.' I guess she was taken aback by my answer. I haven't heard from her since."

Josie's explanation that she didn't want to be around children was actually the least of her reasons for not wanting to prepare dinner. Josie's limited verbal message did not convey the information necessary for Martha to understand her position. More to the point might have been the statement, "Martha, I have changed my mind about preparing a Chinese meal. The main reason is that the preparation time for more than two couples is just too long. I need my Saturday afternoons to recuperate. I'd like to try again when other people aren't visiting."

Talking for yourself

A direct verbal message demands that we speak for ourselves: "I want," "I don't like," "I am not going to." Again, this sounds simple. However, in talking for ourselves, in using the word "I," we are again going against the dictates of the feminine role. Many women are taught that "I" is a dirty word. English teachers inveigh against the word "I." "I" indicates selfishness and self-centeredness, according to many in authority. Only recently, I saw a wall plaque that called "I" the one most useless word in the English language.

The prohibition against the word "I" leads many women to speak indirectly and to minimize their power. We learn to speak through others instead of for ourselves. One way of speaking through other people is to use the word "you" instead of the word "I." Joanna, a second-year law student, was aware that she often fell into this pattern. She shared with the group an incident involving Jerome, the attorney for whom she clerked part time. On this particular occasion, Jerome neglected to add some important information to a document Joanna was preparing. But rather than directly assert herself, Joanna suggested, "Don't you think that you might want to add a section on tariffs?" Joanna explained that she would have felt uncomfortable saying, "*I* think that this document needs a section on tariffs. Why don't you look it over and see what you think?"

Joanna's discomfort with the latter statement in all likelihood stems from the fact that it expresses her own competence. By stating, "*I* think this document needs a section on tariffs," Joanna takes responsibility (and credit) for the idea of adding another section. However, her latter statement is not aggressive or intrusive. As the person in charge, Jerome still has the option of accepting or rejecting her suggestion. In my own view, Joanna's first statement, "Don't you think you might want to add a section on tariffs," was condescending to both her and her employer because it implied that Jerome was too insecure to handle her competence. The use of the word "you" also detracted from Joanna's presentation of herself as a knowledgeable law student.

Besides minimizing her power, the word "you" allows a woman to avoid taking responsibility for her own feelings and desires. Thus the question, "Don't you like this piece of pottery?" may be an indirect way of saying "I like this pottery." The question "Are you sure that you should do that?" usually means "I don't want you to do that." Direct verbal assertion requires that a woman ask a question only when she is actually seeking information. At other times, she must express her feelings and opinions as "I" statements.

In addition to the weakening of a statement by the use of "you," there is another way in which women avoid sending a powerful verbal message. This second way involves substituting the editorial "we" for the individual "I." "We are too tired to go to the movies" really means "I don't feel like going to the movies." "We need to be more considerate" substitutes for "I want you to call me when you are going to be late." Including other people into an assertive statement reduces a woman's directness and with it her individual power and responsibility. And, as we shall see, "we" statements often go further to intrude upon other people's rights. The quick retort "speak for yourself" frequently signals that a "we" message has not been appreciated.

Susan wanted to practice asserting herself to a group of her ski friends with whom she has rented a cabin for the winter. Susan had taken charge of the financial arrangements and had leased the cabin in her own name for the group. Although the lease was due to expire, some people wanted to continue renting the cabin. Susan herself had finished skiing for the season, and she did not want to take legal responsibility for an extended lease.

We rehearsed the situation in the assertive training group, with several members playing Susan's ski friends. Susan approached them and expressed, "I have decided that we won't renew the lease for another month. So we need to set up a schedule to clean up the cabin. We only have a couple more weeks to tie things up." After this initial assertion, Susan listened to feedback from the group. Several of the people participating in the rehearsal told Susan that they had felt irritated about what she had said. She had sounded bossy to them.

I asked Susan to replay the scene talking for herself, using "I" rather than "we." She repeated, "I have decided that *I* don't want to continue to be responsible for the lease, so I am going to tie everything up with the owner of the cabin. I've heard that several people want to keep the cabin until April. It's fine with me if someone else takes over the lease, but *I* don't want to be legally responsible for the cabin any longer." This time Susan took responsibility only for her own feelings and actions. She left the other people free to do whatever they chose to do. Not surprisingly, the other group members no longer felt irritated with her assertion. Susan had left them the space to make their individual decisions.

HONESTY

The second attribute of self-assertion is honesty. By being honest you express what you really feel. Not what you should feel; not what the feminine role would have you feel; not what your listener wants you to feel; not even what you might wish to feel. Honesty involves asserting your feelings exactly as they are, independent of any shoulds or value judgments or role restrictions. The adult Nora in *A Doll's House* also demonstrates honest self-assertion. As Torvald appeals to her that she should remain with him because of her sacred duty as wife and mother, Nora honestly replies,

> I don't believe that any longer. I believe that before all else I am a reasonable human being—just as you are . . . or at all events that I must try and become one. I know quite well, Torvald, that most people would think you right, and views of that kind are to be found in books, but I can no longer content myself with what most people say, with what is found in books. I must think over things myself and get to understand them.

Nora's assertion shows her progression from an external should system to a reliance on her internal feelings. She is no longer conducting her life by the prescription of books or by the judgments of other people. She is instead reowning her own power to control and be in charge of her life.

Karen Horney, the renowned psychoanalyst, has a chapter in her book *Neurosis and Human Growth* titled "The Tyranny of the Should." In this chapter Horney describes how an individual learns to mold herself into an idealized image. The image demanded by a woman's should system may have little or nothing to do with who a woman actually is as a unique human being, but these inner dictates can and do control and direct her behavior.

Imagine the effect on a woman of the following shoulds detailed by Horney. (I have replaced the pronoun *he* by the pronoun *she*.) A woman

> should be the utmost of honesty, generosity, considerateness, justice, dignity, courage, unselfishness. She should be the

perfect lover, wife, teacher. She should be able to endure everything, should like everybody, should love her parents, her husband, her country. She should never feel hurt, and she should always be serene and unruffled. She should always enjoy life. . . . She should never be tired or fall ill. . . . She should be able to do things in one hour which can only be done in two or three hours.

A woman caught in this process allows her should system to override her real feelings. Horney comments that a person may check or inhibit so many wishes and feelings that a general emotional deadness ensues. In every group, I hear women express how their shoulds choke off their feelings. One woman explained in a discussion about this issue, "Now I have a hard time even knowing what I think or what I want. If I don't like something, I ask myself 'Why don't I like it?', 'Shouldn't I like it?'" Of equal importance, I see women overriding their honest assertion because of their should system. For example, Sally said nothing while a friend's two-year old played with and broke several shells in her prized collection, although her stomach was in a tight knot. Sally's "should system" had dictated that "Children are more important than possessions. You shouldn't be so materialistic." Sally was aware of her feelings, but her shoulds inhibited any assertive action.

SPONTANEITY

Spontaneity, the third characteristic of an assertive verbal message, means immediate self-expression. When a woman is spontaneous, she asserts her feelings as soon as possible. Andrew Salter, a pioneer of assertive training, emphasizes in his book *Conditioned Reflex Therapy* that spontaneity is crucial to emotional well being. Salter comments, "When we pause to consider what we have done when we felt happiest, we will recognize that we spoke without thinking. We expressed our innermost feelings. We did not waste time and energy percolating."

Spontaneity is perhaps the most difficult aspect of self-assertion to master. The simple reason is that a person's spontaneous reaction is usually aggressive, not assertive. If someone breaks into line in front of me, my spontaneous reaction might be to trip that person or at the very least to give her or him "a piece of my mind." However, these are aggressive, not assertive, responses. It takes time and practice for me to spontaneously express, "This is a line. Would you please go to the back." To be spontaneously assertive a woman must learn to recognize her internal feelings and then translate those feelings into an assertive message.

Spontaneity is particularly important in expressing negative feelings and setting limits. If I do not express my negative feelings or set my limits spontaneously, one or two consequences will invariably occur. I will withdraw, either by physically leaving the situation or by becoming emotionally distant, or I will explode. If a friend habitually keeps me waiting, and I do not spontaneously tell my friend of my annoyance or state my time limits, I will begin to think to myself, "I really don't like so and so anyway. There really isn't any reason for us to get together so often." In other words, I will begin to accumulate negative feelings and withdraw from interacting with my friend. George Bach, author of *The Intimate Enemy,* has described this emotional withdrawal as "gunny sacking." Gunny sacking means taking a resentment and holding on to it. Gunny sackers do not express their resentment, but neither do they let it go.

When negative feelings are withheld, a second consequence may also occur: an explosion. Like the proverbial straw that breaks the camel's back, one resentment too many bursts the gunny sack. The negative feelings brought out in an explosion are not typically expressed assertively. By this time, assertion has turned into aggression and the response is out of proportion to the triggering event. In fact, it is only when negative feelings are expressed spontaneously that the intensity of the response fits the magnitude of the offense. Holding back feelings when they first occur leads to aggression. Perhaps one reason so many women are labeled (or label themselves) as bitchy is that negative feelings are only expressed when they are at the explosion point.

WHY DIRECT, HONEST, AND SPONTANEOUS ASSERTION?

Since being direct, honest, and spontaneous takes a great deal of effort, you may wonder at this point why it is so important for a woman to acquire this ability. In my own experience, direct, honest, and spontaneous assertion has at least four major benefits that make it worth any time and effort involved. Direct, honest, and spontaneous self-assertion allows you to avoid (1) misunderstandings, (2) emotional withdrawal, (3) hurting other people unnecessarily, and (4) spending energy nonproductively.

To avoid misunderstandings

Misunderstandings frequently arise in day to day interaction. Many of these misunderstandings are never resolved, often because the people involved are not assertive enough to directly, honestly, and spontaneously check out what has actually occurred. In one assertive group, we had the rare opportunity of seeing a misunderstanding checked out and corrected in an assertive manner right before our eyes. Following lunch on the first day of a workshop, I typically ask members (half in fun and half seriously) if they have had any assertive difficulties during the lunch break, and if so, how did they handle them. This particular day I had noticed even before I reconvened the group that one of the women sitting nearest me appeared somewhat disturbed. When I asked my question, she was the first to speak up.

"I'm Marjorie," she began. "I had lunch today with several other women from the group, including Ellen, the woman sitting across from me. And I'm feeling so negative about Ellen right now and feel so much like withdrawing from her that I guess I had better assert myself. I didn't express my feelings during lunch, so this is not a report of success."

Ellen at this point looked surprised at what Marjorie had just expressed. Marjorie continued, "I was still eating my lunch when Ellen said 'It's getting late. Let's head back.' I didn't say 'I can't go now. I haven't eaten my dessert' the way I know I could have. I just gathered up my things and left. But I noticed myself immediately thinking, 'That woman certainly is rude,' and now I have very negative feelings about Ellen."

The moment Marjorie finished what she was saying, Ellen broke in. "Marjorie, I really wasn't aware that you were still eating. I'm usually the last person to finish in any group. In fact, my slowness is something of a joke in my family, so I guess I just asumed that if I was through eating, everyone else was too. I wish you had spoken up."

Fortunately, Marjorie had eventually asserted herself. What might have been a permanent hostility dissolved in the interaction between the two women. Since Ellen and Marjorie were virtual strangers who would probably never see each other again, the cost of nonassertion in this instance would have been a temporary set of bad feelings— cost enough, as far as I am concerned. But in an intimate relationship the cost of misunderstandings may be much higher—years of withdrawal, bitterness, and estrangement.

To avoid emotional withdrawal

The desire to withdraw emotionally, which Marjorie had immediately felt with Ellen, is another common consequence of nonassertion. This withdrawal is a familiar enough experience to have been described in a variety of terms: pouting, sulking, giving someone the cold shoulder, feeling disconnected. When a woman is unable to prevent other people from intruding on her, or when she has no means of expressing her negative feelings, a natural response is to withdraw and become distant. Emotional distancing is a disguised form of hostility. However, it is not a form of self-expression that is likely to solve the problems which have led to the withdrawal in the first place. This form of hostility tends instead to harden into chronic detachment. As a woman unable to say no to her family expressed, only partly in jest, "There are times when I actually wish I were an orphan." Left unresolved long enough, emotional withdrawal can lead to physical withdrawal—a refusal to answer the telephone, a reluctance to initiate contact, separation, or divorce.

I recently heard of a striking example of emotional withdrawal under the most positive circumstances possible—after the parties involved had reopened contact with each other through one woman's self-assertion. Joan had taken part in one of my self-assertion groups several months previously. After hearing another person in the group talk about writing a letter to clear up an old issue with someone, Joan decided that she would write her sister-in-law Marge. Since a negative interchange had occurred between them six years previously, Joan and Marge had not spoken. At the time of their confrontation, Joan had not shared her feelings or her side of the issue with Marge, primarily out of fear of being thought stupid or petty. Now she decided that at least she could express her feelings and explain her reactions at the time of their argument. Joan was overwhelmed with the reply that she received from Marge. Marge praised her for being open and shared her own perceptions of their disagreement. A distance of six years evaporated with Joan's assertion.

Of course, such positive results do not always occur. However, I find that disturbed relationships between wife and husband, between parent and child, between relatives, between friends can often be resolved through direct and honest self-assertion.

To avoid unnecessarily hurting other people

One of the most frequent explanations people give for being nonassertive is that they do not want to hurt another person's feelings. Unfortunately, despite our good intentions, true feelings eventually come out, whether or not we want them to. Expressing oneself directly, honestly, and spontaneously is actually the best way to avoid unnecessarily hurting someone else. This is true because when our feelings first develop, they are typically at a low level. Resentment has not built up. This is the point at which two people are best able to come to a mutual and satisfactory agreement. Furthermore, if our negative feelings are based on a misunderstanding, the misunderstanding can be cleared up right away.

I have had many people tell me that they would like to hear another person's feelings immediately, even if the feelings are negative. Carol, a member of one group, who had just received a negative performance evaluation from her supervisor, was closely in touch with this issue. "I just wish that my supervisor had bothered to tell me even once that I was doing something she didn't like," Carol said. "Now it's written in blood, and I don't have much chance to erase it."

Lavern shared with another group a poignant example of how nonassertion does not prevent other people from being hurt. After being married for three years, Lavern's husband asked her for a divorce. Lavern was shocked. They had had no arguments, and there had been no bad feelings between them that Lavern had known about. When she confronted her husband, he admitted that he had been feeling resentful for a long time. He had not expressed this because he had not wanted to hurt her feelings. After their forced conversation, Lavern and her husband began to talk in earnest, and at the time of the group they had not yet planned a divorce. There was now at least the possibility of working things out. Lavern emphasized how much easier it would have been to solve their problems and how much less painful it would have been for her if her husband had asserted himself much earlier in the relationship.

In day-to-day encounters, other people pick up our negative feelings or our need to set limits, even if we do not assert ourselves. But is is usually much more destructive for a person to have to deal with indirect messages. In working with Liz on setting limits with Tom, a new man she was dating, I found that the fear of hurting another person's feelings was paramount. Liz and Tom lived in the same dormitory, and since they had started dating, Tom always sat by Liz at breakfast. Although Liz liked Tom, she was open to dating other people, and she did not want to be with him so often. She was simply feeling crowded. As Liz explained, "Once I get to know him better, who knows? I might want to see him every morning. But right now I just like to sit by myself and read the paper. I don't feel like conversation that early in the morning with anyone."

In discussing her problem with me, Liz asked "What if I just stopped coming down to breakfast." (Notice that Liz's first alternative to assertion was withdrawal.) "If I were Tom," I replied to Liz, "I would much rather hear your feelings than to have you simply stop showing up. My own interpretations of your behavior might be, in fact probably would be, far worse than what you might tell me. I might think that you were avoiding me and that you didn't want to date me again."

After thinking for a moment, Liz agreed. "I guess he can take my saying that I like being with him, but in the morning I don't feel like conversing with anyone." Liz's choice of being direct actually does Tom a favor. It gives him a clear picture of where she stands. Even when what a woman has to say is genuinely hurtful, that is, she wants to terminate a long-standing relationship, direct, honest communication is the best alternative. The people I have seen in therapy who have been most hurt in relationships are those people who have not been treated directly and honestly by others. When a person is not given an honest response, she or he continues to hope that the relationship *might* work out. Under these circumstances, she or he is not free to let go and move on to develop another intimate relationship.

To avoid energy spent nonproductively

Have you ever had an encounter with someone with whom you did not assert yourself and yet you could not let the situation go? You thought about it before going to sleep, maybe slept restlessly because you could not get the incident out of your mind. You spent a great deal of time talking about the situation to people who had not been involved in it. Your friends, your roommate, your partner—all heard the details. You fantasized in your spare time about what you *should* have done, what you might have said. You found yourself imagining various punishments that might justifiably be visited on the offending party. Your stomach formed a knot for most of the day, and even when your emotion began to subside, you went out of your way to avoid running into the person with whom you were nonassertive. Gestalt therapists call this "unfinished business." Such unfinished business tends to interfere with a person's natural state of relaxation and comfort.

If you have reactions similar to those just described, you might want to take a careful look at the situation and try to balance the costs of not asserting yourself with the risks of voicing your feelings. Look at the energy cost of each alternative. How much time do you spend thinking and talking about your nonassertion? What feelings are involved in asserting yourself? What are the consequences of each alternative?

Nell found herself faced with such unfinished business. She had not been able to let go of her feelings, but neither had she taken any step to change them. Nell's specific problem was that a woman in her apartment complex, who worked as a travel agent, had made the arrangements for a vacation trip to the Bahamas for Nell and her husband Chuck. However, because of poor planning on the travel agent's part, Nell and Chuck had a miserable time. They were without a hotel one night, and they missed a side trip they had particularly wanted to take. Nell was furious with the agent, but she did not want to make a scene, so she carefully avoided any confrontation.

Nevertheless, Nell found herself thinking of the trip instead of working. Each time she thought of the trip, her feeling surfaced again, with full intensity. Nell began to be cautious in her movements around the apartment complex. The travel agent was the last person she wanted to run into.

By the time of the group, Nell had decided that the energy she was spending avoiding a confrontation just was not worth it. She wanted to express the anger she felt in a direct, assertive manner. She did not want to explode or react aggressively. Nell set up the situation to rehearse in the group. Her eventual assertion went something like this:

NELL (rounding the corner and suddenly encountering the travel agent): Hello, June, I've been wanting to talk to you.

JUNE: Nell, I'm so sorry that you ran into so much hassle on your trip.

NELL (ignoring a very strong tendency to say "Oh, that's okay"): Well, June, I'm sorry too, because I was miserable on the trip and I want you to know that I am upset that more care wasn't taken in planning the itinerary.

JUNE: What can I say?

NELL: Well, maybe nothing, but I do want you to know my feelings. I've been angry since I got back.

JUNE: I'm sorry, Nell.

Simply asserting our feelings, even when no concrete change results, is usually sufficient to complete our "unfinished business." The positive consequences of self-assertion in Nell's case may be only that she is now able to let the situation go and move on to address other areas in her life. This is in fact a major value of directness, honesty, and spontaneity. By asserting ourselves in these three ways, we keep our slates clear for whatever opportunities and obstacles we next encounter.

the nonverbal message: how you say it

6

Self-assertion, as you have seen by now, is not a simple action—it is a complex set of behaviors. We have already noted that awareness is a prerequisite for self-assertion. We have seen how anxiety and the way we talk to ourselves interferes with our legitimate expression. We have discussed the importance of direct, honest, and spontaneous verbal communication. Let us now consider the effects of the final obstacle to effective self-assertion: our nonverbal message.

THE NONVERBAL MESSAGE

The nonverbal message is defined not by *what* we say but by *how* we say it. Three people can verbally say exactly the same thing. Yet one person will be listened to, one will be ignored, and one will provoke a hostile response. The difference lies in the nonverbal component of self-assertion.

Our nonverbal message consists of all the physical cues we use to express ourselves. These cues include eye contact, facial expression, tone of voice, voice volume, inflection, body position, gestures, and the use of nonwords. The nonverbal message can either add power and force to a woman's assertion or minimize and detract from her expression. When a woman's nonverbal behavior is not inhibited by anxiety, nonverbal cues generally add strength to her assertion. A woman who freely expresses herself nonverbally finds that a face-to-face encounter where all nonverbal cues are evident is much more effective than a telephone conversation where there are only vocal cues. A written statement has even less power.

Nonverbal cues add strength only when the nonverbal and verbal messages are congruent. When a woman is giving one message verbally and another message with her body position, she confuses her listener. If her words are angry, but her face is smiling, the listener receives a double message. Since the total effect is contradictory, that is, smiling and angry words do not mesh, there is a high probability that the intended message will not be the message received. The intended message may be, "What you are doing bothers me. Don't do it again." However, the message received is, "She is joking. She really doesn't mind what I am doing." Only when both the verbal and nonverbal statements agree is a woman functioning in her strongest position. Since this congruence is achieved by practice, we devote time in each assertiveness workshop to the development of effective nonverbal communication.

Eye contact

Eye contact is invariably the first nonverbal component mentioned when the assertive workshop focuses on nonverbal cues. This is not surprising if you consider the number of folk expressions in our culture related to eye contact. We tend to shy away from someone who has "shifty eyes." We are told never to trust a person who "cannot look us straight in the eyes." Supposedly, "eyes mirror the soul."

Eye contact is indeed a source of power in self-assertion. Direct eye contact signals that we are alert, that we are aware, that we mean what we say. However, many women have learned to fear their own power, and thus they attempt to minimize their effectiveness by avoiding direct eye contact. For example, Margo, a young student in one group, told us that after she introduces herself to someone at a party, she invariably looks down. Margo described this automatic lowering of her eyes as her way of apologizing to the other person. Verbally, she is asserting "I'd like to meet you." Nonverbally, she is saying "Excuse me for being so bold." Sally, a woman in another group, discovered that in facing a difficult assertive encounter she actually closes her eyes for a prolonged period of time instead of blinking. Facing another person with eyelids closed conveys the message, "I would like to avoid you or shut you out," a very different message than the one Sally wants to express.

Why do we learn to avoid direct eye contact? The simplest explanation is that diverting our eyes is one way of avoiding or reducing our anxiety. Take a child watching a horror movie. When the monster is on the screen, the child covers her eyes. This reduces the impact of the frightening scene. The same is true when we come face to face with another person. Blinking our eyes, closing our eyes, looking down, or looking away reduces the impact of an anxiety-arousing encounter.

The group exercise on direct assertive language (which we mentioned in our discussion of the verbal message) provides a vehicle for practicing nonverbal assertion as well. Women find that although almost anyone can *read* an assertive statement, making that statement to someone else, looking the other person directly in the eyes, is much more difficult. Feedback common to this exercise often relates to eye contact. "Sally, you looked up at the ceiling instead of at the person you were talking to." "Eleanor, the minute you finished your assertion, your eyes looked away," or "Denise, you looked at four or five people during your one statement." You may want to return to the sentences you wrote (as well as those in Table 5.1) and practice once more making these statements directly to someone else. This time, focus specifically on your eye contact. When you assert yourself, do you look the other person directly in the eye? Do your eyes shift during your statement? Do you maintain eye contact for a moment after you complete your statement?

In discussing direct eye contact, it is important to note that I am not encouraging women to stare. As with all nonverbal cues, there is a point of maximum effectiveness. Too little eye contact dampens a woman's power; too much eye contact can be viewed as aggressive. It may take several practices before you are satisfied that your eye contact (whether too much or too little) is not detracting from the power of your verbal message.

A side benefit of direct eye contact is that in looking at someone else, we focus less on ourselves. Fritz Perls, the founder of gestalt therapy, spoke of the tendency of people to "turn their eyeballs inward," to focus on themselves rather than on another person. For example, a woman who does not actively look at others may walk into a party thinking, "I wonder how I look." "Am I walking correctly?" "What am I going to say if someone comes over to talk with me?" Her focus is entirely on herself. She is self-conscious. In contrast, a woman who is actively looking outward sees the other people in the room. She assertively decides for herself whom she would like to meet, who looks interesting to her. She takes an assertive, rather than a passive, stance.

You may want to try an exercise in "active looking." The next time you talk with someone, actually try to "see" that person. Observe the color of the eyes, the texture of the skin. Look at the wrinkles and contours of the face. Try to remember something specific about the person you are encountering. When you enter a room, try to really see the people who are there. Try to observe them so that you can later recapture their image. The assertive approach in active looking will lessen your own self-focus and will ultimately reduce your self-consciousness.

Before continuing, I would like to share with you one amusing experience I had in practicing "active looking." I was visiting my favorite sandwich shop, waiting for my order, when I became aware that a young man at the other end of the counter was staring at me. Rather than look away, or look down, as the feminine role prescribes, I decided to look right back. I did look at him for a moment, in a direct, though not aggressive, way. I was surprised at the young man's reaction. He silently but clearly mouthed the word "bitch" to me. Being supportive of myself, I did not label my own behavior in any negative way. Instead, I took the incident as a curious reaction of a man faced with an unfamiliar assertive woman.

Facial expression

Julius Fast, author of *Body Language,* noted "It is considered exceptional, almost peculiar behavior to show what we really feel in our facial expressions." Unfortunately, this statement holds true in many, if not most, situations. We feel ashamed, and taken aback, when someone points out the message that our faces convey.

Our culture urges women in particular not to express themselves through their faces. Recall that one major tenet of the stereotypic feminine role involves an emphasis on beauty and personal adornment. Following this tenet has meant for many women an attempt to inhibit any facial expressions that do not fit with this traditional orientation. The observation to a woman that she is exhibiting something other than a smooth, nonemotional, nonwrinkled facade is frequently enough to stop short her assertion.

Marge, a physician, described such an experience to one group. Several months previous to her assertive workshop, Marge was expressing legitimate negative feelings to a male colleague about a patient whom they had both been treating. His comment to her, "If you could only see the look on your face," left Marge completely unable to continue her strong, forceful assertion. Marge's inability to continue her assertion after her colleague's comment related almost entirely to her acceptance of the unwritten dictate of the stereotypic feminine role: a woman should always be concerned with beauty and personal adornment. Once Marge recognized that she was responding according to a stereotype, she was able to assert, "My face probably looks angry. That's really fine, because I am angry, and I would like to continue our discussion about my anger." By allowing her face to reflect her words, without anxiety or embarrassment, Marge actually added more force to her verbal assertion.

There is no doubt that a woman's facial expression can enhance her power and effectiveness. Unfortunately, as we have noted, the opposite is usually true. A woman is taught to inhibit and disguise her nonverbal expression. The ultimate effect, of course, is to severely minimize the force of her assertion. Since this inhibition is particularly pronounced in expressing anger, let us explain in detail what function this nonverbal incongruence serves and how we can alter it. A good example is that of the woman who smiles when she is feeling angry. Her words say "I am upset." Her smile says "But not really. Don't take me seriously."

This insincere smile associated with the expression of anger has essentially the same function as indirect eye contact. It reduces anxiety. A study by Jack Hokanson and Robert Edelman, which we will detail in the next chapter, showed that women experienced relief from tension produced by another person's aggression only when they made a friendly counterresponse toward that person. An aggressive counterresponse produced anxiety. Similarly, a woman who habitually smiles when she is angry does so because her smile reduces anxiety. Accompanying angry words with a firm facial expression causes tension.

Fortunately, the anxiety associated with the congruent verbal and nonverbal expression of anger can be eliminated. If a woman persists in expressing her anger without smiling, she will find that her anxiety will gradually decrease. To achieve this ease, a woman may need to practice voicing an angry statement to someone else, making sure that she does not smile. Even if in the beginning she experiences no internal feeling of anger, it is important to develop an external congruence in her verbal and nonverbal expression. She will find that she gradually begins to feel comfortable presenting herself without minimizing or disguising her feelings. There may even be an additional benefit to her anxiety reduction. She may find herself really experiencing her anger for the first time.

This occurred when Carla, a piano student, practiced making the statement, "I resent everyone coming into my studio to talk while I am practicing" to one assertive group. Carla's roommates and their friends had repeatedly intruded upon her privacy, even though she had asked them several times to talk somewhere else. Carla's assertions were easy to ignore. Her resentment was softened to almost nothing by an apologetic smile.

Carla practiced her statement six times. With each attempt she smiled a little less. But not until the sixth time was her face firm, with no smile to detract from the power of her assertion. As Carla asserted, "I resent everyone coming into my studio to talk while I am practicing" without any trace of a smile, she experienced something even more important. For the first time, Carla felt her own genuine anger at the intrusion she had tolerated from her friends. Her anxiety about expressing anger had also masked her angry feelings. As her anxiety decreased, Carla was able to experience her anger as well as diminish her smile.

There are numerous other examples of women dampening the effectiveness of their assertion through their facial expression. Take the woman who is practicing a strong, forceful assertion of her limits: "I'm not interested." She closes her statement with her eyebrows raised in a questioning way. Think about the woman interviewing for a job. She is verbally stating that she is a competent person who can function effectively in the position. However, her facial expression does not convince anyone. Even positive feelings are often expressed with contradictory facial messages. At a party, a woman may turn a blank face to the person she finds most attractive because showing her true feelings would make her vulnerable to rejection. Figure 6.1 demonstrates six common nonverbal-verbal contradictions.

Tone of voice

Perhaps no nonverbal component adds more power to self-assertion than tone of voice. Yet many women are totally unaware of the message that their tone conveys. The surprise and chagrin of listening to yourself on tape is evidence of this fact.

Thelma, a young teacher, did not realize what her tone of voice expressed. Thelma was one of the most outspoken women in her assertive group. In interacting with the other women, her voice and general manner conveyed confidence and competence. In fact, Thelma had no difficulty dealing with women. She was taking the group solely because she found assertion with men difficult. It seemed that men always related to her in a sexual way, and she really did not know why. In a rehearsal of a typical female-male interaction, Thelma rehearsed calling a male friend, John, to suggest that they get together for lunch. Since we were in an all-women group, another woman played the role of John.

The moment Thelma began to talk, every other woman in the room knew why she had her particular problem. Thelma's voice, which had been both firm and pleasant in interacting with the women in the group, abruptly changed when she began her rehearsal. Her voice became breathless and seductive. The contrast was dramatic. Simply participating in a female-male exchange evoked from Thelma an entirely different tone of voice, a voice that virtually invited a sexual response from the other person.

If you are sometimes surprised at the response of other people, it may be that your tone of voice sends a message which contradicts or supplants your words. Many women interact with men as Thelma did, in a "little girl" manner.

FIGURE 6.1 Notice how each of these women is giving two opposing messages. Each woman's words say one thing; her face conveys something else.

It goes without saying that regardless of the words used, such nonverbal communication independently evokes a strong response. The same is true when women respond to other people from a parental position. The statement, "Would you please not hum along with the orchestra" can be made with an adult tone of voice, or with the scolding tone of a parent, or with the whining tone of a child. Try the statement each way. The words remain the same, but the effect of the requests on another person will be quite different.

Inflection or change in tone of voice is also an important nonverbal source of information. A contradictory message is often conveyed by a woman's inflection. Betsy made the statement "I really have to leave now." Her words sounded assertive. However, the inflection of her voice turned the statement into a question, "I really have to leave now?" She changed the statement into a question simply by raising the tone of her voice at the end of the sentence. Only after several attempts was Betsy able to "put a period at the end of her statement" by lowering the tone of her voice.

Voice volume

Not long ago I was invited to speak to members of a local women's organization. The president of the group was to introduce me to the fifty or so women in the audience. She had hardly begun her introduction, however, when several women in the back of the room began to shuffle in their seats. Two of the more assertive members spoke up, "We can't hear you back here." The room was large, but the acoustics were not bad. The president of this organization was simply unable to raise the volume of her voice to meet the requirements of the situation. Her effectiveness was limited by her inability to speak loudly.

The plight of the president of this group is a familiar one to women. As with many of the other nonverbal components, women learn to inhibit the volume of their voices. It is not by chance alone that women are more easily interrupted in groups than their male colleagues. The softness of their speech often allows such interruption.

In speaking to the assertive training group about voice volume, I frequently ask, "How many women here are uncomfortable with a loud voice?" Usually twenty-five to fifty percent of the women present acknowledge that they feel tense and anxious when they raise their voice above a certain level. When these women read their assertive statements, much of the feedback directed to them involves suggestions to speak louder. For example, Sonja spoke so softly when she made her assertive statement that the group asked her to *exaggerate* her voice volume when she tried again. Her statement "I don't want you to make commitments for me until I have given my okay" was made the second time with what seemed to be a normal voice volume. Everyone in the group acknowledged how different Sonja sounded this time in comparison to the first time she tried her direct statement. Almost as an afterthought, Anita, another group member, asked Sonja, "You really sounded fine, but why didn't you go ahead and exaggerate your voice volume the way the group suggested?" Sonja appeared a little surprised, before she laughed. "But I did," she said. "In fact, I felt like I was screaming. I'm amazed that the group viewed me as speaking normally." This discrepancy between a woman's self-perception and the perception of other people comes up again and again in assertive training.

One reason so many women experience anxiety about a loud voice is that the stereotypically feminine woman is supposed to speak in a soft, well-modulated manner. Women are punished for being too loud. I remember very well an experience that had a detrimental effect upon my own assertiveness. I was once severely scolded for singing loudly in a school choir and warned that I would damage my voice if I did not stop. Any damage came from my learning not to raise my voice. Only after I became a professional therapist myself did I overcome my own learned inhibition about using—when necessary—a loud voice volume.

Unlearning of the anxiety response associated with a loud voice is aided by an exercise, originally suggested to me by Sandra Enright. The exercise is called "Get Out of My Way." I introduce this exercise with the suggestion that each woman imagines herself in an extreme position. Perhaps a child or an animal is about to run into the street. Another person is blocking her way, and she does not have time for the usual social amenities. She must get past the other person as soon as possible.

In the group, we set up this exercise by having members form a column. Once the column has formed, the woman at the front of the column turns around to face the other members who are in her path. She then goes down the column, confronting each one of them by stating "Get out of my way." The statement is made twice to each person, first softly, then with full force. After a woman completes her assertion, she takes her position at the end of the column, and the next woman begins. The column continues to form until every woman has had a chance to make the two statements to every other woman.

In this exercise, the second statement "Get out of my way" is delivered with full force. This involves not only a strong voice volume, but also direct eye contact, an unsmiling facial expression, and a firm tone of voice. In one sense, this exercise puts together all the nonverbal components we have mentioned thus far in an intense form.

Rarely does a woman need to use this very high level of expression in dealing with another person. This exercise is mainly an exercise in "stretching limits." If a woman feels comfortable with the voice volume called for in this exercise, she will feel comfortable with the loudness required to speak in front of a large group. If she can go down this column of women without smiling or laughing, she will find that expressing herself firmly when she is angry is not so difficult. If a woman can stand in this column while nine or ten other women vehemently scream at her to get out of their way, she can effectively confront a person who tries to intimidate her by raising her or his voice.

Body stance

Jan, a young secretary, recalled to one group the time she was told by another woman, "Never stand up when you are around a man. You will intimidate him because of your size." Jan, who is 5 feet, 9 inches, took the comment to heart. As she explained to the group, "I always maneuvered to sit down whenever I talked to a man. Instead of walking into a man's office, I made sure that he came into mine. I never once walked with a male colleague to the coffee machine." Because Jan was taller than the average woman, she was told to limit her body position to a narrow range of seated interactions. It is inconceivable to think of a man being instructed to limit his power and mobility in this way.

Our body stance is an extremely important part of our nonverbal message in that it communicates the basic attitudes we have about ourselves and other people. Slumping shoulders and a lowered head may reflect a negative self-image. A protruding jaw may communicate hostility or defiance. A friend of mine once visited a psychiatrist who conveyed an aggressive attitude through his body stance. At their first meeting, this psychiatrist sat facing my friend with his feet on top of his desk. The soles of his shoes stared into her face. This body position and the nonverbal message that it broadcast destroyed any chance for my friend to hear a verbal communication of empathy and understanding, even if it had been expressed.

By recognizing that what we say with our bodies often gives a stronger message than what we say with our words, we can often decipher why another person is responding negatively to us. Our supposedly assertive message is perhaps being overshadowed by a critical gesture such as a pointed, accusing finger. Or perhaps we are standing with our hands on our hips. At other times, we may be squirming or physically backing away. The person we are talking to may or may not be able to say what is producing a negative emotional response. Frequently, however, when a person is able to analyze the negative reaction, she or he tells us "It's not so much what you're saying, as it is the way you're saying it."

Nonwords

The difference between effective and ineffective assertion sometimes lies in the final nonverbal component: the use of nonwords. Nonwords are defined as sounds or words that add no meaning to what a person is saying. A cough, a sigh, and words such as "okay," "ah," "really," or "you know" are frequently inserted simply to "fill" a sentence. These fillers can detract strongly from the power of our assertion. An example with which you are probably familiar is that of the speaker who connects all her or his sentences with "and uh." Ultimately the "and uh" attracts more attention than the content of the speech.

Again, in practicing direct assertive statements, the existence of nonwords is sometimes found to be the factor that detracts from a woman's nonverbal assertion. The interesting aspect of nonwords is that a woman may be completely unaware she uses them. Even when she is aware that she is inserting "fillers" into her assertive statements, they are difficult to eliminate.

Nonwords serve at least two functions. First, they reduce the intensity of emotional expression. When a woman forces herself to omit a nonword, she will frequently experience her feelings in a different way, in a more intense, possibly more anxiety-producing way. This was the case with Judith, whose assertive statement was directed toward Sybil, the assistant stenographer whom she supervised. Sybil had taken a particular afternoon off, against Judith's specific instructions. The assertive statement that Judith first made in the group was this: "I am really, you know, angry that you, you know, ignored my instructions. It has, you know, caused me no end of problems." When Judith finished making her statement to another member of the group, she looked questioningly toward me and shrugged her shoulders.

"How do you feel?" I asked.

"I don't know" she replied. "Not very satisfied. Kind of a 'so what' feeling."

Judith, as the group pointed out, had used "you know" three times in her assertive statement. We asked her to try to say just what she wanted without adding any fillers at all. It took Judith two more attempts before she could make the statement "Sybil, I am angry that you ignored my instructions. It has caused me no end of problems." In terms of the power and force of her statement, there was no comparison between Judith's first and last attempt. The interesting change to me, however, was Judith's report that her last statement alone connected with her own internal feelings of anger. The phrase "you know" had all but taken the meaning from her assertion.

Nonwords also serve the function of reducing any silence that would occur if gaps between phrases were not filled by *uhs* or *and uhs* or *okays*. The absence of these filler sounds would lead to brief pauses as a woman formulated her statement. However, these pauses are not distracting. They can in fact actually add strength to self-assertion. The silence interspersed in the statement "I would like for you (pause) not (pause) to give your secretary instructions through me" gives me a message of definiteness and confidence. When a woman in the assertive group has allowed herself to pause when she is formulating her thoughts without resorting to nonwords, the group has consistently given her positive feedback.

SUMMING UP

We had a chance in one group to see the cumulative effect of several nonverbal cues on the power and effectiveness of a woman's self-assertion. Sally was involved in a business partnership with Alan, a man she was dating, and his friend George. After several major business reversals, Sally decided that she needed to become more assertive about the direction in which the business was moving. Up to now she had let Alan handle the affairs with George. However, she was unimpressed by the plans for next year's operation, and she wanted to voice her objectives to several ideas. At the same time, Sally felt that if she came across in an aggressive or parental manner, she would accomplish nothing.

Sally chose another woman to play the part of George and began the rehearsal. Sally told George that she wanted to speak with him about the business, that she was unsatisfied about some of the decisions which had been made for next year, and that she wanted to explain her reasons. She then told George why she objected to the plans, verbally presenting her ideas in a clear, logical way. But the woman playing the role of George had a grand time ignoring and discounting everything Sally said. "Don't you bother about that. It's nothing for you to be concerned about," George replied time after time.

When we stopped the rehearsal to give Sally feedback, almost everyone had something to say. Sally had clearly minimized her assertion and her power through her nonverbal behavior. One group member pointed out that Sally was sitting (almost reclining) far back in her chair with her body turned sideways. Furthermore, she had looked down over her right arm toward the floor during most of the interaction. Another person commented on the softness of Sally's voice and how slowly she expressed herself. The total message that her nonverbal behavior conveyed was one of fatigue, or nonconcern, or helplessness. Although her words were strong, George had little problem ignoring them.

When Sally began again, she sat facing George. Her back was straight, she faced him directly, and she maintained good eye contact. She made an effort to speak louder and to hasten the pace of her speech. The contrast with the first rehearsal was dramatic. Besides changing the nonverbal behaviors that the group had mentioned, Sally had spontaneously begun to gesture and her voice had acquired a full rich tone. George was not able this time to ignore Sally's remarks. Her nonverbal power made ignoring her impossible.

You may want to review the nonverbal components of self-assertion by asking yourself the questions presented in Table 6.1. The more comfortable you are with direct and honest nonverbal behaviors, the more effective your self-assertion will be.

TABLE 6.1 Nonverbal Components of Self-Assertion

Eye contact
Can you look another person directly in the eyes?
Do your eyes shift away when you are making an important assertive statement?
Are you able to maintain eye contact for a moment after you complete your statement?
Do you lower your eyes when you are expressing negative feelings or saying "no?"
Can you accept a compliment with full eye contact?

Facial expression
Can you keep your face firm when you are expressing negative feelings?

TABLE 6.1   Nonverbal Components of Self-Assertion *(cont'd.)*

Are you uncomfortable when your face looks angry?
Do you try not to let your face mirror your emotions?
When you are happy to see someone, do you convey your pleasure in your face?
Do you avoid smiling or frowning because you are concerned about wrinkles?
Do you find yourself smiling when you do not feel like smiling?

Tone of voice, inflection, voice volume
Are you reluctant to use a firm tone of voice?
Do you become uncomfortable around "loud" people?
Are you frequently ignored when you say something?
Do other people interrupt you when you are talking?
Do you frequently find yourself in the position of appealing to others in a little girl voice, rather than expressing yourself from an assertive position?
Are you able to speak or ask a question in front of a large audience?

Body stance
Do you minimize your effectiveness by slumping or holding your head down?
Do you freely use gestures to express yourself?
Do you have difficulty knowing what to do with your hands?
Do you antagonize other people with critical gestures?

Nonwords
Are you afraid of silences?
Are you aware of nonwords you frequently or habitually use?
Do you interfere with your assertion by excessive movements or sounds?
Are you afraid to speak slowly?

assertion versus aggression: how to express negative feelings effectively

7

I had an interesting conversation one evening with John, a friend of mine. He had seen me talking about assertiveness and women the previous week on San Francisco AM, a television talk show, and was somewhat confused. Perceiving me as a very feminine woman, he could not reconcile how I could endorse self-assertion for women. I was intrigued by his confusion and asked him to describe the picture he conjured up when he thought of an assertive woman. His response was immediate. "Screaming, bitchy, lethal, vindictive, nonloving, manipulative, sarcastic, backbiting, fingerpointing, accusing, someone who would make me feel guilty, Elizabeth Taylor playing in 'Who's Afraid of Virginia Wolfe.'" I could understand his dilemma. John could not reconcile his view of me as a caring person, someone with a naturally soft voice and gentle style, with his idea of assertiveness.

Such a misinformed view of self-assertion is held by women and men alike. Assertion is frequently mistaken for aggression. The assertive woman is seen as someone who has acquired the ability to stand up for herself at the expense of losing her warmth, compassion, and sensitivity. John's comments made me even more aware of how important it is for women to distinguish between assertion and aggression. This is true because so many women, in trying to steer as far as possible from being aggressive, inhibit entirely appropriate and legitimate forms of self-assertion.

The confusion between the two words stems in part from the fact that in being assertive, a person does at times express negative feelings. Assertion, as we have already defined it, is the direct, honest, and spontaneous expression of any feeling. All of us at one time or another feel annoyed, resentful, frustrated, or angry. All of us experience the physiological concomitants of these negative feelings. Our blood pressures rise. Our hearts beat faster. Our muscles become tense. Whether we are assertive or aggressive in conveying these negative feelings depends on *how* we express ourselves. In this chapter we will explore this *how* in further detail.

PASSIVITY, ASSERTION, AGGRESSION

In dealing with negative feelings, a woman has essentially three choices: (1) she can inhibit her expression and say nothing, or she can give so many "hints" that no one knows what she is talking about; (2) she can attack and intrude upon another person by labeling them, moralizing to them, putting them down; or (3) she can directly, honestly, and spontaneously express her own feelings and opinions. Passivity, aggression, assertion—these are her alternatives.

In his book *I'm Okay; You're Okay,* Thomas Harris provides one framework that clarifies the attitudes underlying these three response possibilities. Harris describes three basic life positions that develop in childhood and influence all subsequent interaction. These life positions are concisely summarized as: I'm okay—You're okay, I'm okay—You're not okay; I'm not okay—You're okay. Assertive, aggressive, and passive behaviors are reflected in each of these respective life positions.

The person who is generally passive or inhibited frequently has an attitude that goes something like this: "You're okay, but I'm not. Therefore, I'll be very careful of what I say around you. I'll make sure that I don't offend or displease you, even if you do something that hurts me. I will not assert myself with you because I do not have that right."

On the other hand, the person who responds aggressively functions from the position, "I'm okay, but you're not. Therefore, I'll feel free to intrude upon you, to call you names and to attack you. Since you're not okay, you deserve to be treated badly."

Only the person who operates in an assertive manner has the attitude: "I am okay *and* you are okay. I will freely reveal my feelings to you. I won't allow you to take advantage. But you have the same privilege. You can freely express your feelings to me. I will not attack you for being who you are." Figure 7.1 illustrates these three positions.

When a woman states her *feelings* as fully as possible, she is being assertive. This is equally true whether the feeling expressed is anger or affection. Statements such as "I feel annoyed," "I resent what you just said," and "I am furious at you" are all assertive statements. They simply reveal what is felt ˙or experienced at the moment. If a woman goes one step further and attacks or intrudes upon someone else, then she is responding aggressively. Thus, statements such as "You're really immature," "You're a slob," or "If you were a good person, you wouldn't do that" are all aggressive. Each of the above statements intrudes upon another person by attack, name calling, or moralizing.

A woman has, of course, a third alternative of remaining silent. She can inhibit her expression of negative feelings. This is viewed by many women as the safest alternative. Unfortunately, passivity has some rather severe penalties. The woman who swallows her negative feelings, who pushes them down and tries to hide them, will generally find herself withdrawing from the person she is annoyed or angry with. She may withdraw by escaping the situation— "I have a headache and think I will go home now"—or avoiding it—"I don't think that I will see Pat again. She just seems too preoccupied with herself."

When escape or withdrawal appears to be impossible, as in a marriage or a business arrangement, a woman will tend to back away on an emotional level. She may express the emotional distance she feels by sulking, by withdrawing her affection from the other person, or by losing interest in sexual contact. This distancing may even occur without awareness, so that a woman abruptly notices that her feelings toward the other person have changed. Of course, if negative feelings go unexpressed for long periods of

126

FIGURE 7.1 Which life position fits you? Are you passive, assertive, or aggressive in your interactions with other people?

time, a woman may physically escape the marital interaction through divorce, or she may leave an unsatisfactory
business arrangement by finding another job. Table 7.1
directly contrasts passive, assertive, and aggressive responses in several specific situations.

Activity is not aggression

The failure to distinguish assertion from aggression has
led many women to inhibit highly desirable qualities of
forcefulness and strength. To be definite in one's own
opinions or to express one's own feelings or ideas forcefully is not to be aggressive. Ruth, a member of one group,
had difficulty with this distinction. When Ruth first came
into assertive training, she described herself as being
overly aggressive. As a free-lance writer, she frequently
met with potential clients and presented samples of her
work to them. "I come on as if I really know what I'm doing,"
Ruth told the group. "I guess that you might say that I'm
very forceful in presenting ideas." Still not getting any indication that she was aggressive, I asked Ruth to give me a
specific example of a situation where she had responded
aggressively. Ruth replied, "Just several weeks ago, a
male colleague of mine was presenting some material
that I felt was inaccurate. I asked him if he would be more
specific, and he called me an aggressive, critical bitch!"

The intrusive response of this one man alone may have
led Ruth to label herself as aggressive. More likely, however, the man's comment simply reinforced an idea that
Ruth already had about herself. Ruth had probably learned
to mistake forcefulness for aggression. In our society, when
a woman behaves in an active rather than a passive manner, she is more often than not labeled aggressive. It is
unfortunate that our culture is structured so that in social
interaction with men, a woman normally takes a passive
position. She has doors opened for her. In a restaurant,
her meal is ordered by her escort, paid for too, in all likeli-

hood. She waits to be called; she waits to be asked out. The subtle (or not so subtle) message given to women is that femininity means passivity.

Anger is not aggression

It is also crucial for women to distinguish between anger and aggression. Anger is a legitimate human emotion that can be expressed in one of three ways: passively, assertively, or aggressively. In other words, aggression is only one of three possible ways of responding to our angry feeling. But in our society, women are not expected to express their anger in any way.

Anger is, in fact, as much a "taboo" emotion for women as sadness is for men. Our society allows men to experience and express their anger, but women learn very early that anger (the feelings or the expression) is not acceptable. Young girls learn that expressing anger is neither polite, ladylike, or feminine. It is a lesson that lasts. Virtually every psychological comparison of adult women and men has shown that women are less aggressive than men. Women express less anger than men both verbally and physically, although, as we have noted, women tend to be equally hostile in their attitudes toward other people. It should be noted that in most psychological experiments, the focus has been on the aggressive expression of anger. Unfortunately, we have no separate data on the assertive expression of anger since the two terms have only recently been adequately distinguished.

Psychological research has also shown that women and men respond in a different manner to hostile provocation from other people. Hokanson and Edelman performed an interesting experiment that documented this difference. In their experiment, both women and men were given painful shocks by another subject, who was actually an accomplice of the experimenters. Blood pressure readings were taken on the women and men to see how they

TABLE 7.1

Situation: I am asked by telephone to be in charge of a charitable campaign in my neighborhood. This is a responsibility I do not want to accept. I respond:

Passively	Assertively	Aggressively
I say "yes," then slam down the telephone.	I really don't want to take on that responsibility this year.	Don't you realize that other people are busy?

Situation: A friend is talking on and on, and I have to get dinner. I respond:

Passively	Assertively	Aggressively
I tell my son to go ring the doorbell. Then I say "I've got to hang up now. Someone's at the door."	I have to go now. I need to start dinner.	It's six o'clock. You know I have to get dinner. You don't think about anyone but yourself.

Situation: I am seated in the window seat on an airplane. A honeymooning couple in the seats beside me are waiting for everyone to leave before getting up. I have to connect with another plane. I respond:

Passively	Assertively	Aggressively
I sit until they leave. I get a stomach ache.	Would you mind letting me get past? I have to make a close connection.	Are you two ever going to leave this plane.

responded to being shocked. As expected, both women and men evidenced a significant increase in blood pressure.

The women and men who had received the shocks were then allowed to counterrespond, either by shocking the accomplice, by ignoring the accomplice, or by making a friendly counterresponse. Blood pressure readings were

TABLE 7.1   *(cont'd.)*

Situation: I am not pleased with the service in a restaurant. I respond:

Passively	Assertively	Aggressively
I leave a penny tip.	I don't feel that I was given adequate service.	You are the rudest waitress I've ever encountered.

Situation: My husband has not been helping me clean up the dishes after we have had guests for dinner. I respond:

Passively	Assertively	Aggressively
I make a show of cleaning the dishes—banging several pans to-gether. Then I stalk to bed without saying goodnight.	I don't want to clean up by myself. I expect you to do half.	With sarcasm: I just love to wait on you and your friends. It's my life's ambition.

Situation: My male friend arrives to pick me for our date thirty minutes late. We have missed the first part of the movie we planned to see. I respond:

Passively	Assertively	Aggressively
I say *nothing,* not even hello, as we ride to the movie.	I am annoyed that you are thirty min-utes late. I don't like to miss the begin-ning of a movie.	You are so incon-siderate. You shouldn't make com-mitments you can't keep.

again taken to see how the hostile, friendly, and ignoring reactions had affected arousal level.

When the male subjects shocked the accomplice, their blood pressure immediately decreased. There was a catharticlike effect, whereby taking aggressive action immediately led to a reduction of tension. This was not at all true of the female subjects. When they counteraggressed against the accomplice, their blood pressure went even higher. Apparently, for women aggression provided no catharsis or relief. Only when a woman made a friendly counterresponse did her blood pressure return to the preshock level. Expressing anger was, for the average woman, associated with anxiety. Submission was associated with relief.

Hokanson and Edelman went one step further and looked at how these different physiological reactions were established. This time, whenever the male subjects responded aggressively toward the accomplice, they were punished. After several trials, the men no longer experienced relief after aggression. Instead, they learned to respond with anxiety when expressing their anger. We can assume that a woman's heightened anxiety at expressing anger is also learned. It is unlikely that a woman instinctively associates anger with anxiety. Our culture teaches her to do so.

HOW TO EXPRESS
NEGATIVE FEELINGS ASSERTIVELY

Directly expressing negative feelings is a difficult assertion for many people (women and men alike). Since anger, resentment, and annoyance have not been considered appropriate feminine emotions, however, this difficulty is compounded for women. When first beginning to assert negative feelings, many women are concerned over the counterresponses of other people. Certainly, if a woman aggressively attacks someone else, she can expect to receive a negative reaction in return. However, the chance of a negative counterresponse is minimized if she can express herself assertively. Assertiveness here involves at least two considerations: the distinction between "I" messages and "you" messages and the use of "muscle."

"I" messages versus "you" messages

You can see from Table 7.1 that assertive expression generally involves what might be called "I" messages. *I* feel, *I* resent, *I* am angry. "I" messages convey that I have feelings and that my feelings are my own responsibility. In contrast, aggressive expression usually involves "you" messages. Another person is attacked or labeled in a negative way. *You* should not do that. *You* are bad. *You* are a rude person.

Dr. Thomas Gordon was one of the first psychologists to recognize the importance of "I" messages. In his book *Parent Effectiveness Training,* Gordon urged parents to share their feelings with their children by way of "I" messages rather than scolding them with "you" messages. For example, instead of "Don't you have any manners? You sound like a couple of hyenas," Gordon would encourage a parent to say something like "I don't like so much noise in the livingroom." Gordon emphasized parent-child communication, commenting that adults generally send "I" messages to other adults. Although this may be true in "polite company," my own experience is that adults frequently send "you" messages to other adults. Employers send "you" messages to employees; wives send "you" messages to their husbands, and *vice versa*. In fact, the probability that a person will send a "you" message when angry is so high that consistent practice and attention is necessary to alter the habit.

Take Susie as an example. Susie's best friend Claire abruptly canceled plans to go to a concert with her when Claire's boyfriend Dan dropped by. Susie was annoyed, but she passively accepted Claire's explanation without objection. However, in the assertive group Susie practiced expressing her true feelings. Much to her consternation, she kept slipping into "you" messages. Rather than "I felt annoyed when our plans were canceled. I would like for that not to happen again," Susie moralized to Claire, "You shouldn't have canceled our plans. You should have known that I couldn't find anyone else to go with me. You were just inconsiderate!"

Even after three practices, Susie continued to tell Claire what she should and should not do. Her fourth attempt to express her feelings to Claire occurred in reality. Her practice had apparently helped, because the following week Susie told the group that she had successfully asserted herself without once using the aggressive message *you should*.

Why so much emphasis on the "I"—"you" distinction? Before answering that question, I would like to take just a moment to do a brief experiment with you. If I were to say to you, "You're wrong," what would your reaction be? How would you respond? How would you feel? If you are like many women, your reply might be, "Who do you think you are?" or "No, I'm not." You might feel angry or defensive or want to withdraw. If, on the other hand, I were to say to you, "I disagree," how would you react? Again, if you respond as most women, you might feel, "That's okay" or "You're entitled to your own opinion." You would probably feel less negative (maybe not negative at all) about my latter statement. The simple shift of a statement from a "you" message to an "I" message can result in a great difference in another person's feeling. In my own experience, aggressive expression (a "you" message) almost always leads another person to counterattack or defend. A "you" message feels like an intrusion. Alternatively, "I" messages offer no intrusion or put down. An "I" message allows the greatest chance for increased understanding.

Eric Berne's system of Transactional Analysis provides a useful framework for examining the differences between "you" messages and "I" messages. According to Berne, every person operates from each of three positions: a Parent Position, an Adult Position, and a Child Position. In other words, each person has a Parent part, an Adult part, and a Child part. Our Parent part consists of all the shoulds and should nots we are taught by our parents and society. Our Child part represents the feelings experienced by us when we are children. Our Adult part acts as a computer, helping us to make decisions based on our current experience as well as on past information.

When anger is expressed from the Parent, it is usually by moralizing, scolding, or name calling. The Parent typically relies on "you" messages. "You shouldn't do that" or "You don't ever do anything right" or "You're a bad (selfish, rude, childish, and so on) person." When we hear a Parent remark, most of us remember the scolding "you" messages from our own parents, and react back as angry children, "Don't tell me what to do" or "You're just a nag." Alternatively, negative feelings expressed from the Adult position will usually call forth a complimentary Adult response from the other person. The statement, "I don't like to be teased" typically leads to the counter Adult response of "I'm sorry. I'm really just expressing my affection for you."

Let us analyze the interaction of Jill and James in terms of Parental "you" messages and Adult "I" messages. Jill and James have been married for a little over a month. Tonight for the first time since their marriage they are going out to dinner and then to the theater with friends. After leaving the restaurant, Jill takes James aside, and the ensuing dialogue takes place:

JILL: You were really rude to me in the restaurant. I wasn't even finished with my dessert when you suggested to everyone else that we leave for the theater. You need some training in etiquette. (Here Jill is speaking from her critical Parent position. She does not reveal her feelings but instead lectures James from her parental rule book of shoulds and should nots.)

JAMES: You're never satisfied. All you do is nag. Next time, I won't even take you and your friends out. (James responds as any

135

attacked child by defending, counterattacking, and then withdrawing.)

Jill and James do not speak for the rest of the evening. A small but important misunderstanding has escalated into their first marital quarrel. Jill begins to question the value of sharing her feelings with James. James vows to himself that he will not be treated like a child again.

Were both Jill and James to replay the situation in an assertive manner, a different result would be likely:

JILL: I was upset that you suggested that we leave before I was finished with my dessert. I would like you to ask me if I'm finished before suggesting that we leave. (Notice that Jill simply states what she does not like without attacking James' character or putting him in a Child position. Furthermore, she takes responsibility for her own needs and tells James what she would like to occur in future situations. James is not left with the duty of solving Jill's problem for her.)

JAMES: I'm sorry, Jill, I really didn't realize that you hadn't finished. I guess I was anxious to get to the theater. I'll try to check with you first next time. There's one thing I'd like to ask you to do though. If I forget next time, it's not intentional, so just speak up and tell me to slow down. I won't get mad. (James corrects Jill's possible misperceptions about the intention of his remark. He gives her some information as to his position at the time, that is, "I was anxious to get to the theater." He acknowledges both her feelings and her request for him to change his behavior. James also asserts his own desire for Jill to feel free to express herself at the moment.)

Through an assertive dialogue (using "I" rather than "you" messages and stating feelings rather than attacking), Jill and James have a better understanding of each other. Rather than closing off communication, the sharing of negative feelings has enhanced their understanding of each other.

Translating feeling into expression: In the assertive training workshop, one question is frequently asked: "How can

I express my negative feelings? There are many times when my feelings are so intense that all that I experience is rage. When that happens I can't think of anything to say." Expressing negative feelings assertively is a skill that can be learned. Assertive expression involves taking a gut feeling and translating that feeling into an "I" message. This kind of translation takes practice. When provoked, the spontaneous response of many women is to attack the aggressor either verbally or physically. Yet since most women fear the consequences of such an attack, they stifle their expression and do not react at all.

This was the case with Chris, a nineteen-year-old college student majoring in English. About ten minutes before her assertive workshop began, Chris was treated in a way she did not like. She had been unable to respond assertively to the incident. Chris admitted that the only response she could think of was an aggressive one. "I wanted to walk over to the man and kick him in the shins. Instead, I said nothing."

Chris described the situation to the group:

> I was talking to Mary, a friend of mine about taking the assertive training class. A man was standing nearby, and I guess he overheard our conversation. When I asked Mary where the ladies' room was, he broke in, "Why don't you just go to the men's room. It's over there." It was his sarcastic way of equating assertiveness with masculinity.

As we discussed Chris' alternative to kicking the man in the shins, one group member suggested, "If it were me and I had simply put my gut feeling into words, I would have said to the man, 'I really resent that comment!' He would have known my feelings without my having to attack him or dissect his personality."

Why not attack?: Ellen, another woman in the group, countered with the question, "Why not attack? He deserved it. Why not tell him he's a male chauvinist pig? Why take

care of his feelings? You'll never see him again anyway." Ellen's question essentially asked, "Why limit self-
expression to being assertive?"

This is an important issue. In every group, a similar
question is asked. Ultimately, each woman must answer
the question for herself. My own view is that any feeling
can be expressed assertively. I can express my anger,
even my rage, in an assertive manner. Therefore, I really
have no need to respond aggressively. Aggressive reactions usually take place when a person feels that she or
he has no alternative but to act aggressively. Feelings
build up to the point where there is no choice. Examined
from this perspective, it can be seen that aggression does
not emanate from a position of power and control but from
one of impotence. The woman or man who reacts hyster-
ically or who periodically has an aggressive outburst (a
temper tantrum) is not the person who is generally respected or listened to.

Moreover, for many women, aggressive expression
leaves a bitter aftertaste. After the anger of the moment
subsides, guilty self-punishing thoughts begin to surface.
"Why did I have to explode?" "I really went down to his
level." "Maybe another reaction would have caused him
to change his attitude." When a woman has responded
assertively, there is no need for guilty recriminations.

Muscle

The second parameter to consider in expressing your
negative feelings is the level of muscle. Muscle is a concept I have found very useful with all self-assertion, but
particularly with the expression of negative feelings. I first
began to use muscle as an assertive technique after talking one afternoon to a friend of mine named Karen.

Karen, in the course of our conversation, told me about
an experience she had when flying back to San Francisco
from a vacation in the East. Her vacation had been fun,

but she was saturated from talking with other people and also exhausted. All she wanted was to spend her return flight relaxing, maybe sleeping, maybe reading a book. However, Karen soon found that the man sitting next to her had different needs. He was in the mood to talk. Now, Karen did *not* assert herself. She did not say, "I'm tired from my trip and don't feel much like talking today." Instead, she took the passive or indirect approach and began to "hint" to her uninvited traveling companion that she did not want to talk. She perfunctorily answered several of his questions. She stared intently at her book, trying to signal him nonverbally that she was not interested in carrying on a conversation. Her indirect action had no effect. Feeling extremely annoyed, and by now at the boiling point, Karen shouted, "I don't want to talk!" The man appeared stricken, and although Karen apologized for the intensity of her response, she felt guilty for the rest of the trip.

Karen's response, "I don't want to talk" *was* assertive. She stated her feeling with an "I" message. She did not attack or name call. However, Karen used a club to rid herself of her annoyance when a feather would probably have done the job. In other words, Karen used too much muscle. The intensity of her response did not fit the demands of her situation.

The degree of muscle is an important aspect of self-assertion. As I am using the term, muscle essentially means strength. A woman will usually feel uncomfortable with her assertion unless the level of muscle fits the intensity of the event. I personally prefer to begin my assertions at the lowest level of muscle. Not only do I use the smallest amount of energy I need, but I also ensure that I do not inadvertently intrude upon another person. If the first level of muscle does not suffice, I am perfectly willing to move on to a higher level. Thus, if someone were kicking the back of my chair in a movie, I would turn around and politely request, "Would you please not kick the back of my chair. It's bothering me." This is level-one muscle, and most people would respond by ceasing their kicking. In many cases, the person would not have realized that she or he was bothering me. A more intense response would have been unnecessary.

If the intrusion persisted, if the person behind me continued to kick my chair, I would go to level-two muscle. "I don't want you to kick my chair again." This statement would have been expressed with increased verbal and nonverbal intensity. My words would be straight to the point. My voice volume, tone of voice, and facial expression would all be conveying more force. Whereas this level of muscle would initially have sounded rude, it is now appropriate to the situation in which another person continues to intrude upon my territory.

Backing up words with action: If the individual continues to kick the back of my chair, I would move to the third level of muscle. "If you kick my chair again, I am going to get the usher." At the third level of muscle, I let the other person know the consequences of failing to comply with my request. Although going to the usher initially would have been unnecessarily severe, now this action fits the circumstances.

At level-three muscle (even at level-two muscle), many women begin to back down. They decide that the issue just is not worth facing a confrontation. They fail to use the power at their command for fear of "creating a scene." A common question about this third level of muscle reveals both the anxiety and the confusion it generates. "What is the difference between a consequence and a threat?', someone will ask with concern. On the gut level, of course, a threat is a dirty word. No one wants to be accused of making a threat. For this reason alone it is important to recognize that a threat and a consequence are not the same. A threat is aggressive; a consequence is protective. A consequence simply adds to our power to prevent another person from taking advantage of us.

At the fourth level of muscle, I would carry out the consequence. If the person kicking my chair did not stop, I would indeed go to the usher. If I fail to back up my consequence with action, I am simply teaching other people that my words do not matter. Figure 7.2 illustrates the four muscle levels.

As we have noted, moving from a lower level of muscle means changing both the verbal and nonverbal components of self-assertion. Nonverbally, as I have already mentioned, increased muscle may mean a louder voice volume, a firmer tone of voice, and a more serious facial expression. Verbally, different words convey an increase in muscle level. "I would rather" is lower muscle than "I want." "I insist" or "I demand" is higher muscle yet. Our assertion is most powerful when the level of verbal and nonverbal muscle is sufficient to handle the situation.

High-level muscle: There are obviously some situations where a person is not able to progress from one level of muscle to another. The magnitude of the situation and the intensity of the emotion calls for the immediate use of high-level muscle. Jean, a graduate student in biology, shared an apartment with two other women. Jean was conducting an experiment for her masters thesis and had a litter of white mice as subjects. She kept the mice in her closet so she could carefully regulate the number of hours they were exposed to light. Jean had warned her roommates never to go into the closet, because by turning the light on or off, they could upset her research. One afternoon, Jean came back from class and found her roommate Lois rummaging in her closet. Lois had turned the light on, perhaps destroying Jean's experiment. Lois looked up when Jean came in, but she offered no apology or explanation. In fact, as Lois left the room, her only comment was "I was

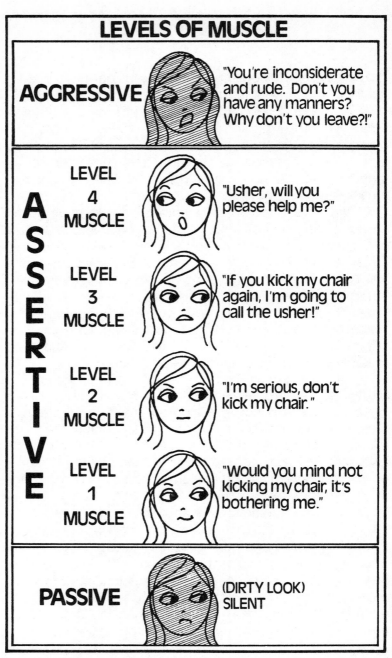

FIGURE 7.2 Without being either passive or aggressive, a woman has a wide range of responses available to her. Different muscle levels allow her to fit her response to the intensity of the situation.

looking for one of your sweaters to borrow." Jean was livid with rage. She was also speechless, totally unable to express her anger. She spent the night upset, unable to go to sleep.

Although a week had passed since the incident occurred, Jean continued to feel unable to express her feelings, even in a role-playing situation. Jean asked if anyone else in the assertive group could demonstrate how they would handle the encounter because she honestly did not know what to say. Technically, Jean's inhibition was caused as much by a behavioral deficit (a term used by behavior therapists to describe the absence of an appropriate response) as by anxiety. Even if Jean had been perfectly calm, the lack of knowledge about what to say would have kept her in a passive position. The problem here for Jean, as for many other women, was that she had never seen another woman express anger without losing something in return. She had never had a *model* of a woman who was effectively assertive in expressing her negative feelings.

Susan, another member of the group who also had some difficulty expressing anger, volunteered to play out the situation with Jean. Jean decided in the first rehearsal to play the role of her intrusive roommate.

JEAN (walking toward the door):   I was looking for one of your sweaters.

SUSAN (in a "reasonable" tone of voice):   Jean, I told you that I didn't want you to go into my closet because I was doing an experiment and didn't want it to be disturbed.

By the time Susan had completed her sentence, Jean had walked out of the room. Susan quickly saw how she had let her "reasonableness" get in the way of expressing her anger. In terms of power and impact, telling someone what you *think* is very different from telling them what you *feel*. In Susan's next practice, she relied more on her feeling response and less on her logic.

JEAN (walking out of the room):   I was looking for one of your sweaters.

SUSAN: Jean, I don't want you ever to go into my closet again. I am furious with you. I never want you to do that again.

JEAN: What did I do?

SUSAN: My experiment may be ruined. I am just disgusted. I mean, never do that again. Is that clear?

Jean nods, acknowledging Susan's statement.

Notice that Susan not only expressed her current feelings, but she also told Jean what she expected in the future. Susan's forceful words as well as her firm tone and stern facial expression frightened some of the group members. Many of them had never seen a woman use her anger in a powerful way.

Expressing anger without anxiety

Before a woman is completely free to express anger (or for that matter, to hear another person express anger), she must become comfortable with both anger's verbal and its nonverbal aspects. A woman must be able to increase her voice volume without anxiety. She must be able to maintain a firm facial expression. She must be able to confront another person with direct eye contact. She must feel comfortable with strong forceful language. Many women respond with anxiety to at least one of these components. Some women find that anxiety is triggered by all the components. This anxiety can prevent a woman from ever really experiencing angry feelings. It can even cause her to substitute crying for angry expression.

Margaret, for example, worked part time as a secretary to help with her college expenses. One day Margaret's supervisor severely criticized her for misplacing a file. The criticism was unjust. The file was not Margaret's responsibility, and she knew nothing about the incident. Margaret recognized that her internal feeling state was rage. This had not been the first time she had felt unjustly accused. In fighting to hold back her anger, Margaret began to cry. The intensity of her feelings demanded some release, and crying was the less frightening alternative.

When women substitute crying for expressing anger, they are sometimes rewarded. Most men will stop their provocation, even give in to a woman's wishes when she begins to cry. But the woman is the loser in the long run. Her indirect approach strengthens the traditional view that women are overly emotional and excitable. It reinforces the argument that women cannot be truly responsible.

The woman who wants to express her anger as anger needs both permission and practice. Permission is necessary because within the confines of stereotyped femininity, anger is not allowed. Practice is needed because until a woman learns that the floor does not swallow her up, the roof does not cave in, or people do not run away when she expresses anger, she will continue to experience anxiety. This learning is emotional, not intellectual. Women obviously know on an intellectual level that expressing anger does not lead to a catastrophe. However, when a woman first attempts to assert her anger, she may *feel* that something terrible will happen.

Within the assertive training group, we usually have one exercise where every woman has the opportunity to practice expressing anger. Preferably this initial practice involves a nonpersonal situation or a situation low on a woman's hierarchy. In learning to express negative feelings, a graduated approach is important. The exercise I mentioned involves members sharing various anger-provoking experiences, one of which is chosen for group practice. By re-creating the intrusive situation through role playing, each woman is allowed to practice asserting her negative feelings. Those women who have had the least difficulty expressing anger begin first. They serve as models for those women who follow. Among the provoking situations chosen by the various groups have been the following:

1. Before moving out of their home, Judy's neighbors dug up *her* rosebushes to take with them.
2. Lynne told her physician that she wanted to be referred to as *Ms.* Atkinson. He sarcastically replied, "If you are *Ms.*, then call me Drrr (a mispronunciation of Dr.).
3. Phyllis was practicing the piano in her apartment. Friends of her roommate came into the practice room and began talking. When Phyllis asked them politely to leave, they refused.

As each woman practices voicing her anger, the remainder of the group gives feedback about her voice volume, facial expression, and assertive stance. Many women repeat the rehearsal several times before they are able to maintain a firm, strong voice and can refrain from smiling. The differences between the first attempt and the second or third are often dramatic. Many women within the group actually begin to feel their anger for the first time as they become freer in their self-expression.

You may want to practice responding to one of the anger-provoking situations described above (or to one of your own). You can practice alone or, better yet, act out the situation with a friend. If you have felt uneasy with your anger, begin by adding one component at a time. Start off by simply expressing your angry feelings assertively with "I" messages such as "I resent," "I don't like," or "I am angry about." This is not as easy as it sounds. Some women find that they must write out a brief script to keep their verbal message assertive.

Once you have mastered this first step, try to express your negative feelings by looking directly at your friend or, if you are practicing alone, by looking in the mirror. Notice any tendency to look away. At the end of your assertion, try to maintain your eye contact for a brief period of time. This lets the other person know that you mean what you say. In the third practice, increase your voice volume until it is stronger than usual. Make sure your voice is firm and to the point. When you complete your assertion, does your tone go up or down? It will go down if you are making a firm statement and not asking a question. Finally, try putting the components together. Do not be afraid to be intense or to have emotion. Remember that anger is a legitimate feeling. The more you practice the assertive expression of anger, the easier it will become.

Spontaneity—little things are important

Even though the ability to express anger at high levels is important, I want to emphasize that once a woman begins asserting herself, she may actually find herself experiencing fewer feelings of anger and resentment. In being assertive, negative feelings are expressed spontaneously, before they have had a chance to accumulate and build up. Instead of telling another person "This is the hundredth time that you have been late" (with a hundred resentful feelings behind the statement), the assertive woman takes care of her resentment on the first occasion when the feelings are at a low level. Instead of exploding "If you do that again, I'll kill you" after her feelings have reached the boiling point, the assertive woman requests, "Please don't use my typewriter again without asking." Once the feelings are expressed, the resentment typically evaporates. The woman who is chronically hostile is not the woman who is able to freely and spontaneously express her negative feelings.

By taking care of our annoyances as they arise, we rarely need to go beyond level-one or level-two muscle. By reacting immediately we ensure that our reactions are appropriate to the intensity of the frustrating situation. But what if a woman has not been assertive in the past? What if she has accumulated a store of resentments and hurt feelings? Such a situation is not uncommon. Because of unexpressed resentment, many women experience every new situation against the backdrop of prior frustrations. Under these circumstances, any spontaneous reaction will tend to be aggressive. Take for example the woman who finally decides to tell her friend not to bring her pet with her when she visits. The next time her friend drops by with her dog, the woman may explode, "Don't ever bring that dog here again!" Her high muscle response is based on many visits, not just one. She may later find that her friend is hurt and confused by her expression. Her accumulation of anger did not permit a lower level response.

How does this woman handle such a situation assertively? How does she keep her pent-up hostility under control? The issue here is really one of timing. If a person has allowed resentment to build up and knows that one more intrusion may spark an explosion, an alternative approach is to take the situation into one's own hands. In other words, a discussion about a problem can be initiated *before* the problem triggers the backlog of resentful feelings. A woman is then acting rather than reacting. The woman in the previous example might take the initiative and call her friend. Since she is not angry at having just encountered her unwelcome guest once again, she can express her feelings at low-level muscle. "Jane, something has been bothering me, and I wanted to let you know. I'd like you not to bring your dog when you visit. My house isn't set up for pets, and I feel uncomfortable when he's here."

ONE FINAL WORD

The distinction between assertion and aggression is not complete without a specific focus on the concept of intrusiveness. In some assertive training groups, members are given homework assignments that are supposed to help them become more assertive. Illustrative of this practice is the assignment to "Buy fifty cents' worth of gas from a service station attendant, then demand that the attendant wash the windshield." This assignment seems intrusive to me. First, it is artificial. The woman ordering fifty cents' worth of gas, when she actually has money or does not need fuel, is being dishonest. Under these circumstances, her action takes advantage of someone else. The service station attendant is inconvenienced without genuine reason. The action, as I see it, emanates from the aggressive attitude "I'm okay, but you're not." In my own view, there are enough situations where a woman can legitimately assert herself. There is no need to create such an artificial encounter. In the next chapter on setting limits, we will look at intrusiveness from another angle, specifically at how to keep other people from intruding on us.

setting limits: learning how to say no

8

As I have mentioned, in every assertive training group I have members participate in an exercise that involves making direct assertive statements. Each woman individually composes several direct statements related to situations where she would like to be more assertive. As we practice making the statements to each other, I am always struck by how many of these direct sentences involve some kind of limit setting. Not expressing negative feelings, not practicing self-initiation, not expressing positive feelings. The statements invariably say "no" to other people.

Limit setting is one of the most difficult areas of assertion for women. As we have seen, saying no to the requests and demands of other people is in direct conflict with the other orientation of traditional femininity. In our culture, women have been taught to be polite, to be unselfish, to subjugate their own needs to the needs of others. In playing out this culturally prescribed role, a woman can end up taking care of everyone but herself.

WHAT DOES LIMIT SETTING INVOLVE?

Setting limits means defining for yourself, "This is who I am." It means deciding for yourself, independent of the external demands of other people, how you wish to spend your time, to what use you want to devote your energy, and how much privacy, emotional space, and time alone you need. Setting limits is also a way of teaching other people how you expect to be treated. A limit essentially puts a boundary between you and another person. This boundary defines the parameters of your relationship—the closeness of your interaction, what you do together, the time you spend together, how you relate as two distinct people. This limit also defines your personal space—the time you spend alone or with other interests and involvements. The limits a woman asserts typically have three important characteristics: they are individual, they are changing, and they are signaled by feelings.

Limits are individual

Limit setting, like all self-assertion, is a means by which a woman defines her own uniqueness. One woman's limits will be different from another's. For example, Hilda enjoys visitors. Her style is free and relaxed, and she likes people to drop by spontaneously. If a friend comes to Hilda's home uninvited, it is an unexpected and completely welcome surprise. Kathy, on the other hand, is a more private person. She enjoys visitors also, but she likes to plan for them in advance. Kathy frequently works in the evening— she is a law student—and when someone comes over without calling, she feels resentful. Kathy's time/privacy limits are much tighter than Hilda's.

Neither woman is wrong. Neither woman should change or alter her limits. Kathy and Hilda are simply two unique people, two people who are different. For Kathy and Hilda to be friends, however, they will have to make their limits clear to each other. Otherwise, when Hilda drops by unexpectedly, Kathy will begin to feel intruded upon. Hilda will not know that Kathy does not share her very open time limits unless Kathy tells her.

Limits are changing

A second aspect of limits is that they change—with different people, different situations, and different circumstances. As Mildred indicated, "At times, I can allow touch. At other times, I cannot. This changes, according to where I am at the moment, and I feel fine about that." Many of my friends learned that my limits changed once I began writing a book. For example, when I went out with a friend for lunch, I no longer had time to sit and converse afterward. If things were not going well one day, I had to say no to invitations that would have been welcome under other circumstances. I had to turn down requests from people who were less important to me so that the time available to me could be spent with those people who mattered most. In other words, my limits, especially those regarding time, underwent a complete alteration as I committed myself to my writing.

A woman's limits can also change as time passes. Karen drove by every morning for a full six months to pick up a friend and coworker whose car had broken down. As Karen described the situation, "At first, I genuinely didn't mind. I was glad to help out. But her house is really, really out of the way, and as time went by (with me, of course, saying nothing), I felt more and more intruded upon. I guess I just couldn't admit that my limits had changed."

Limits are signaled by feelings

The third aspect of limits is that they are based on feelings. I can usually tell when I need to assert my limits because my face becomes hot or my stomach begins to knot up. My body signals that something is not right for me. If a woman tunes into her feelings and accepts them, she has a clear blueprint for asserting her limits. Unfortunately, as we have seen, most people do not accept their internal feelings as valid. Their external "should" system interferes.

Stanley Milgram conducted what is now a well-known experiment relative to the internal-external issue. Milgram's study examined the amount of shock a subject would willingly administer to another person when instructed to do so by someone in authority. The study found that the majority of subjects (sixty-two percent) obeyed the authority's command even to the point of delivering what they *thought* was 300 volts of shock to another person. The 300-volt shock was given even though it was clearly labeled as dangerous. It was given even when the victim (actually an accomplice of the experimenter) cried out in pain that he did not want to continue participating in the experiment. Yet—and this is the aspect of the study most relevant to our discussion—the subjects obeyed orders and gave painful shocks to another person over "powerful reactions of tension and emotional strain." As Milgram notes, "Persons were observed to sweat, tremble, stutter, bite their lips, and groan as they found themselves increasingly implicated in the experimental conflict." Very few subjects, however, listened to their own internal emotional response when authority demanded, "You have no choice, you must go on."

Milgram also used a group of female subjects in one of his experiments. He initially thought that female subjects might give the victim less severe shock than male subjects. We know that women tend to express less aggression than men on a voluntary basis. On the other hand, a study by Bem, which we shall detail later, has shown that women who conform to the traditional feminine sex role have more difficulty than men standing up against external pressure. Milgram found this latter tendency to dominate. Women were just as obedient as men. Sixty-five percent of the women gave the victim maximum shock. Interestingly, however, this one group of women reported higher tension associated with their compliance than any of the twenty groups of obedient males Milgram had tested. Thus women refused to heed even more powerful internal signals than men when they were put in a position where obedience was expected, in a situation where they *should* obey.

The *should* that overrides a woman's feelings often comes from her own self-talk. "I *should* be a good hostess, even though my guests are intruding on my need for privacy." "I *should* be polite, even though my housekeeper is scratching my floors." "I *should* always be available to talk to my friend, even though I have a business deadline to meet."

Shifting from an external "should" system to an internal "feeling" orientation involves the recognition that feelings

155

are valid. As Karen noted just after taking an assertive training class, "It has been a revelation to me to accept the fact that my feelings are important, just by the fact of my feeling them, no matter how insignificant they may seem." Until a woman does accept her feelings, she will find it extremely difficult to recognize, much less assert, her limits.

THIS IS WHO I AM

The first important aspect of limit setting is defining for yourself and for other people "This is who I am." Limit setting contributes to this definition by stating what does *not* fit with you as a unique person. This self-definition can be best illustrated, in Figure 8.1, by two circles representing Person A and Person B. In the first illustration, Person A and Person B are completely alone in their own space. There are no demands or intrusions on either person from the other. Although everyone needs a time to be alone, to have privacy, the two individuals at the top of Figure 8.1 are completely isolated from each other. Their need for contact is being totally ignored. Limits allow A and B to define the extent of contact they desire.

The second drawing in Figure 8.1 demonstrates a relationship between A and B where there is some mutual contact. The darkened area represents the time A and B spend together (or any shared aspect of their relationship, for that matter). If both A and B feel comfortable with this degree of contact, there is no problem. However, let us say that A feels comfortable sharing this amount of time with B, but B wants more contact with A. Person B will try to increase this contact by initiating more activities with Person A.

If A is assertive, B's attempts to increase the time spent together will be met with limit setting comments such as "I don't have time tonight to go out" or "I need some time alone tonight." However, if A is nonassertive, she will not

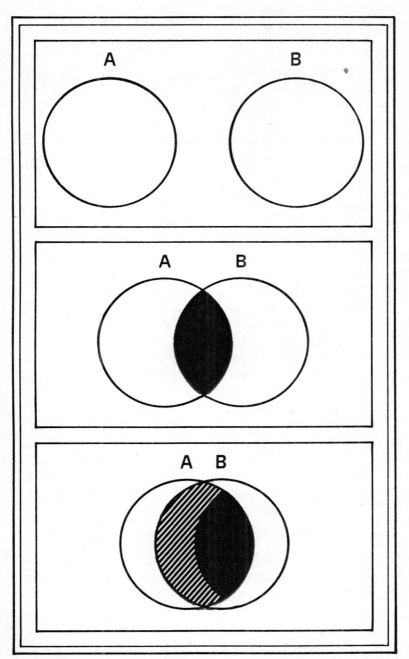

FIGURE 8.1 The top drawing represents two people with no personal contact. The second drawing illustrates a mutually desirable interaction. The diagonal lines in the third drawing demonstrate where person A has allowed person B to intrude into her space.

honor her own time limits. *B's* advances will not be stopped. *A* will allow *B* to intrude. This intrusion is illustrated in the third drawing. The diagonal lines represent the increased time not desired by *A*.

The result? *A's* feelings will signal intently that an intrusion is taking place. Resentment will build up. If Person *A* continues to be nonassertive, she will either withdraw or explode. Person *A* may hint at limits to Person *B*, and if these hints are ignored, Person *A* may stop answering phone calls from *B*. There will be a stress on the entire relationship. Person *A* may finally aggressively attack *B*. *A* cannot ignore her limits without cost.

If *A* is nonassertive with everyone else in the same manner she is nonassertive with *B*, she may begin to lose her sense of personal identity. A situation may develop where the external influences in her life override her own feelings. Cathy, a young mother, found herself in this position. She admitted, "I took assertion training, because I was allowing other people to take control of my life. I found myself relying more and more on my husband to decide how to spend money, how much to save, how to spend time. I was relinquishing control of my *self.* I began feeling depressed and began wanting to escape and withdraw. I had none of the zest that I had when I determined my own course." Such a pattern of not asserting limits, if it becomes habitual, can result in a life always lived for others rather than for oneself.

THIS IS HOW I EXPECT TO BE TREATED

The second vital function of limit setting is teaching other people how to treat us. Women frequently allow themselves to be treated in a negative manner, mainly because of a fear of setting limits. As Gloria described,

> My husband and I went to a restaurant and were told that since we didn't have any reservations, we couldn't eat there. My husband noted that there were five vacant tables and asked if there would

not be a way to fit us in. He wasn't aggressive or rude; he just asked a question (and got us a table, by the way). But when he didn't accept that we couldn't eat there and confronted the maitre'd, I got so uncomfortable that I retreated to the door and left him standing alone. My fear of creating a scene kept me from making sure that I was being treated fairly.

Unfortunately, like Gloria, many women learn to rely on other people to take care of them. They continue the plight of Nora in Ibsen's *A Doll's House,* moving from the protection and control of their fathers to that of their husbands. A basic tenet of the feminine role, in fact, demands that a woman rely on a male provider for support. But because men are allowed to carry the burden of self-assertion, many women never learn how to take care of themselves. I recall one woman, recently widowed, who was having difficulty asserting herself with her son. She was doing all his ironing (although he was twenty-five) and paying for his long distance calls. This problem with her son was a totally new one for her. For twenty-four years, whenever her son had gotten out of line, her husband had set him straight. Having never been assertive before, she was now at a loss about what to do.

In letting other people know how you expect to be treated, you need first to know your rights, and second, you need to refuse to be treated in a manner that ignores those rights. Self-assertion involves fully accepting the position "I'm okay." My mother recently wrote me a letter in which she detailed an experience she had had. Having tuned in more to her own self-assertion through our discussions, she has kept me informed about any assertive experiences in her life. She wrote:

About my assertiveness: The waiter at this fashionable restaurant seated us at a corner table that had a very good view and was away from the traffic. Then the head waiter, after our order had already been taken, came over and wanted to move us to a less desirable place. He said a mistake had been made. I asked if our table was

159

reserved. He said no. We were about to move, when I decided we were just as important as anyone else, so I told the other people at the table that I didn't want to move. Everyone agreed, so I informed the waiter that we would either stay there or leave. Naturally, he let us stay.

By refusing to be treated in an unfair or unequal manner, my mother maintained the basic position "I'm okay." She also saved herself the inconvenience of having to change tables.

The positive consequences of limit setting with strangers usually occurs immediately, as in the previous example. However, with acquaintances, friends, and intimates, the positive consequences of stating how you want to be treated may continue for long periods of time. For example, if I ask a coworker not to interrupt me when I am dealing with clients, I prevent myself from being interrupted on sixty additional occasions. If I refuse an unwelcome committee assignment, I save myself twenty-four dreaded bimonthly meetings. In other words, by setting my limits the first time something bothers me, I will usually not have to face the annoyance a second time. If I fail to assert my limits, I can be almost certain that the disturbance will be repeated.

HOW TO SET LIMITS

In setting limits, a person quickly discovers that some methods work better than others. Some methods lead to success; others lead to difficulty. In this section I would like to discuss several ways of setting limits that optimize a woman's effectiveness. Among these methods are

1.   Making your limits clear
2.   Using partial limits
3.   Employing the necessary muscle
4.   Setting meta-level limits
5.   Separating intent from effect

Making your limits clear

The first method—making your limits clear—is not always easy. The main problem is that you yourself have to understand what is bothering you about a particular interaction. This may involve a careful analysis of what feels comfortable and what feels uncomfortable to you in the situation. For example, Stella had a neighbor, June, who visited her each night around six o'clock. Stella worked all day, and it seemed to her that the moment she arrived home, June dropped by. Furthermore, June's conversations were full of complaints. She was unhappy about her in-laws, and Stella was the only person she felt she could talk to. June typically stayed thirty to forty minutes and most of the interchange focused on her in-laws. Stella liked June and wanted to maintain their relationship, but she no longer looked forward to their visits. Stella knew that she was becoming resentful, but she did not know exactly why.

In discussing the situation with Stella, we came up with four separate issues concerning June's visits:

1. The length of the visits (typically thirty minutes each)
2. The number of times June came over each week (almost every night)
3. The timing of the visits (around the time that Stella was preparing dinner)
4. The topic of conversation (mostly complaints about June's in-laws)

In separating the various issues, Stella realized that what was really bothering her was the content of their conversation. She and June had always visited nightly, and she had not been bothered until recently when June's in-law problems began to dominate the conversation. Identifying where she felt uncomfortable allowed Stella to tell June, "I'd rather not talk so much about your in-laws.

I think you're going to have to confront them and set some limits with them before the issue can be resolved. I just realized that we spend most of our time talking about them, and I'm feeling uncomfortable with that."

To assert her limits clearly, Stella found it necessary to ask herself the question, "What do I really want to change about the situation?" Until she was clear about what she wanted, Stella was unable to assert her feelings to June. Any message lacks power if it does not clearly and directly express the genuine underlying feelings.

The use of partial limits

One benefit which comes from making one's limits clear is the realization that limit setting is not an all-or-nothing proposition. For example, by setting her limits with June, Stella was not cutting off communication entirely. She was in fact setting a partial limit, a limit relating to only a part of their interaction. Most limits are partial. They are necessary under certain circumstances but not others. Partial limits frequently allow some satisfaction to both people involved.

Sandy, a high school counselor, had a problem situation where the use of partial limits provided an effective solution. Gina, one of the students whom Sandy counseled, was very much in need of contact with another person. Gina did not have any support from her family, and she had no friends in school. She was a painfully shy teenager, who had opened up to Sandy alone. The problem was that Gina came by Sandy's office every day after school and talked for long periods of time. Sandy did not want to forbid Gina to stop by her office since it was a positive reaching out to another person on Gina's part. However, Sandy knew that she could not devote so much of her working time to Gina; she had reports to write and other things to do. Sandy resolved the situation by setting a partial limit with Gina each time she came by. "I'm interested in talking with you, but I have only ten minutes to spare today." After asserting this limit, Sandy reported back to the group, "I'm actually surprised at how well it worked. And Gina, to my great relief, does not seem upset that I now limit our interaction to the time that I can comfortably talk."

The use of muscle

Perhaps the most important aid in setting limits is the freedom to use the necessary muscle. In setting limits, you may find that you must rely on more than one level of muscle. Occasionally you may even find that to protect your own interests and prevent other people from intruding, you must go from level-one muscle to level-four muscle. To review briefly, level-one muscle involves a polite, low level statement of your limits, or a low level request for someone to stop intruding on you. Level-two muscle intensifies your request by increasing both its verbal and nonverbal intensity. At level-three muscle, you inform the other person that their continued intrusion will result in a consequence. At level-four muscle, you carry out that consequence.

In using muscle, a woman must be conscious of those situations where she has legitimate power (those situations where she can bring in a consequence if the intrusion persists) and those where she has no legitimate power. For example, if I am sitting in the nonsmoking section of a commercial airplane and someone next to me lights up a cigarette, then my limit-setting statement "This is the nonsmoking section, would you please not smoke" is backed up by all the legitimate power that I need, the full power of the federal government. If I do not have my limit enforced, it is not because I do not have the power to do so. It is because I choose not to or because I am afraid to use that power. If, on the other hand, I am in a restaurant and ask the person at a table close to mine,

"Would you mind not smoking? It's bothering me," I have only the power of my person behind me. The individual smoking the cigarette can reply "Yes, I do mind," and that is within her or his rights. I can of course raise my muscle to level two, but unless there is a law against smoking in a public place, I have no further consequences on which to draw.

Why assert at all when there are no consequences to back up my assertion? Simply because most people do not want to intrude on others; most people want to be pleasant and reasonable. For that reason, most people will honor a polite request—regardless of whether or not it can be enforced. I have a good friend who occasionally asks a person smoking a cigar in a restaurant if he would mind not smoking. She has never had to move beyond level-one muscle in her request, and her request has always been granted.

Returning to a situation where a woman does have consequences, such as in the nonsmoking section of a commercial airplane, it should be noted that even in a clear-cut situation a woman may have to be persistent in her assertion. Letti found this to be the case. In her work as a state consultant, Letti travels a great deal. She is a nonsmoker. In fact, she is allergic to cigarette smoke, so she carefully books her flights in the nonsmoking section of the airplane. You can imagine Letti's annoyance when on a particular flight two men on either side of her began to smoke. Further, these two men fell into that small minority of people who do not seem to mind ignoring the rights of others. Letti politely asked if they would please not smoke. She repeated her request by explaining that she was allergic to cigarette smoke. Again, no effect. She informed the two men that she would be forced to call the flight attendant if they did not stop smoking. Her level-three request was also ignored. Finally, Letti called the stewardess and informed her that the two men were smoking in the nonsmoking section. The stewardess replied, "Well, these men were unable to get a seat in the smoking section, that's why they are smoking here." After having gone through four muscle levels, Letti gave up. She spent an uncomfortable, frustrating, smoke-filled hour before arriving at her destination.

After describing Letti's situation to assertive groups, I often ask, "What could Letti have done?" Some suggestions are aggressive: "Put the cigarettes out in their ears." Others are more passive: "Move to another seat." But I rarely hear the suggestion that Letti could continue to assert herself by confronting the stewardess. In other words, Letti may need to go through the four muscle levels with the stewardess as well.

Why is this alternative so difficult? First, simply by expressing her own limits to the passengers, Letti has already ignored two injunctions of stereotypic femininity: the injunction that a woman live for others rather than for herself and the injunction that a woman inhibit all forcefulness, assertion, and power strivings. If Letti continues to assert herself, she will encounter more and more frequently the negative self-labels that occur when a woman goes against the stereotypic feminine role. She will feel that she is "creating a scene," being "bitchy," "rude," "unfeminine," "selfish," or "petty"—all labels with which women inhibit their legitimate self-assertion.

If Letti had not stopped herself, if she had chosen the assertive alternative and expressed her limits to the stewardess, the dialogue might have gone something like this:

LETTI: Would you please ask these two men not to smoke?

STEWARDESS: Oh, they were unable to get a seat in the smoking section; that's why they are smoking here.

LETTI (increasing her voice volume and expressing herself with a firmer tone): That may be. However, I sat in the nonsmoking section so that I would not be near cigarette smoke. I would like you to ask these men to put out their cigarettes or to move. (level-two muscle)

STEWARDESS: Well, the plane is full, and the flight is not very long.

LETTI (with her anger beginning to show in her voice and in her facial expression): Are you saying that you refuse to enforce the federal regulation against smoking in this airplane? (checking out her perception with an implied consequence, that is, level-three muscle)

STEWARDESS (backing down): Well, no, if you're that serious about it. I guess you gentlemen will have to stop smoking.

If at this point the stewardess still refused to back down, the dialogue might have continued:

STEWARDESS: Yes, that is what I'm saying.

LETTI: Then, I want your name, and I want to speak to the head stewardess. I believe that there are severe penalties imposed when federal regulations are ignored.

STEWARDESS (backing down): That won't be necessary.

It is unlikely that Letti would have needed to assert herself further. You may ask if such a prolonged interaction would be worth the effort. It certainly would be to me. For me, the cost of nonassertion is much greater than the cost of assertion. Letti's encounter, however, is unusual. In my experience, in asserting myself over this same issue three or four times in the past two years, I have never encountered any opposition that forced me to go beyond level-one muscle.

The final consequence: letting go: There are situations where in moving to level-three muscle, the only consequence that a woman has is the consequence of leaving or letting go. We are not talking here about a passive avoidance of self-assertion. We are talking about a final consequence under our control that can be used when persistent self-assertion has failed to change a toxic situation. An illustration may convey the difference between

166

letting go as a passive solution to a problem and letting go as a powerful assertive consequence.

Faye, a dental hygienist, had worked for two years for Dr. A., a dentist who had a reputation for aggressive outbursts with his staff. Faye was terrified most of the time lest she make some mistake or say something to trigger one of his scathing attacks. In the past month Dr. A. had blown up at Faye twice over a file she supposedly misplaced. On both occasions Faye expressed to Dr. A. that she did not like being talked to in such a manner, but her assertion just upset him more. Faye wanted the assertive group she was attending to help her come up with a solution to her problem. She was beginning to feel that because of her anxiety, the quality of her work in the office was slipping.

In exploring alternatives with Faye, I asked her if she had considered changing jobs. She admitted that in her field there were jobs available and that she would have no problem getting one. But she did not want to "give up" and then feel like a failure.

In speaking further with Faye, it became clear that she was confusing "giving up" with "letting go." Faye had remained in her job for two years, and she had made several attempts to change Dr. A.'s behavior toward her. It seemed to me that Faye was now subjecting herself unnecessarily to a toxic environment, an environment where she was not thriving, an environment where, if anything, she was moving backward. Faye's only remaining consequence in the situation was to state that if the outbursts continued, she would resign. And if the situation did not change, Faye could regard her leaving as an assertive action. If, of course, Faye had left a good job without ever asserting what she did not like about it, her "leaving" would not have been assertive. Leaving under these circumstances would have been a passive avoidance of self-assertion.

Setting meta-level limits

Scene: Carol has set up a rehearsal to practice setting limits with her roommate Penny.

CAROL: Penny, do you have a moment to talk?

PENNY: Sure.

CAROL: I want to bring up something that's been bothering me and see if we can work it out. I've been upset about your leaving clothes and personal articles in the living room.

PENNY: Well, I don't like your leaving your stockings in the bathroom either.

CAROL: Then perhaps we could both say what is bothering us and work out some kind of a housekeeping arrangement that we can agree upon.

PENNY: I'm satisfied with my housekeeping habits. You're just too picky.

CAROL: That may well be, Penny, but it's important to me to have the living room uncluttered in case guests come to visit. Would you be willing to try to keep your things picked up?

PENNY: As I said, I'm satisifed with things as they are.

At this point in her rehearsal, Carol looked toward me for help. "What do I do now?" she pleaded.

"What are you feeling?", I asked.

"I'm frustrated," Carol answered. "I don't like the response that I'm getting. I'm trying to be reasonable, and I'm just getting cut off at every point.

"Maybe you need to move the focus of your assertion away from the issue of whether or not Penny's clothes are kept out of the living room to the issue of your feelings about the interchange you are now having with her. In other words, move to a meta-level," I suggested. Step back and take an objective view of your interaction and your feelings. Then, comment on what you see.

CAROL continued: Penny, I'm feeling very uncomfortable about the way this discussion is going. I'm not trying to attack you or put you down. I realize that you and I have different habits. I just want us to work out a mutually satisfying agreement. I value our relationship, and I don't what this to come between us. Is there something that you are upset about?

PENNY: Yes, I guess that I am upset. This just isn't the right time for me to talk. Can we talk tomorrow?

CAROL: Sure.

According to Webster's dictionary, *meta* is a prefix meaning "after, beyond, or higher." Thus a meta-level assertion develops after an interaction has begun. Carol's statement to Penny, "I am beginning to feel very uncomfortable about our discussion" initiates limit setting on a meta level. Carol comments on the feelings and concerns that have developed over and above the original issue. Figure 8.2 illustrates meta-level assertion in pictorial form. Notice in particular that a meta-level limit is a comment about how a person is being treated at the moment. Meta-level assertion frequently prevents a person from getting stuck in a negative or nonproductive interchange.

Here are some other examples of meta-level limits:

1. I don't want to go any further until you stop the name calling.
2. I can't respond to you unless you are willing to tell me your feelings.
3. Please stop taking care of me. I have a right to base my behavior on the reality of the situation.
4. I can't listen to you or try to understand when you use that tone of voice.

Separating intent from effect

I had a horrible, awful day today, taking a final exam, hassling with a department store that had overcharged me $120.00, then rushing to pay some bills which were overdue so that my service would not be cut off, Anita began telling her ongoing assertive group. Anyway, by the time I got home, I was fighting back tears. I got a phone call from Greg. He wanted to tell me that he had found out from a realtor what my former house sold for and that I had made too low a sale. He had also found that I had sold my stocks too

META LEVEL ASSERTION

FIGURE 8.2 In meta-level assertion, a person comments on the feelings and concerns that have developed over and above the original discussion.

soon, because they were now making a terrific profit. It was the absolute worst time for me to hear what Greg wanted to tell me. I didn't think I could get much lower today until he called. Quite frankly, when we finally hung up, I was very angry with him. I know he meant well, so I couldn't exactly tell him how angry I was. I initially tried to let him know my limits. I told him that I had had a bad day, but I guess that wasn't direct enough.

As we talked, I became aware that Anita was letting Greg's good intentions stop her from setting her limits in a clear, direct manner. When I shared this observation with her, Anita asked, "But what could I say?" She then immediately answered her own question. "I know Greg's intentions were good, but I just wasn't in a place to hear any bad news today." Anita's statement, as she herself suddenly realized, separated Greg's *intention* to be helpful from the actual *effect* his conversation was having on her. Separating the *intent* from the *effect* frees a woman to state her limits without putting another person down. Anita did not need to attack Greg personally to let him know how she was feeling.

We immediately set up a rehearsal in the group to integrate Anita's insight into her actual behavior. The dialogue went something like this:

GREG: Hi Anita. How are you?

ANITA: Well, Greg, I don't want to go into it, but I've had a very bad day.

GREG: Oh, well, I just wanted to tell you that I saw the realtor that I told you about and you won't believe what your house sold for. You're going to be disappointed.

ANITA: Greg, I'd like to hear about it another time, but right now I'm just not in a good emotional place. I've had too many hassles today.

GREG (ignoring Anita's limit): Well, I went to a lot of trouble to find out that your house sold for . . .

ANITA (interrupting): Greg, I know your intention is to help me, and I would like to discuss it with you another time, but right now I'm really feeling down and I just can't handle any more bad news.

GREG: Well, you've got a lot of it coming. You know that stock that you bought . . .

ANITA (raising her muscle): Greg, stop! I don't want to hear any more right now. Please respect my limits on this.

GREG: Oh, you really don't want to talk about this right now.

ANITA: That's right. I don't want to talk about it.

PITFALLS TO AVOID

Having discussed several ways to make limit setting more effective, we can now turn to some of the pitfalls to avoid. These include:

1. Reinforcing what bothers you
2. Attempting to be reasonable
3. Making excuses
4. Responding by reacting
5. Engaging in a "rescue operation"

Reinforcing what bothers us

Rosalind, a head nurse, complains that many of the nurses under her supervision tattle about the behavior of their colleagues when they could settle the matter by discussing it between themselves. Rosalind feels that this tattling to her not only interferes with her own duties, but that it puts her in the position of being a parent to everyone. Whenever someone comes to her, however, Rosalind typically says, "Thank you for telling me about this."

Paula, director of a physical therapy unit, describes an assistant, Pat, who never shows up at team meetings. Although Paula deeply resents this behavior, after every meeting she takes Pat the materials and instructions that she handed out to the other group members. Pat is not forced to face the consequences of not participating as part of the team (that is, she is not reprimanded, and she always has the materials to do her job). In fact, Pat actually receives special treatment because of her absence.

Both Rosalind and Paula are reinforcing or rewarding behaviors that they do not like. They are following undesirable behaviors with positive consequences. Naturally, this behavior tends to increase in frequency. Tattling followed by a thank you or absences that result in special attention will almost certainly occur again.

Because women are taught to be polite, to nurture, and to take care of others, they often fall into the trap of reinforcing other people for imposing on them. Perhaps the most common example of nonintentional reinforcement is that of the woman who finds herself listening to the problems and concerns of another person, long past the time that she desires to do so. Not only is this woman unable to assert "I have to go now," but she actually nods politely, smiles, and says "um huh," encouraging the other person to continue talking while she seethes inside. The first step in setting limits for some women, in fact, may be simply to stop reinforcing behavior that is bothersome to them.

Trying to be reasonable

A second pitfall to avoid is that of trying to be "reasonable," as demonstrated by the following exchange:

SALESPERSON (drawing a ball-point pen out of his pocket): This is a very good pen that I would like to sell you today. I know you will like it. It is guaranteed to last for at least a year.

CUSTOMER: Thank you anyway, but I don't need a pen right now. I never use them.

SALESPERSON (incredulously): Never use a pen?

CUSTOMER: You see, I type all of my letters.

SALESPERSON: Ah. But once you have typed your letters, you will need this pen to sign your name.

The above role-playing interaction actually occurred in one assertive group. It demonstrates how trying to be reasonable is not an effective way of setting limits. Reasonableness rarely works because for every reason I give for not wanting to do something, you can give an opposing reason back. Reasonableness frequently leads to interminable arguments.

Liz found herself having such arguments with her two teenagers about the issue of their bringing visitors into the house without her knowledge. A typical interaction with her son Phil went something like this:

LIZ: Phil, you didn't tell me George was going to be here. I never know when someone is coming over. I want you to stop doing that. Someday, I may not be dressed.

PHIL: I never bring my friends over early in the morning or late at night. You're always up. You've never not been dressed.

LIZ: Yes, but what if I plan to have company over myself? You and your friends would be in the living room, and I would have no place to go.

PHIL: Yes, but if that happens, we can go outside.

LIZ: Yes, but that's a hassle. If it's raining, you can't go outside and anyway, I don't want to be ,policing you and telling you to leave.

PHIL: Well, you bring your friends over uninvited.

The dialogue could go on much further, with Liz and Phil countering reason for reason. Liz left such encounters feeling very ineffectual and impotent.

Liz was unaware that the most powerful expression of limits, one that cannot be argued with, is the expression of feeling. The validity of a person's feelings cannot be denied. Someone may counter with "You shouldn't feel that way," but you can always reply, "Maybe not. But that *is* how I feel." When Liz asserted to Phil, "I don't want you to bring friends over without telling me," the following dialogue ensued:

PHIL: But why not?

LIZ: I feel uncomfortable not knowing who is here.

PHIL: But why?

LIZ: I don't really have a good reason, Phil. I just feel uneasy, and I would like you to tell me before inviting anyone over.

PHIL: Well, I don't see why you have to feel that way.

LIZ: I don't know either, but I would like you to let me know when someone is coming over. It's important to me.

In comparing setting limits by trying to be reasonable with setting limits by honestly stating one's feelings, the group member playing the antagonist (Phil, in this case) is usually the person most convinced of the ineffectiveness of being reasonable. The antagonist frequently observes, "In the first rehearsal, I could have gone on forever. I felt that I had you under my control. The second time, when you just stated your feelings, I could hardly think of anything to say. I simply couldn't argue with you."

Making excuses

A third tactic to avoid in setting limits is making excuses. Excuses allow a woman to avoid expressing her honest feelings. A woman may tell herself that she makes excuses to keep from hurting someone's feelings or to avoid offending someone. What she is more probably doing is minimizing her own anxiety about defining herself as a unique human being. Sue illustrated this practice. Sue did not want to go to the symphony with Mary because she did not enjoy concerts. But Sue told Mary that her husband had made other plans. By using her husband as an excuse, Sue did not need to let Mary know an area (going to the symphony) where they were different.

Anyone who has resorted to making excuses knows that an excuse provides at best a hit-and-miss solution to the problem of setting limits. For example, an acquaintance may ask me to do some volunteer work. She may want me to meet with twenty other people to stuff envelopes for an upcoming campaign. If I do not want to go, I can make the excuse, "I don't think that I will be able to get a baby-sitter, and I'll be the only one home that night." "I've gotten out of it," I may think to myself. Then my acquaintance can counter, "No problem. We have someone to babysit at the campaign office." I am now stuck. Once an excuse has failed, I have no opportunity to try again.

Making excuses is an ineffective form of limit setting for a second reason. When I make an excuse, I can be assured that I will have to deal with the situation again. The second time will invariably be more difficult. Having been dishonest with another person, having placed another person in the position of extending herself or himself twice, I will feel guilty and anxious about setting my limits. Many women find themselves in this position with men who ask them out. They do not want to put the man down or hurt his feelings, but neither do they want to go out with him. The compromise solution: an excuse.

Agnes, a young teacher who took one of my assertive workshops, wrote to me about one such incident. Agnes met a man at a party, talked to him part of the evening, and then gave him her phone number. Agnes wrote, "All is fine, right?" and then answered her own question "No! You see, I really have no interest in dating Paul. He has called me five times in the past two weeks, and either I'm busy or ill with the flu. In other words, I've been putting him off. The flu was real, but it was also an excuse not to make plans with him or tell him how I really feel. The result? I'm anxious every time the phone rings for fear it is Paul. Paul, by now, is getting rather upset with my put offs. I'm getting upset with Paul, because I don't like being in pressured situations. Conclusion: The next time Paul calls, I have to lay it on the line and tell him I'm not interested in dating him. It would have been so much easier to do that in the beginning."

Responding by reacting

In one of my assertive workshops for women and men, Tom described his difficulty in setting limits with friends

176

who called him for help (without pay) whenever they had any plumbing problems. Tom, who had once been a plumber, found it very difficult to refuse to help friends who telephoned with panic in their voices saying they were up to their knees in water. In fact, Tom felt that asserting himself under such circumstances would be impossible. Tom's situation provides a good vehicle for contrasting responding by reacting and responding by initiation.

In any situation where your limits have been intruded upon and you expect the intrusion to continue, you can assert yourself by *reacting*—by waiting until the intrusion occurs once more—or you can assert yourself by *initiating*—by speaking up before the intrusion has had a chance to reoccur. In a case like Tom's, limit setting by initiating is the simpler alternative. If Tom tells each friend he has assisted in the past, "I'm letting everyone know that I'm not available any longer to help out with plumbing emergencies," he will not be faced with asserting himself under guilt-producing circumstances, that is, when his friend's basement is overflowing. The same is true when a woman knows that if an intrusion occurs again, she is likely to react with too much muscle. If Carolyn expects her husband to leave his clothes on the floor again, she can assert her limits by initiating a conversation with him before he does so. Her chances for a productive interchange will be much greater if she responds by initiating rather than by reacting.

A similar issue involves the timing of your limit-setting statements. If a friend telephones and you do not have any time to talk or you can only spare five minutes, it usually works best to initiate, "I don't have time to talk right now" or "I have to stop in about five minutes," rather than to react "I have to interrupt. I'm late for an appointment." Asserting ourselves in advance feels more comfortable to most of us than interrupting someone who has just launched into a long story.

The emphasis here on setting limits by initiation rather than by reacting is not intended to speak against spontaneity. In certain guilt-inducing or anger-provoking situations, responding by initiating may simply be the more effective alternative.

Engaging in a rescue operation

SECRETARY: I don't drink coffee, but I always clean up the office area before I leave.

GROUP MEMBER: But why?

SECRETARY: Well, if I don't, it's sticky in the morning.

GROUP MEMBER: But you don't drink coffee. Why do you care?

This brief interchange illustrates a good example of a feminine "rescue operation," a term frequently discussed by family therapist Shirley Luthman. Although Luthman uses this somewhat differently, the term in my own view is descriptive of the inordinate responsibility for others that a woman caught up in the stereotypic feminine role takes upon herself. The rescue operation derives from two basic tenets of traditional femininity: the expectation that women will emphasize nurturing and life-preserving activities and the injunction that women live for others rather than for themselves.

The need to rescue and/or take care of other people is a major obstacle to setting realistic and appropriate limits for oneself. Carol, for example, found her rescue operation interfering with getting her job done. Carol worked in a large computer center as a programmer. Other people used the computer, and knowing less about it than Carol, they often asked her questions. Because Carol was the one person on the staff who always politely responded to any requests for information, she was of course asked more questions than anyone else.

Carol set up this situation to role play in front of her assertive training group. Her first rehearsal, which follows, clearly told part of her problem.

QUESTIONER (looks around the room and fumbles with some papers)

CAROL (looking at the person through the corner of her eye):   Do you need some help?

QUESTIONER: Well, yes. Do you know. . . .

On seeing this brief interchange, the group was dumbfounded. Not only had Carol not set her limits with the questioner, she had actually volunteered her services. The strength of Carol's "rescue operation" was such that a look of distress was sufficient to provoke a reaction.

The feeling of responsibility to take care of other people runs deeply through the experience of many women. At times the rescuing takes place at deep personal cost. As a woman who has had to fight a strong tendency to rescue others myself, I was very pleased after completing one assertive training workshop, when I received the following letter from Diane. In her letter, Diane describes how she had begun dealing with her own rescue operation in setting limits for herself.

My first strong assertion came about last week when I said "No, I really don't feel I can get any more involved in Nancy's life." To understand how dramatic a change this is from my unassertive self, I need to give some background on my complete lack of assertiveness in this area.

I spent four and one-half years living with a brilliant man who unfortunately was an alcoholic. On nine different occasions, I put up with his drinking bouts. He had lost his license because of drunk driving. Therefore I became his driver. This included waiting outside bars for literally hours. When he decided he had had enough drinking for awhile, I took him to the hospital (three different ones) for detoxification. Then I picked him up three or four days later, only to find the first stop after the hospital was the corner bar. This went on for the four and one-half years we were together, ending in his suicide.

During this time, my wants were almost completely squashed. I complained to very few people, and then only a little. I was the "nice" wife, nursing and protecting and going along with the wishes of a man who, during most of that time, was out of the world of reality. His suicide, instead of releasing me from my unassertive position, heaped guilt on my head. Because I had not asserted myself toward David when he was alive, it was impossible to do so when he was dead. I felt it necessary to seek professional help for the depression, guilt, and anger inside of me. Because I didn't assert myself and untangle myself from this situation by saying, "This is it if you continue to drink," I spent three years paying off debts he had incurred.

Not too surprisingly, those four and one-half years have left me with an overreaction to anyone who is drunk. I am immediately filled with an almost uncontrollable anger. I shake from anger and feel my heart racing when I must deal with someone who is drunk. One of the people I have dealt with when she is drunk is my husband's sister Nancy, who is also an alcoholic. I have been the "nice" person as I sit and try to get her to drink coffee, put on her clothes, or go to the nearest detoxification hospital. All the while I feel the unexpressed anger that built up over those years of marriage.

The events leading up to my assertive step were as follows. Nancy usually calls about once a week to chat when she is not under the influence of alcohol. By Thursday I had not heard from her for over a week. I called her psychiatrist and found out she had missed her last two appointments and had not answered her phone calls for over a week. I went to her apartment house and her car was in the garage, but I saw no sign of life at her apartment. Previously, under such circumstances I would have entered her apartment and then I would have been involved in getting her to the hospital. Wednesday night I decided I would not walk into this unpleasant situation. Thursday I called the manager of her apartment and explained I feared she might need assistance.

The security guard entered her apartment and found her incoherent and very drunk. I relayed this information to her psychiatrist, and he wanted me to go over to her apartment to try to sober her up. This would be a replay of all those years with David continuing on and on. After thinking about the problem for some time, I informed the psychiatrist and the apartment manager I didn't feel I could get any more involved and I would not be going over to rescue Nancy.

After asserting myself I felt relieved and at long last freed from my subservient place in the lives of these two people. Contrary to what I expected, the doctor and the apartment manager both accepted my statement without any argument or explanation. I realized it was because I had a right to do what I felt was best for me.

The rest of the afternoon and evening I had twinges of "not being a nice person" and "everybody, especially Nancy, certainly won't like me," but I had no regrets for what I said. It is as though a new pathway has opened in my forest of emotions. I think it was easier to assert myself to two strangers. It probably would have been harder if I had had to be assertive to Nancy in person, but I hope I have progressed up the ladder of assertiveness to the place where I can also assert myself directly to Nancy. What a pity I did not have this courage years ago.

don't let criticism stop you

Fear of criticism is perhaps the most potent of the many factors that have an inhibiting influence on self-assertion. Take Donna, a young student, for example. Donna does not offer any opinions in class because she fears that someone might call her ideas stupid. Look at Nancy, a secretary. Nancy does not tell her roommate Vivian she would like the ice trays filled after the ice has been used because she is afraid Vivian will counter with something critical about her own housekeeping habits. The examples are everywhere. Betty is afraid to return a dress that does not fit because she fears a hostile reaction from the sales clerk. Alice does not pursue her interest in taking ballet because she is afraid someone might laugh at her.

Criticism is an especially frightening consequence for a person who accepts two common irrational assumptions. *Assumption number one:* For me to be "okay," it is absolutely necessary that I am liked by and approved of by everyone. *Assumption number two:* For me to feel good about myself, I must never make a mistake. The negative effects of these particular irrational beliefs have been thoroughly documented by Ellis in his book *Reason and Emotion in Psychotherapy.* Ellis has actually based his system of Rational Emotive Psychotherapy on the harmful effects of such beliefs.

Without doubt, the two assumptions affect both women and men. However, there is some evidence that women may be influenced more than men by the assumption that an individual's self-worth is dependent on the positive responses of other people. In *The Psychology of Women,* Judith Bardwich notes that "being loved" is more important to developing girls than to boys of the same age. And most women tend to view themselves from the vantage point, not of what they have achieved, but of the affection they have received from other people.

If a woman's "okayness" depends on her pleasing other people, she will frequently feel bad about herself. To please everyone is an impossible task. As I jokingly tell women in my assertive workshops, "I could sit in a corner and never say a word that could possibly offend anyone." Still someone would say, 'I don't like that woman sitting in the corner. She's not assertive enough.'" My point, of course, is that no matter how hard a woman tries, she will not be liked by everyone. Since every woman will confront criticism of her assertion, it is important that she learn to respond assertively to criticism.

RESPONDING ASSERTIVELY TO CRITICISM

The inhibiting influence of criticism was highlighted for me recently when one assertive group chose to devote an entire evening to the issue. The group began with a discussion of how people typically respond to criticism. "I can tell you how I respond," offered Lee, a graduate student in English. "When I'm criticized, no matter what the criticism is, I apologize. I say, 'Yes, that's true and that really is awful and I'm a terrible person.'"

Cynthia, a computer programmer, observed, "I get a lot of criticism associated with my job. Every programmer in my company does. But I'm not at all like Lee. Whenever I'm criticized, I become defensive. I start to explain why I'm doing what I'm doing. If that doesn't stop the criticism, I start attacking the other person. I really don't even hear what the other person says. I just try to demolish them before they demolish me."

Lucy, a laboratory technician, added, "You know, I really don't know how to handle criticism in any way. I once lost a job because I let my employer believe that the criticism he had heard about me was valid. It wasn't true, but there was no way at that time that I could stand up for myself and tell him so."

The responses of Cynthia, Lucy, and Lee are fairly typical. Even though these three women respond in different ways to criticism (Lee apologizes, Cynthia defends and counterattacks, Lucy says nothing), the effect is the same. Each woman ends up feeling bad about herself. Lee accepts feedback about herself that does not fit her view of who she is. She apologizes about something that she does not intend to alter, thereby giving an erroneous message to the other person. Cynthia's automatic defensiveness keeps her from hearing criticism that may be valid. Her tendency to counterattack does not allow her to compromise or respond to the needs and feelings of another person. The perceived threat of the criticism makes an open response impossible. The consequence of Lucy's habitual silence is already evident. She once lost a job because of her nonassertive stance.

Fortunately, criticism does not invariably lead to negative feelings about oneself and other people. When a woman responds in a nondefensive, nonapologetic, and nonattacking manner, she frequently finds that the criticism directed toward her loses much of its sting. The purpose of this chapter is to demonstrate how a woman can deal with criticism in such an assertive manner.

There are five basic ways a woman can respond assertively to criticism from another person:

1. Accept the criticism
2. Disagree with the criticism
3. Set limits with the person who is criticizing her
4. "Fog" away the criticism
5. Delay her response

As with all self-assertion, the alternative a woman chooses will depend on her feelings at the moment. All the above responses are assertive in that they allow a woman to state her honest feelings without attacking the other person. All responses allow a woman to maintain the basic position, "I'm okay. You're okay."

Accepting the criticism

In the assertive workshop I usually ask each woman to write down one realistic and one unrealistic or preposterous criticism about herself. You may want to do the same. These self-criticisms are useful in learning how to respond to criticism from other people. Make both criticisms "you" messages: "You are lazy," "You are selfish," "You are wrong." This is how most people give us negative feedback.

In the group, after writing the realistic and preposterous criticisms and putting her name at the top, I ask each woman to hand the messages to two other women. Thus Paula hands one criticism to Kathy and another to Nan. Later, when the group practices how to respond assertively to negative feedback, Kathy and Nan will each criticize Paula with the criticisms that Paula herself has written. Table 9.1 outlines how to do this exercise in a group setting.

When a criticism is realistic, your most powerful assertive response may be a simple acceptance of the criticism, an acceptance that does not apologize, does not defend, and does not put yourself down. Thus if someone criticizes me, "Pam, your report is not well written," and I feel this criticism is valid, I can assertively reply, "You're right. I'm going to brush it up tonight." If my reply is stated with direct eye contact and a firm tone of voice, I convey to the other person verbally and nonverbally, "I did not write a perfect report, and I plan to correct it. However, being perfect is not a condition of my okayness. I can make mistakes without feeling bad, inferior, or wrong." In contrast, if I reply to the criticism about my report, "Oh, I'm really sorry, I just can't seem to get it together. I had company last night, and I wasn't able to get anything done," I would be accepting and even accentuating a not okay position.

TABLE 9.1   Dealing with Preposterous and Realistic Criticism

---

1. Think of one realistic and one unrealistic or preposterous criticism about yourself. Write each criticism on a separate piece of paper. Put your name at the top of each piece.
2. Exchange one of your criticisms with the woman on your left; exchange the other criticism with the woman on your right.
3. When the exercise begins, take your turn giving and receiving criticism.
4. When you are criticized, accept your realistic criticism and disagree with your preposterous criticism. Practice affirming yourself after you disagree. If appropriate, set limits with an aggressive criticism.
5. Note your reactions. Was it easier for you to accept criticism or to disagree with it? How did you feel when you affirmed yourself? Were you able to set limits with your critic? How did you feel criticizing another person?

In responding to realistic criticism, some women find that a simple acceptance or acknowledgment that the criticism is valid has the paradoxical effect of putting an immediate end to the criticism. If Tom criticizes Miranda, "You're always late," and Miranda agrees, "You're right, Tom. I am late most of the time. I really am working on being on time," Miranda usually will find that an acknowledgment is all Tom wanted to hear. Had Miranda responded to Tom's criticism "You're late again" with the excuse, "Yes, but I was busy finishing my report," it is very doubtful that the criticism would have stopped there. Tom's counter-response would probably have gone something like this: "Well, you're not the only person who has other things to do. I made an effort to get here anyway. Why didn't you?"

In most cases a "yes, but" excuse tends to escalate a conflict. The forthright acceptance of criticism is an assertive alternative to such defensiveness. This alternative is difficult only for the woman who accepts the irrational assumption "I must be perfect to be okay." If this assumption is challenged, many women find a great deal of power in allowing themselves to be, perhaps for the first time, an imperfect member of the human family.

Disagreeing with criticism

There are times when criticism does not fit. There are occasions when criticism is based on false information. If this is the case, it is important *not* to accept the criticism. It is important to disagree. Yet many women find it impossible to challenge a criticism they feel is invalid. A compliment may be dismissed "You must be kidding," but a criticism is swallowed without question. How many of you have had the experience of being in a situation where everyone was friendly and complimentary except one person? In terms of your feelings, did the twenty positive responses or the one negative response have the most effect? Many of us would find that a critical reaction has much more influence than a positive one.

In the exercise on responding to criticism, I discovered that many women do not permit themselves to say "I disagree." Doris, for example, accepted her first criticism "You're always late." Then when her second criticism— "You never do anything for me"—was directed to her, she agreed again. In fact, she apologized, "I'm sorry. What would you like me to do?" Because her second reply had a discordant ring to it, I asked, "Is that what you really wanted to say?" "No!", Doris vehemently replied. "I wanted to say 'I disagree with your statement. It just isn't true.'"

Why do we have such difficulty disagreeing with criticism? In exploring this issue, I have found that many women equate disagreeing with attacking another person. Our culture tends to have the viewpoint that if you and I do not agree in every significant respect, then either you are not okay or I am not okay. You are wrong or I am wrong. There is no room for both of us to be different. But this is simply not so. Only when two people stop trying to be identical can they begin to experience their own unique-ness. Looked at from this framework, disagreeing is not judging "You are bad," it is stating "I differ from you."

Criticism that is too broad: Have you ever noticed how many critical remarks contain the words "always" or "never?" "You're *always* late." "You *never* think about me." Disagreeing with such criticisms may simply mean refusing to accept such a broad negative evaluation.

One of the difficulties in responding to overly broad criticism is that many people accept a categorical inter-pretation of their behavior. They agree with the premise, "If you are not absolutely perfect, then you are guilty of whatever criticism is offered." In other words, you are either one-hundred percent considerate or you are incon-siderate. You're a good housekeeper, or you are not. You are well organized, or you are sloppy. Lazarus emphasizes the importance of looking at behavior in relative rather than in categorical terms in his book *Behavior Therapy and Beyond.* In no area is a relative approach more im-portant than in dealing with criticism.

In responding to criticism that has some grain of truth but which is overly broad, a focused disagreement works best. A focused disagreement allows a woman to view her-self in relative terms. A focused disagreement allows her to accept the valid aspects of a criticism while separating herself from the erroneous portions. I have found that many women find it very liberating to determine for themselves what they do and do not accept from a critical remark.

Audrey described an incident to one group that allowed us to examine how focused disagreement works. Audrey was confronted with a criticism that was partially true but that was much too broad. Audrey was talking to a coworker, Diane, when their supervisor came into the office and crit-ically remarked, "Don't you two *ever* start on time?" Audrey felt that the criticism was intended more for Diane than for her since Diane was often late for work, but the criticism was given jointly, and Audrey felt bad about it. At the time the remark was made, Audrey felt that she could not disagree. She *was* talking when she should have been at her desk. Yet her discomfort came, in part, from feeling that the criticism was unfair and that she did not like being viewed in that way. In sorting out what she really wanted to convey, Audrey came up with the simple statement "Today, I *am* late getting started. Today really is the exception, however. I'm usually at my desk at nine." Audrey focused her disagreement on the part of the remark that was invalid. She did not defend herself or make excuses. She simply clarified the facts.

Criticism based on value judgments: There are also times when a criticism is not based solely on a factual incident but on a broad evaluation and interpretation of the meaning of that incident. This happened with Carrie, a young accountant who upon graduation went to work for a large, rather impersonal accounting firm. During tax season, Carrie was frequently asked to work overtime. One Monday, when her husband was ill, Carrie refused to work past the normal five o'clock quitting time. In refusing the overtime assignment, Carrie did not give her supervisor the full picture. She did not explain that her husband was ill, but neither did she feel that this was necessary. Several weeks later, Carrie met with the firm's personnel officer to go over her quarterly performance evaluation. She was somewhat shocked to hear that her immediate supervisor had criticized her by saying that she did not seem committed to the firm. After thinking for a moment, Carrie was certain that her supervisor, Michael, was annoyed that she had once refused to work overtime and that this one incident had provoked the interpretation "not committed to the firm." However, rather than disagree or set the record straight, Carrie told herself, "Michael is entitled to his own opinion. He can believe what he wants to believe."

When Carrie told her group about this incident, everyone was of one mind. In this situation, the opinion of Carrie's supervisor was not totally his own business. It was also Carrie's concern since the criticism could have a direct effect on her career. Several women in the group emphasized how important it was for Carrie to set the record straight. Although Carrie knew what she really wanted to say, it took some practice before she comfortably asserted, "I strongly disagree with Michael's observation that I am not committed to this firm. I believe this criticism is based on the fact that I refused to work overtime on one occasion. My husband was ill that night, and it was actually very difficult for me to work at all that day. Except for this one occasion, I worked overtime for the firm every time I was asked. As you are probably aware, this amounted to approximately thirty nights of overtime."

Note that Carrie's reply is at level-two muscle. Her words "I strongly disagree" and the *specific* facts that she cites add to her statement. The focused disagreement of criticisms based on value judgments works best when a woman clearly states specific incidents that lie behind the judgment. Then she can disagree, as Carrie did, that the facts support such a broad evaluation.

Person-oriented versus behavior-oriented criticism: Focused disagreement is also useful when criticism fails to distinguish between who we are and what we have done. Karen received the criticism "You are a pushy woman" from a male faculty member who was registering students for classes. Karen was able to reply, "Well, I am certainly pushing to obtain my undergraduate degree, but no, I am not a pushy woman." By her comment, Karen was able to differentiate her behavior in one situation from her general approach to life.

There are other times when a woman is saddled with criticism that was once valid but is no longer appropriate. Cynthia, a social worker, faced a yearly performance evaluation which invariably contained a statement to the effect that she was a nonassertive person. "I'll admit that the first three years in my job, I was nonassertive," Cynthia explained. "However, since that time, I have changed a tremendous amount. To cite just one example, I fired my social work aid under very difficult circumstances. Yet, I stood my ground throughout the entire procedure. The old view of me no longer feels right, and I'd like to change it." Cynthia went on to add, "The focused disagreement which I would like to make is to my social work supervisor. I would like to tell her that I was nonassertive when I first began this job. However, that no longer is the case. I think the way that I assertively handled the difficult situation with my aid demonstrates that I have changed!"

Cynthia's last statement goes beyond focused disagreement. Cynthia also stated her new position as it is now. She acknowledged and affirmed herself as a person who does respond assertively.

Self-affirmation: When a woman states, "I can't accept that criticism" or "I disagree with what you just said," she is essentially blocking a not okay message from another person. But a woman can go one step further. She can actively describe how the criticism does not fit. She can affirm her okayness by stating her own opposing viewpoint. This is illustrated in Figure 9.1.

To go back for a moment to my original example, if someone said to me, "Pam, your report is not well written," and I did not agree with this observation, I could assertively reply, "I don't agree." I could also go one step further and affirm, "In fact, I spent a great deal of time researching the issues, and I am quite pleased with the way that I have presented them."

193

FIGURE 9.1 When criticism is unrealistic, a woman comes from a powerful position when she not only disagrees but also affirms her own positive view of herself.

If you are wondering how anyone could make the above statement, remember that old negative labels of "conceited," "bragging," and "overly confident" quickly surface when a woman speaks positively about herself. The important issue is do we determine our own behavior and our own values or do we give someone else that power? It may surprise no one that a woman's usual tendency is to invest her power in other people. In contrast, self-affirmation allows a woman to state, "I can evaluate and support myself. I am not at the mercy of other people. I do not allow other people to determine how I view myself."

Dale, a well-established, highly respected bank officer, shared with me an incident that occurred early in her career. This incident provides a clear example of self-affirmation. After Dale attended a meeting with a group of bank executives, she was asked to read the notes she had taken. When she had read her notes, one of the executives asked, "Is that all of the business we conducted today? You don't take very good notes, do you?" Dale's reply, "I actually haven't had much experience taking notes for other people. I have always been used to participating fully in the discussion" is a striking example of self-affirmation. Not only did Dale not accept the message "You're not okay," but she let the group of executives know that she saw herself in a positive way, equal in all respects to everyone else in the group. Contrast Dale's reply with a self-deprecating comment such as "I'm really sorry. I am a terrible note taker."

Self-affirmation serves an important function, even when a woman is not criticized directly. Self-affirmation can put a halt to a woman's own self-criticism. In one situation, Helen was having dinner with her close friend Rochelle. During cocktails, Rochelle excitedly related to Helen that Norrie, a mutual acquaintance, had in record time established her own boutique. Rochelle's remark, although not intended as a criticism, nevertheless evoked in Helen a wave of anxiety and self-approach. New businesses were a sensitive subject to Helen since she herself had decided to open her own small shop.

Helen, however, had not found her business in record time. She was in fact moving slowly, carefully gathering the information she felt she needed to make a wise decision. Recognizing her feelings, Helen was able to say, more to herself than to Rochelle, "I'm really happy for Norrie. My style is different from hers though. I need to take my time and find something that I am sure suits me." Through her self-affirmation, Helen acknowledged "I'm okay." You may want to try out the self-affirmation responses to criticism listed in Table 9.2.

Limit setting

As I listened to women in various assertive training groups deal with realistic and preposterous criticism, it soon became evident that "I disagree" was not a satisfactory response to some of the hostile attacks women had directed against themselves. Criticisms such as "You're a terrible mother," "That was a stupid comment," "You're a very boring person," or "You are fat and ugly" evoked feelings that needed to be resolved over and above the issue of whether the criticism was valid. These feelings necessitated the setting of limits with the husband, friend, employer, boss, or acquaintance who was doing the criticizing.

You may recall that setting limits involves teaching another person how we expect to be treated. This includes teaching another person how to give us negative feedback. Since aggressive criticism can and often does harm a person, it is very important that a woman know and assert her limits in this particular area.

In one class that I was teaching, I asked each member to describe an incident where they were nonassertive and the consequences of their nonassertion. Bonnie, one of the class members, gave an excellent example of the type

---

TABLE 9.2

Criticism	Disagreement and Self-Affirmation
You're too demanding.	I don't agree. I think I'm learning to be assertive.
You spend too much time in your work.	I can't accept that. I feel that I'm doing something important to me.
You're selfish.	I disagree. At last I'm trying to take care of myself.
You can't get close to other people.	That's really not true. Relating to others is one of my strongest points.
You're overly concerned.	No. I feel that I devote my full attention only to issues that need that amount of concern.
You're never organized.	I find that I am very organized with those activities which are important to me.

---

of destructive criticism each of us occasionally encounters. I would like to share with you Bonnie's description, which she ingeniously titled *Portnoy's Complaint.*

> Several months after I had completed reservation and ticketing training with one of the national airlines, I accepted a position with a travel agency. My employer, Mr. Portnoy, knew my qualifications as a travel agent—99.1 average and no experience—so he informed me from the outset that I had a lot to learn and that when he finished training me I'd definitely know the travel business.
>
> As I prepared for my first day of work I was quite excited. I really wanted to become a first-rate travel agent.
>
> My first assignment seemed relatively routine, and I accepted with confidence Mr. Portnoy's request to book three specific flights for his clients. Unfortunately, the airline reservation agent informed me that those three flights were fully booked. After hearing that news I confidently strode into Mr. Portnoy's office to get alternative instructions.
>
> "I told you to get me flights!" he shouted, loud enough for the entire office to hear. "Do you have any flights? No?!! I don't need stupid people around this office! When I say flights, I want flights!!!"

Stunned, I walked shakily back to my desk. "How can I get those flights when I've been told that they're fully booked. I really must be stupid! I don't know what to do!"

Fortunately another employee came to my rescue and told me to book alternate reservations as close to the original departing time as possible. A clear, simple alternative that Mr. Portnoy could have pointed out to me.

My entire working experience in Mr. Portnoy's office was filled with incidents similar to this first one. I never stopped Mr. Portnoy when he called me stupid. I never once pointed out the fact that what I lacked was experience rather than intellect. I simply remained silent and allowed my self-confidence to be torn from me by his continuing abuse.

I became so nervous, unsure, and apprehensive that my performance never improved. In fact, it actually deteriorated. My anxiety rose with each passing day, until one day I went home "sick" never to return to the travel business.

As Bonnie mentioned in her vivid description of aggressive criticism, had she been assertive, she would have set limits with Mr. Portnoy by immediately stopping him when he used the term "stupid." "Wait just a minute," she might have said, "I resent being labeled 'stupid.' I lack experience, not intellect." From Bonnie's description of Mr. Portnoy, it is not inconceivable that he might have fired her. No catastrophe for someone with Bonnie's credentials. On the other hand, Portnoy might have reconsidered his abusive behavior. Had he been unresponsive to her limit setting, Bonnie could have raised her muscle. If level-two muscle was also ineffective, she had within her power an important consequence. She could resign.

Fogging

Manuel Smith, author of *When I Say No I Feel Guilty,* has formulated a method of dealing with criticism that he terms "fogging." Fogging is a response to criticism that does not say "yes" or "no." If I am fogging, I neither agree nor disagree with a criticism. Instead, I briefly acknowledge that a person has criticized me and then quickly move on to another subject. The analogy I like to use in explaining fogging is this: If I walk through a fog bank, I am not changed by it in any way. The fog has no effect on me or on the direction I am traveling. A whimsical contrast to walking through fog is walking through a briar patch. If I walk through a briar patch, I am pricked and scratched. I have to spend a great deal of time unhooking my clothes from the snagging briars. I have to walk very carefully to keep from getting caught, and I am exhausted when I finally get out of the area. But if I walk through fog, nothing touches me.

How do I change a potential briar patch into a fog bank? I can use some basic expressions such as "You *may* be right," "I *can* see how you *might* think that," or "*Sometimes,* I *may* be selfish." Notice the italicized words. These words allow me to avoid accepting or disagreeing with a criticism.

I usually give the following example of fogging to assertion workshops: If someone said to me, "Pam, you're a selfish person," I could fog by replying "I *may* be selfish *sometimes*" or "That *may* be true." The accusation of being selfish does not particularly bother me.

I was giving this favorite example to one group when one woman said, "I couldn't fog away the label 'selfish.' It really has too much feeling behind it for me." I immediately realized and shared with the group that neither would I want to fog away the criticism "Pam, you're stupid" by replying "You may be right." My emotional response would demand that I set limits with this particular criticism. In my own opinion, fogging is most useful when a criticism does not evoke a strong emotional reaction. This brings us back to the recognition that self-assertion flows from an individual's internal response. Fogging is simply another alternative for a woman to use in conveying her feelings.

Delaying

The fifth and final method of dealing with criticism is delaying. There are times when criticism takes a woman completely by surprise. She feels confused; she does not know what she wants to say. This experience occurs less and less frequently as a woman becomes more assertive, but it is nevertheless an experience that must be considered.

Again, a woman can respond assertively in such a situation simply by indicating the confusion, surprise, and/or disappointment that the criticism provokes. At that moment she does not respond to the content of the criticism. Thus, a woman might say, "I'm really confused about that criticism. Let me think about it for a few minutes."

Giving oneself permission not to respond immediately to criticism in no way contradicts the goal of being spontaneous. My spontaneous reaction may be, "I don't know how to respond to that. Let me consider it and get back to you." Feeling free to express our feelings of confusion or our inability to respond means that we are less likely to accept a criticism which does not fit or let someone get away with an aggressive attack. By backing up for a moment to examine our feelings, rather than simply reacting from panic, we can most effectively sort out and respond to the realities of the critical message.

PUTTING IT TOGETHER

Teresa, a psychiatric nurse, wanted to try out her new skill in dealing with criticism and see if she could actually use the various assertive alternatives that had been discussed. Because she wanted a relatively intense experience, we set up an exercise called "centering," where Teresa stood in the center of a circle composed of the other group members. The group agreed to criticize Teresa with both realistic, unrealistic, and aggressive criticisms.

As you may imagine, responding to criticisms that come spontaneously from someone else causes much more anxiety than dealing with those criticisms you yourself have written. For this reason I use "centering" only after the exercise on realistic-preposterous criticism has been completed. Centering provides an exaggerated critical situation in which a woman can test her mastery of the assertive concepts.

Teresa asked that the group's criticisms toward her relate to a decision she had made in one encounter group several months previously. Teresa's decision not to talk during that particular meeting about herself or her problems had led to a critical confrontation with the other group members. Because she had been unable to withstand the group's criticism, Teresa had revealed much more about herself than she had wanted to reveal.

Picture Teresa in the center of a circle composed of other group members. The centering went something like this:

GROUP MEMBER 1: You aren't talking much tonight. (Mildly critical)

TERESA: I know. I really feel like just sitting here and listening. (Accepting the criticism)

GROUP MEMBER 2: You never say anything in the group.

TERESA: Well, I disagree. Today I have been exceptionally quiet, but I usually contribute to the group. (Focused disagreement, self-affirmation)

GROUP MEMBER 3: You'll never get anything out of the group if you don't talk about yourself.

TERESA: You may be right, but I really don't feel like talking tonight. (Fogging, setting limits)

GROUP MEMBER 4: You're just a distant person. You don't want to get close to anyone else.

TERESA: I can't accept that. Getting close to other people isn't one of my problems. (Disagreeing, self-affirmation)

GROUP MEMBER 5: If you would just get off your high horse and come down to reality, you might see yourself as you really are.

TERESA: Wait just a minute. I really resent what you just said. I don't want to talk about this further. (Setting limits)

GROUP MEMBER 6: You're getting defensive.

TERESA: I'll have to think about that, but right now I don't want the group focusing on me. (Delaying, setting limits)

the
professional
woman

10

WANTED: INSURANCE EXECUTIVE

Competitive, ambitious person with leadership ability needed to head our Investment Division. We want someone who is self-sufficient and dominant. The position requires strong analytical ability. This is the perfect job for an independent, self-reliant individual.

WANTED: INSURANCE EXECUTIVE

Affectionate, childlike person who does not use harsh language needed to head our Investment Division. We want someone who is cheerful and eager to soothe hurt feelings. The position requires gullibility. This is the perfect job for the tender, yielding individual.

The adjectives in these advertisements were chosen randomly from the Bem Sex-Role Inventory's Masculine and Feminine Items respectively. You will recall that Bem found that qualities viewed as desirable for a woman differ from those considered positive for a man. In composing both Wanted: Insurance Executive ads, I simply drew items from the two sets of diverse adjectives and placed them into the framework of a standard job advertisement. The question "Which advertisement fits reality?" really does not need to be raised. It is obvious that only those qualities described in the first advertisement (desirable masculine attributes) are consistent with those expected in a professional position. An advertisement composed of positive feminine qualities seems at best humorous, at worst ludicrous.

The contrast highlighted above demonstrates the diverse demands and expectations under which the American working woman operates. The traditional qualities and characteristics considered desirable for women are not those thought important for the competent professional. This matter affects a not insignificant number of women. In 1973 almost forty-four percent of working-aged women were employed. Between 1950 and 1973, the labor force participation of women rose by one-third.

The increasing number of women workers in the United States labor force, however, find themselves facing what V. K. Oppenheimer terms two separate labor markets: a male market and a female market. They find a labor market segregated into female and male jobs on the basis of sex-role definitions. The most common jobs for women—being a nurse, teacher, or a secretary—are those that involve nurturing or caring for the needs of someone else, behaviors entirely consistent with the "other orientation" of stereotyped femininity. On the other hand, qualities that women are supposed to possess are not those which are desirable in higher paying "masculine jobs." The advertisements at the beginning of the chapter provide an exaggerated case in point.

The impact of stereotyped notions of what is suitably feminine and what is suitably masculine must not be underestimated. In this chapter we will examine the effect of stereotypic femininity on the women professional—particularly upon the woman not choosing to conform to the traditional feminine role.

THE PROFESSIONAL VERSUS THE FEMININE ROLE

My first interest in the incompatible roles that women face came directly from my own personal experience. As an undergraduate student, I remember being warned by a male psychology professor that the more years of college a woman completed, the less chance she had of getting married. The dilemma at that time felt very real to me—a woman must choose marriage or a career. The feminine role, unlike the masculine role, does not permit her to have both. A friend of mine recently shared that she had had a similar experience. She had no encouragement (except from her parents) in her desire to become a medical doctor and few, if any, role models showing her a successful combination of doctor, wife, and mother. People kept telling her, "'Why be a doctor? You'll get married anyway." Unlike her male colleagues, she was not expected to have both a profession and a marriage.

The professional-feminine role conflict affects even the woman who has been able to establish herself in a profession. As one woman put it, "When I'm at work, I seem to be wearing a sandwich board. One side says 'mother' and the other side says 'professional woman'. I never know which side of the board someone else is reading." Another woman described to me how she walked out of the professional role when she left her office and changed into a totally opposite set of behaviors when she arrived home. The confusion between roles can be intense. A woman must often learn an entirely new way of relating if she is to become a successful professional. The task is not easy. "I was a secretary for eight years before I became a manager," Nancy told me, "but I find that I still have the tendency to cater to everyone else's beck and call. I forget that I am now the manager."

In no area is the feminine role-professional role conflict demonstrated more clearly than in the symbolic issue of who will take the notes in a professional meeting. Taking notes (or making coffee or performing any other caretaking function) is an expected part of the female sex role. However, a woman who habitually fulfills this nurturing function can and frequently does interfere with her own professional position.

For example, consider the following situation. John, the manager of a large chain of department stores, is holding a monthly meeting with his assistant managers: George, Alex, Carl, and Sue. The meeting is being held to consider a new proposal about employee benefits.

JOHN (turning directly to Sue):   You don't mind taking notes, do you?

SUE: No, of course not. (Although silently to herself Sue thinks: "How dare you suggest that I take notes. It's just because I am the only woman here that I am asked to do it.")

FIGURE 10.1 The professional woman frequently gets caught in the traditional feminine role. Although functioning in a position of authority, she is expected to be caretaker of everyone else's needs.

In one assertive workshop, we took the note-taking issue and practiced how to deal with it. The difficulties involved in this particular situation and the various coping strategies that were employed to deal with it provided the group with a detailed look at this symbolic dilemma.

Elaine, a consultant with a state consumer agency, was the first to volunteer. Elaine explained that she was the logical candidate for this particular rehearsal, since she had actually attended the assertiveness workshop because of the note-taking problem. In trying to get out of taking notes herself, Elaine had offered her own secretary's service. Jan, Elaine's secretary, resented being pulled from her own work and brought into another office to take notes, so she suggested my course to Elaine. Elaine's first rehearsal went something like this:

MANAGER: You don't mind taking notes, do you?

ELAINE: You know, I really don't take very good notes. I find that I can't effectively concentrate on more than one thing at a time. Why don't I find someone else to take them?

MANAGER: Okay, fine. Why don't you have your secretary come in?

ELAINE (stopping the rehearsal): That's what happened to me last time. That's why I'm here. I'm trapped!

Elaine's trap in this instance is her automatic "rescue operation". With her offer "Why don't *I* find someone else to take them?", Elaine stepped in to rescue the manager— to solve his problem for him. The knowledge that she was supposed to give an *assertive* response did not interfere with her habitual "service" position.

Before asking Elaine to try again, I checked out one additional issue with her. "Do you really think that your notes are not good?" Elaine smiled, "No, my notes are always·very good." The next logical question—"Then, why did you put yourself down?"—did not need to be asked. Every woman in the room understood what Elaine's statement was all about. Only by minimizing her own competence had Elaine been able to assert her desire not to take notes.

Self-minimization is a common tactic of women. We have learned not to assert ourselves from a position of strength but from one of weakness. This tactic is certainly not reserved for the professional woman alone. As a young mother in one group put it, "When I try to set limits, I always put myself down. I say something like 'You know what a neurotic, fussy housewife I am, but would you please take your feet off my antique table!' " Self-minimization, as we shall see, is one aspect of the stereotypic feminine role that can do great damage to the woman professional.

Elaine began her second rehearsal:

MANAGER: You don't mind taking notes, do you?

ELAINE: I really feel put down that you asked me to take notes. (Aside to the group, "You bastard!")

Elaine's assertion was direct and honest and, except for her side comment, not aggressive. She simply stated her feelings. She did not attack the manager. The feedback from the group was generally positive. But several women suggested that Elaine's response (even without the aside) may have been at level-two muscle, that it was too high for an initial assertion in that situation. Elaine acknowledged that she had allowed a great deal of hostility to build up and asked the group, "What would be a lower level alternative?"

Janet, an elementary school teacher, suggested, "Why not say 'I would rather not be responsible for notes.' That would make the same point, but I don't think that the words would have as much emotional impact. I personally wouldn't want to get into the male-female issue."

Betsy, a secretary, offered a second alternative. "How about 'I would be glad to take notes this time, but if this is going to be a regular procedure, I don't want to be responsible for them at every meeting. Let's assign a different person to take notes each time.' "

Jill, a free-lance artist, argued, "Why mince words. I would be even stronger than Elaine in my assertion. I would say 'As a woman, I resent being asked to take notes.' We would have the issue out once and for all."

Each of the above alternatives is assertive. No one offered an aggressive counter such as "You are really not with it, are you?" The exact words Elaine eventually chooses to use, however, will depend entirely upon her own feelings at the moment and her own personal style. The same is true for you. Your assertion will reflect your own style and your own manner. What is important is that you get across what you feel in a way which does not put down someone else.

The professional woman is of course struggling over much more than who will take the notes or who will make the coffee. She is struggling against all the constraints of her prescribed sex role. Because of the difficulty of this struggle, some women have given up completely. They function without ambivalence in the traditional feminine role. Other women, in reaction against the confines of stereotypic femininity, have resolved their turmoil by shifting roles. They fulfill the expectations of stereotypic masculinity, priding themselves on "acting like a man" and "thinking like a man." As Ann, the payroll manager of a San Francisco bank, revealed, "I almost never say anything about my feelings anymore. My requirements for myself—to be always cool and level-headed—are probably much more severe than those of any man in my office. But I'm afraid of being classified as a 'hysterical woman' so I steer myself completely in the other direction."

Moreover, even when women are themselves comfortable with their own behavior, external pressure for them to conform to either the stereotypic feminine or the stereotypic masculine role is intense. Carolyn was faced with this pressure during an interview for a job as a programmer. After' she had been hired, the man interviewing her explained, "I am not a male chauvinist. I'll treat you like I do anyone else. And that means that I expect you not to cry." Carolyn nodded and said nothing. In the group, however, she was able to put the feelings that she had wanted to express to him into words. She asserted, "I do not cry in order to manipulate anyone else. I cry only from hurt or pain and that is a part of myself that I do not want to change." Carolyn's latter statement clearly defined that she intended to be herself, a complete human being, unhindered by either a rigid feminine or a rigid masculine sex-role definition.

Functioning without inhibition in a professional position requires that a woman rid herself of three traditional feminine constraints: the fear of success, the reluctance to exercise legitimate authority, and the tendency toward self-minimization. The rest of this chapter will examine each constraint in more detail.

THE PURSUIT OF SUCCESS

Jeri Scott is a professional woman. In fact, she is one of the few women managing a regional advertising staff for a large nationwide newspaper. When asked what she envisioned herself doing in ten years, Jeri replied, "I can see myself as editor of a small town newspaper." Jayne Townsend, president of the San Francisco chapter of the National Organization for Women and director of her own consulting agency, is asked the same question. She projects that in ten years she would like to be mayor of a small community outside San Francisco.

Both these women have shown superior achievements up to now. Nevertheless, both see themselves in ten years as leaders of *small* outlying communities. In telling this story during one assertive workshop, Jeri explained, "After we had both made our ten-year projections, Jayne made the observation that if we were two men, in the positions we now hold, we would not settle for small town leadership.

I would be striving to become publisher of *The New York Times* and Jayne to be mayor of San Francisco, or even governor of California."

The research of Matina Horner provides a possible explanation of Jayne's and Jeri's behavior. In her 1968 doctoral dissertation at the University of Michigan, Horner gave female and male students the single clue, "After first term finals, Anne (John) finds herself (himself) at the top of her (his) medical school class." Horner asked men to write a story based on John. She asked women to write a story about Anne. Horner intended to look at female-male differences on the achievement motive, which is defined as "an internal standard of excellence, motivating an individual to do well." Horner felt that many women equated intellectual achievement with loss of femininity, and so evidenced a "motive to avoid success." If this were indeed the case, then that motive would conflict with the motive to achieve.

In examining the responses to her hypothetical description of Anne or John, Horner found that more than sixty-five percent of the women students told stories which reflected anxiety or concern about Anne's success. The most frequent stories recounted that social rejection followed Anne's success. Other stories questioned Anne's normality as a woman, and some stories even denied that Anne was really in a successful position. On the other hand, fewer than ten percent of the men tested had negative or anxiety-ridden stories to the "top of *his* medical school class" clue. These results confirmed for Horner the now familiar "fear of success" syndrome in women. Apparently, women develop a motive to avoid success that inhibits them in competitive stituations.

Subsequent research on fear of success reviewed in a 1973 article by David Tresemer, has questioned whether Horner's study reflected a true motive for women to avoid all success or simply a fear of sex-role inappropriateness.

In other words, success in the male-dominated profession of medicine may have seemed inappropriate to the women students. The traditional feminine role in our society has not encouraged women to assume a position of leadership in this area. It is of some interest to note that when men write stories about Anne, the stories contain even more fear of success imagery than those which women write. Men apparently view Anne's success with even more trepidation than do women.

Eleanor Maccoby and Carol Jacklin, in their comprehensive book *The Psychology of Sex Differences*, have suggested that a person's behavior is governed by her or his view of what is appropriate or inappropriate. Both women and men seem to view Anne's success in medical school as inappropriate behavior and write stories that reflect this underlying concern. The extent to which social inappropriateness governs behavior is documented in several experimental studies. For example, Thomas Wolf found that young girls play with "masculine" toys only after they see another female child playing with them. Watching young boys play with "masculine" toys does not influence their behavior.

Sandra Bem and Daryl Bem have also examined the influence of a women's view of sex-role appropriateness on her behavior. The Equal Employment Opportunities Commission asked Bem and Bem to examine how sex-biased job advertisements affect women's interest in certain jobs. Sex-biased advertisements are those written to appeal only to one sex. In advertisements biased against women, the job titles are male, and the pronoun *he* is the only one used. Unbiased advertisements use both female and male pronouns, and job titles do not contain the suffix *man*. For example, the unbiased advertisement for Telephone Lineworker says, "We're looking for Outdoor People! Are you a man or woman who likes fresh air and exercise?"

The result of Bem and Bem's study was clear-cut. Whereas only five percent of the women indicated an interest in jobs advertised in a sex-biased format, twenty-five percent were interested in jobs advertised witout bias. In other words, when jobs were not advertised in a manner that indicated they were inappropriate for women, women responded with interest.

The influence of what is viewed as appropriate and inappropriate sex-role behavior was further documented in a second experiment by Bem and Bem. This study demonstrated that sex-segregated want ads actively discouraged women from considering jobs. Whereas only forty-six percent of the women reading an ad would apply for a job when it was listed as "male interest," eighty-eight percent of women *preferred* the same job when it was listed without a limiting heading.

In short, the influence of sex-role stereotypes on the attitudes and behaviors of women is quite dramatic. The woman who wants to realize her full potential must recognize that she has been conditioned to see certain areas as off limits. The "fear of success syndrome" will only come to an end when women look beyond such artificial sex-role limitations and begin to take on positions of more responsibility and more power.

The power of "I want"

"I want" is definitely not a statement that fits the prototype of stereotypic femininity. It is, in a sense, exactly opposite to the other orientation that is characteristic of the traditional feminine role. A man can say "I'm out for number one" without censure, but an orientation toward self is considered inappropriate for a woman. Shirley Luthman, Codirector of The Family Therapy Institute in San Rafael, California, is one of the first women to recognize the power of the statement "I want." Luthman shared with a class that I attended her personal view of the power that comes from acknowledging one's own desires. She feels that once a person is completely in touch in her or his gut with "I want," she or he can then sit back and wait for events to move in the desired direction. There is no mysticism in this statement. Until a woman acknowledges her needs and desires, she cannot recognize or reach out for opportunities as they arise. My personal experience also bears this out. For example, only when I acknowledged to myself that I would like to appear on one of the morning television shows in San Francisco did I initiate any action to put myself there.

I worked recently with Tina, a woman who had decided to return to school to obtain a degree in business administration. Tina began psychotherapy because she found herself constantly confronting obstacles (many of them self-generated) that interfered with her career plans. What Tina and I came to observe as we worked together was her reluctance to acknowledge that she wanted a career *for herself.* Not "It would be nice to have a profession if my marriage fails" or "I could be of more help to my husband if I knew more about business," but simply "I want a career, regardless of whether I stay married or get a divorce." Once the "I want" was clear, Tina began to work for herself. Having a definite, concrete goal in mind, she began to take the steps needed to accomplish her objectives.

THE EXERCISE OF AUTHORITY

The second feminine constraint interfering with the professional woman is the reluctance to exercise legitimate authority. A good example of this occurred in a class I attended several years ago, which had as participants professional psychologists, social workers, and psychiatrists. Most of the participants were women. At the beginning, the class divided into five small discussion groups, and each group chose a leader. Four of the five leaders were men. A coincidence perhaps. Yet functioning as a leader or presenting oneself as an authority is extremely difficult for many women.

The difficulty in exercising authority is not limited to the problem of leading a group. It is also apparent in the woman who is unable to tell her housekeeper what she wants done, and in the woman who does the work of her subordinates because she does not want to seem bossy. It includes the woman who tells the assertive group that she prefers to express her ideas through a man, rather than express them herself, and the copy editor whose suggestions to authors are full of apologies when, in fact, making suggestions is part of her job.

With Joan, an attorney, the problem of asserting legitimate authority was the major focus of therapy. Although Joan was in a position of power (the highest ranking attorney in a group of five), she found herself doing almost all the unpleasant and tedious assignments. She went to most of the committee meetings with other agencies, leaving the four male attorneys time for more direct work with clients. In addition, Joan found herself frequently backing down from orders she had given, instead doing the jobs herself. Within the group, Joan described an encounter with Howard, a new attorney in the agency. Howard had attacked her the previous week because she had required him to take charge of a time-consuming but necessary report. Their confrontation had left her virtually speechless. Joan practiced expressing, "Howard, I want to talk with you about the situation last week. For me, it is unfinished."

She also rehearsed responding to criticism from her male colleagues. To the attack, "Joan, you mumble," she replied in a loud, clear voice, "Yes, sometimes I do. Can you hear me now?" To the criticism, "Joan, you're too gullible," she disagreed, "That isn't true. After working years in this office, there is no way that I could be gullible. I do believe in reasonable doubt." Initially, Joan's eyes went down and her voice trailed off as she made these strong assertions, but with practice her statements sounded confident and forceful.

How authority is minimized

The change in Joan's bearing as the group progressed was dramatic to observe. Her assertion of authority became difficult to ignore as her verbal and nonverbal messages became congruent. When she asserted, "I want you to do this report," there were no lowered eyes and no hesitant, tentative voice giving the opposite message, "But I can easily be persuaded to change my mind". When she said, "I want to share the committee work equally," there was no apologetic smile to say, "But don't take me seriously." Joan's clear message, as the group progressed, was tied to her growing acceptance of the position, "I am the authority." Once a woman accepts the exercise of authority as personally appropriate for her, she can begin to confront the external obstacles by which her authority is reduced. This diminuition of authority can occur through the

1. Use of names
2. Acceptance of sexist language
3. Forfeiting of one's own agenda
4. Acceptance of nonperson status
5. Failure to assert one's credentials

The use of names: A woman's authority can be minimized by a simple introduction. In our society, status is conveyed by the use of surnames and titles. For example, children are called by their first names, but children usually refer to adults by their surnames. Susie or Johnny talks to Mr. Jones or Mrs. Smith. The practice is continued even into adulthood, where a "lower status" person is called by her or his first name and a "higher status" person by her or his surname. Women are more frequently in a lower status position than men, and their first name is more generally employed. When people are on a mutual first-name basis, or when both parties interact through surnames, an equal relationship is generated, at least on a superficial level. But when one adult is referred to as Mr. or Dr. and the other as Martha, an unequal interaction is set up. The use of names is of both practical and symbolic importance. And in this situation, as in many others, a woman determines to a large extent by her own behavior how she is treated by other people.

One of the first cues that gives another person an indication of our basic attitude toward ourselves is our self-introduction. Jackie Smith, executive secretary to the head of a manufacturing company, called James Johnson, vice-president in charge of personnel. Jackie wanted to obtain specific details about the company's new affirmative action program. She had been given the authority to check out the program by the company president. This assignment had been a genuine accomplishment for her, since she had been actively seeking more responsibility. When she called, the vice-president was not in his office. She asked his secretary, "Will you please tell Mr. Johnson that Jackie called in regard to the affirmative action program?" Later in the day Mr. Johnson returned the call, but not to Jackie. He telephoned directly to the president of the company. In other words, Jackie was bypassed. She angrily telephoned James Johnson and asked why he had not contacted her directly. He replied, "I assumed that you were calling for your boss and felt that there was less chance of confusion if I went directly to him." Jackie managed to utter the single reply, "I see," and hung up.

When Jackie told this incident to the group, we were struck with how careful she was to refer to the company vice-president as Mr. Johnson and how naturally she introduced herself as Jackie and left a message in her own first name. In short, she herself set up an unequal relationship. As executive secretary to the president, she had been with the company for over eight years. She knew as much about the company business as any executive there. Yet her message was dismissed as inconsequential. If Jackie had presented herself on an equal name basis, it would have been less likely that her authority would have been overlooked.

At this point, you may want to look at areas where you operate on an unequal name basis. Do you refer to your doctor by her or his first name if your doctor relates to you on a first-name basis? Do you initiate calling people by their first names, or do you wait for them to set the name pattern? Would you feel uneasy relating to someone you have always called Mr. or Dr. on a first-name basis?

Sexist language: Not infrequently, the woman professional finds her authority undermined in a second way: by sexist comments and sexist language. This may range from a woman being referred to as "sweetie" or "honey" to women being viewed as perpetual "girls." Commonly, a woman's legitimate assertion of anger or resentment is dismissed by vulgar references to menstruation or menopause. "She's having her period" explains all.

Confronting sexist comments is a major assertive task. This assertion is especially difficult because sexist remarks are often subtle, and they are frequently embedded in "joking" interaction. Upon hearing a sexist remark, a woman's gut level response may be a feeling of annoyance, accompanied by the perception of herself in a one-down position. Since the overt message is humorous, however, she may hold back from expressing her legitimate resentment. She may fear being labeled a "bad sport," "too sensitive," or a "woman's libber." Thus she offers an embarrassed smile at sexist comments for lack of having another response available. Of course, this smile may actually reinforce the comment.

When a sexist remark is allowed to pass unchallenged, a woman may find herself in a perpetual one-down position. Haig A. Bosmajian's article "The Language of Sexism" discussed the importance of women themselves determining who they are rather than allowing men to do it. If a woman tolerates the appellation "kiddo," she is accepting a less-than-adult status in a professional interchange. The woman who allows her employer to call her "sweetie" is going to have a very difficult time asserting negative feelings or setting limits. "Sweeties" do not refuse to make coffee or work overtime. "Sweeties" do not get raises or well-deserved promotions either.

Asserting our feelings about sexist language is basic to positive self-presentation. Sexist language is, in fact, only a subset of any comments that put a woman into a "not okay position." Many other remarks that lack a sexist element can lead a woman to adopt the attitude "I'm not okay." To not accept a one-down position, an assertive response is necessary. The response can be initially at low-level muscle: "I feel uncomfortable about what you just said," or "I would rather you not call me 'sweetie'." Many times this is all that is necessary. At other times, a statement will need to be repeated at a higher level of muscle: "I don't like being called 'kiddo'" or "I resent hearing women referred to as 'broads.'"

Keeping to your own agenda: In watching women deal with professional issues in the assertive training group, there is one behavior that never ceases to amaze me. This is the tendency of women to give up their own agenda and follow the agenda of someone else. By agenda I mean, quite simply, a woman's own set of priorities. It is very difficult for many women to assert themselves without deferring to the agenda of someone else. This is a third way in which women minimize their own authority.

Let us take Joanna as an example. Joanna holds the position of personnel manager for a small company. The president of the company does not have a secretary, so

Joanna occasionally performs minor secretarial duties. Joanna's complaint is that she has not been treated in a professional manner by the manufacturing manager of her company. She describes the following interaction with him which led to her negative feelings:

MANUFACTURING MANAGER (talking in the doorway to some guests): Joanna, do you have a note pad? I need to write something.

JOANNA: No, I'm sorry, I don't.

MANAGER: How come you secretaries never have a note pad?

JOANNA: Perhaps it's because I'm not a secretary.

MANAGER: What are you?

JOANNA: I am the personnel manager.

MANAGER: Oh, they're just the same.

Joanna stopped her assertion at this point. She did not want to express her resentment in front of the visitors. But her resentment did not go away. In the group, she decided to rehearse initiating a discussion with the manufacturing manager about this issue.

JOANNA: I want you to know that I was bothered by our encounter the other day when you asked for a note pad. Why did you refer to me as a secretary?

MANAGER: Well, you type, don't you? I really don't see the big deal. And besides, I really didn't like you challenging me in front of the guests. I think that is poor office practice.

JOANNA (confused): Well, I really don't think that I was rude to you. I actually didn't say everything I wanted because of the guests. But I'm sorry if I offended you.

In this brief interchange Joanna tossed her power away at two points. You may want to refer to the dialogue once again and try to pinpoint where Joanna's power was lost. Because Joanna did not stick to her own agenda (which was to have her legitimate position recognized), the value of the exchange, in terms of her feeling of accomplishment, was nil.

You may have noticed that Joanna first sidetracked her own agenda when she asked a question instead of making a statement. Finding an answer to "Why did you refer to me as a secretary?" was not really what she wanted. She wanted to tell the manager that she did not like her professional position being ignored. By asking a question rather than voicing her feelings, Joanna tossed away her power. Her second departure from her own agenda came when she deferred to the manager's complaint instead of pursuing her own. The moment he complained, "I really didn't like you challenging me in front of guests," Joanna shifted from her own purpose. In defending herself, she came from a position of weakness rather than one of strength. By the time the interaction ended, *Joanna* had become the offending party.

Had she kept to her own agenda, Joanna would have acknowledged the manager's complaint but continued with her own assertion. To the comment "I really didn't like you challenging me in front of the guests," she might have replied, "Well, that may be. However, what I want to discuss is the fact that I was referred to as a secretary when I am the personnel manager. I want you to acknowledge my position and refer to me by my appropriate title." In the latter statement, there is no diversion to the manager's concerns.

The brief acknowledgment "That may be" is a form of fogging. We have already examined this technique developed by Smith in his book *When I Say No, I Feel Guilty* in our chapter on criticism. To review briefly, when a woman fogs, she acknowledges another person's comment without getting caught in it. Fogging rids her of the necessity of defending or counterattacking. Thus Joanna fogs "That *may* be" to the manager's criticism and continues to assert her own agenda. She could have used other fogging phrases such as "You *may* be right," "I *may* have *seemed* inconsiderate," or "I *could* see how you *might* have felt that" and then continue to assert herself, "However, . . ."

222

There is a third way in which women throw away their power. They fail to complete their assertion. In other words, they lose their agenda by "stopping short." One group member, Jane, a high school teacher, wanted to practice expressing her negative feelings to her principal. The principal had come into Jane's classroom unannounced and taken down Jane's bulletin board, offering no explanation for this action except, "I knew you were no longer on that topic." Jane wanted to practice confronting her principal about this incident, so we set up the situation to rehearse.

JANE: I want to talk with you about some incidents that I feel have been interfering with our relationship. I thought that you might also have some things to bring up.

At this point, Jane stopped. The group member playing the principal began "Well, yes, there are certain issues that have been bothering me. . . ." Several other women in the group broke in and cautioned Jane, "Stop! You've just thrown the ball right into your principal's lap." Jane had given up her agenda by stopping short with her assertion. In her second attempt, she was careful to state initially exactly what *her* complaint was. "I want to talk with you about some incidents that I feel have been interfering with our relationship. Specifically, I was very bothered that the material on my bulletin board was removed without my knowledge or permission." By fully stating her own agenda, Jane makes sure that her priority issues will be dealt with before another issue surfaces for discussion.

Women as nonpersons: We already noted that women receive less recognition than men and that nonrecognition (nonreinforcement) is one source of female depression. This lack of recognition permeates all society and is a fourth way in which a woman's authority is minimized. As Bosmajian noted, even our language relegates women to the position of nonpersons. A woman's existence is lost in the assumption that managers, doctors, senators, and supervisors are men. Cultural blindspots, areas where the tendency to stereotype is so great that there is a distortion of reality, influence women and men alike. The woman professional constantly encounters such blindspots. An interesting example is that given by Mildred Hamilton of a woman vice-president of a major New York firm who went out to greet a businessman. The businessman was so caught up in the perception "woman equals secretary" that he handed the vice-president his overcoat! I have personally had the experience of telephoning someone, giving my name—"This is Dr. Butler calling"—and having them reply "Would you tell Dr. Butler that Mr. Smith is busy right now?" The automatic assumption "Doctor equals man" was strong enough to override my statement "This *is* Dr. Butler."

The issue of woman as nonperson goes back to our emphasis on the stereotypic feminine role. A woman is viewed according to cultural stereotypes even when these stereotypes do not fit. In an article in *Physician's Management,* Joyce Sloan Anderson commented on a question her doctor had asked her: "Are you still teaching?" The question sounds innocuous until you look at it from the other side—from Joyce Anderson to her doctor—"Are you still practicing medicine?" The question exposes the subtle message that women are constantly confronting. Women are supposed to rely on men; they are not to take their own professions seriously; they are not meant to function in positions of authority; and, if the message is pushed to its logical conclusion, they are not full and complete human beings.

Credentials: Helen is the assistant sales manager of a small drug company. When Bruce, the sales manager, is away from the office, Helen is in charge. But there is a problem. As Helen explains, "Bruce gets frequent calls when he's out. I know that most of them are business calls, so I always ask 'Can I help you?' Usually the response is 'No!' Just that, 'No!' I guess what I really resent is that people assume that I'm not qualified to answer their questions."

After presenting her problem, Helen agreed to rehearse the situation for the group. We felt that by hearing her response we could provide feedback as to why her offer of assistance was being ignored. Helen's first rehearsal was very brief. She asked "May I help you?" and the customer said "No thanks, I'll call back." Helen, with a sigh of resignation, said "That's what happens all right." The brief practice was of some use, however. The group member who had played the customer suggested, "I would naturally say no. I wasn't just responding that way because of the rehearsal. I would assume that you were the secretary and were not involved in the company sales."

Helen had allowed her authority to be minimized by failing to state her own credentials. Even though she did not like being disregarded, she disliked even more the idea of asserting her title "assistant sales manager." Helen was very reluctant to present herself as the person in charge. The extent of her conflict was clearly evident from her startled response to the group's question, "Why not say 'This is Helen Jones, the assistant sales manager. I am in charge when Mr. Smith is out of the office. May I help you?'" Helen replied "But I don't want to *flaunt* my position."

The negative self-label "flaunt" did not escape the attention of the group, and it was quickly brought to Helen's attention. One member told Helen, "By stating your credentials, you are merely giving necessary information about yourself to your customers. You aren't flaunting anything." Helen agreed that she was minimizing her authority by not asserting her position, but she added, "It's going to take some work to change that habit!" She is correct.

Asserting one's own credentials runs counter not only to the prohibition against being an authority but also to the third casualty of stereotyped femininity: positive self-presentation.

POSITIVE SELF-PRESENTATION

Women frequently minimize their own strength and accomplishments. It is in fact rare to hear a woman speak out about her own abilities. Presenting oneself in a positive manner is not reinforced by our society. Children are punished for talking positively about themselves. Feelings of power are squelched by derogatory appellations such as "bragging" or "big shot." Women learn to fear their own competence and to become anxious when they experience their own power. There is danger in feeling too excited or too good.

In the assertive workshop for professional women I typically ask each woman to introduce herself in a positive manner. I suggest that for the purpose of this exercise, no one is to say anything negative about herself. Women in the group frequently report that this one exercise creates more anxiety than all the other group exercises combined. I concur with their opinion. When I first began modeling positive self-presentation for the group, I also experienced a high level of tension accompanied by an unfamiliar blush. I also confronted a barrage of negative self-labels after I had completed my own self-affirmation. Does the group think I am bragging? Does this sound self-centered? Am I coming on too strong?

Of course, most times a woman never experiences the full-blown anxiety reaction that accompanies positive self-presentation. Quite simply, the anxiety is not experienced because most women rarely reveal positive accomplishments or dwell on feelings of pride and achievement. As one successful artist admitted to me, "I really never feel good about my success. The moment I have com-

FIGURE 10.2 "By the way, aahh, this isn't really important, and I ah don't know why I'm bringing it up, but I was ah, just awarded the Pulitzer Prize."

pleted one thing, I have already started worrying about another."

The class exercise on positive self-presentation provides some clear examples of the automatic tendency toward self-minimization. Susan, a twenty-five-year-old EKG technician, was one of the first women in her group to try to introduce herself in a positive manner. She recounted her present activities to the group in this way: "I am an EKG technician. I supervise two other people, and I have written several professional papers." Susan's self-presentation was punctuated with long pauses, her eyes focused on the ceiling and on the floor. After stating three pieces of information about herself, Susan stopped herself and said, "That's about all that I can think of."

Janice, another group member who had been listening intently, commented, "Susan, you stated some of your credentials and accomplishments and that sounded good, but you never told us how your own ability was involved. I would like to hear what you personally had to do with being appointed supervisor." On the group's suggestion, Susan began again. "I am an effective EKG technician. I am able to supervise two other technicians in a way that gets the work done but allows them a lot of independence and freedom. I have just written a paper "The Personality Correlates of Heart Disease," which has been accepted for presentation at a national conference. Last year I won an award for my presentation. I convey ideas clearly and thoroughly. My research has led to some interesting and important conclusions."

In her first presentation, Susan minimized her own accomplishments, not only by failing to state how her own ability was involved, but also by her lack of specificity. Initially she neglected to share the concrete details of her accomplishments. When Susan told the group the title of her paper and that she was presenting it before a national conference, we were all impressed. In fact, several group members commented that they would be very interested in talking to Susan later about her findings. Far from socially isolating her, Susan's positive self-presentation actually led to her connecting with several other people.

In addition to failing to assert their own abilities and specify their accomplishments, women minimize their competence in another way: they present themselves as passive bystanders in their own lives. Betty, a thirty-year-old student completing her doctorate in sociology, began her positive self-presentation with the statement, "I have been able to manipulate my way through a difficult doctoral program where only sixty percent of the students graduate." She continued, "I enjoy teaching and I enjoy writing. In general, I find that my work is very interesting." Betty presented herself almost totally from a passive orientation. "I enjoy writing," rather than "I write well." "I enjoy teaching," rather than "I am a good teacher. I am able to help students recognize and use their abilities." "I manipulated" rather than "I worked hard." The failure of a woman to view herself as an active instigator who influences what happens to her can have profound psychological consequences. As we have seen, the feeling of having control over one's life is an important antidote to psychological depression.

A fourth example of self-minimization was illustrated by Dr. J., a psychologist and a director of a counseling center. Dr. J. chose to describe her life in this way: "I was a psychology major in college. I liked the subject very much, so I applied to graduate school. Surprisingly, I was accepted. I learned a lot and grew a great deal during that time. Since I graduated, I have been a counselor. I have learned a great deal about people during that time. I now have an opportunity to serve as director of a counseling center, which I know will teach me even more. In my spare time, I have taken up ballet, but only for my benefit. I would never think of performing." Dr. J.'s last statement really summed up her entire self-presentation. Throughout the exercise she carefully avoided presenting herself as an authority. In describing her professional career, from graduate student to director of a counseling center, she maintained the role of "eager student." This particular form of self-minimization ensures that a woman will not be viewed as a competent professional.

You may want to try this exercise yourself. First, write down a list of your own positive characteristics and accomplishments. If you are thinking "I don't have any," then this is a particularly important exercise for you. If you are unable to think of yourself in positive terms, you have probably fallen into the all-or-nothing trap: either you are one-hundred percent reliable or you are unreliable. Consider thinking another way about yourself. If you continue to have difficulty listing your positive attributes, ask several friends to tell you what they consider your strong points to be. If you are like most women, you tend to minimize your own abilities. A friend may give you a more accurate picture of your strengths. Once you have listed five or ten positive attributes, go over your list asking yourself the following questions:

1. Are my positive traits or achievements confined to one area alone? Do I emphasize only the personal area or only the professional area?
2. Do I simply list an achievement, or do I describe how my own ability is involved? Contrast "I'm a good mother" with "I have a great deal of patience with my children which allows me to teach them and at the same time make learning fun."
3. Am I specific about my accomplishments? Rather than stating "I am a volunteer," can I specify "I donated over fifty hours of my time collecting money for charity?"
4. Do I present myself as a passive onlooker rather than as an active instigator in my own life? Do I *enjoy*

teaching, or do I teach in an interesting, enthusiastic manner?

5. Do I reduce the impact of my presentation through subtle apologies and qualifiers such as "I can't believe," "because of luck," "a little," or "kind of?"

As a second step, state your positive characteristics and accomplishments to yourself in the mirror. Be aware of your nonverbal as well as your verbal message. Do you have an apologetic tone in your voice? Do you convey a feeling of embarrassment through lowered eyes or nervous laughter? Do you indicate your uncertainty about the validity of your statements by the frequent use of qualifiers? Once you are comfortable with this step, try out your positive self-presentation in front of a friend. Ask yourself the same questions, and if you like, take advantage of your friend's feedback.

Positive self-presentation is crucial for the professional woman. Whether you are reentering the work force after taking time off to start a family, interviewing for a better job, or asking for a raise or a promotion, you will find that other people respond to you according to how you present yourself. Table 10.1 lists a number of statements other women have used in the exercise on positive self-presentation. You may also want to try out these positive self-affirmations.

As you have probably realized by now, fear of success, fear of authority, and self-minimization overlap to a considerable degree. Since this is true, change in one area often leads to change in another. A woman's comfort with her own authority will be reflected in her positive self-presentation. A woman who does not fear her own success will function comfortably in a position of authority.

The job interview

There is no place where positive self-presentation is more important than in a job interview. Yet the prohibitions

---

TABLE 10.1   Positive Self-Presentation

---

1. I am an excellent teacher. I go beyond the expected requirements to make learning an exciting experience for my students.
2. I establish and maintain good rapport with my coworkers. For that reason, I am able consistently to get projects done and meet deadlines.
3. I'm the best writer my company has had. My press releases have been used more than anyone else's.
4. I am extremely dependable. When I say that I will do something, I do it to the best of my ability.
5. I'm a very good speaker. I am able to be witty, entertaining, and informative. In a public relations job, this is an important asset.
6. I am a outstanding secretary. Not only am I competent in secretarial skills, but I am also well organized and able to keep material flowing smoothly.
7. Through my years of experience, I have developed an effective way of translating a client's needs into a successful finished product.
8. As a mother of four, I have learned to deal with crisis situations in a level-headed and effective manner, a quality I can put to its best advantage in this position.
9. As a volunteer, I have extensive experience in financial management and fund raising. The campaign I managed last year was the most productive to date.
10. Because I have had complete responsibility for the introduction of a new business, I feel my salary should be increased accordingly. As you know, I was completely in charge of all introductory publicity and public relations for the airlines.
11. Now that Mr. Smith is leaving, I would like to be given the chance to take over the other accounts. I have developed comprehensive programs for a number of clients and feel that I am now ready to take on more responsibility.

---

against presenting oneself as competent follow women even into this crucial area.

In the assertive workshop, women frequently use the exercise on positive self-presentation as an opportunity to practice interviewing for a job. Jackie, the executive secretary in a previous example, had the goal of moving into a job where she had more responsibility. Thus she focused on describing her job-related abilities and strengths in a positive manner. Jackie asserted: "I have been an executive secretary for over eleven years. One of my strengths is that I am a good organizer. I worked, for example, with a university project to provide housing for visiting students. This involved a lot of calling and matching resources with need. I feel very good about that project." The project, as it turned out, had been Jackie's own initiation. She did not work with the project; she established it. Jackie's self-presentation was positive even at her initial try, but she did not begin to present the full force of her abilities and accomplishments.

At the group's followup two weeks later, Jackie explained that she took into consideration the feedback of the group concerning her tendency toward self-minimization. "I wrote a letter of application a few days after the workshop. When I first saw the job announcement, I thought to myself 'I can't apply for that.' But then I asked myself 'Why not?', and the words just seemed to flow. I wrote what I have accomplished, and what my abilities are, without trying to hold back. I want to read the letter to all of you. What pleases me most is that I described my abilities without ever using the same word twice." Jackie continued, "I'll read the job description to you and then my letter of response. The advertisement read:

EXECUTIVE SECRETARY
ADMINISTRATIVE ASSISTANT
TO PRESIDENT

Highly motivated individual with solid business background sought as executive secretary and administrative assistant to chief executive officer and president of major corporation. Involves all phases of executive responsibilities with great growth potential for aggressive, take-charge individual. Send resume and references to:

Jackie replied:

I am the Executive Secretary-Administrative Assistant described in your recent Wall Street Journal advertisement.

I am single, attractive, assertive, and self-motivated, with strong organizational and administrative abilities. Highly disciplined research and analytical strengths facilitate my ability to make value judgments and decisions. In my eleven year career of assisting top-level executives, I have successfully

> developed and functioned in the position of Conference Coordinator for a large Midwestern university.

> conceived a special events/student housing program within the community, which is now an ongoing project

> coordinated a United Crusade fund-raising campaign, which increased returns thirty percent over previous years

> administered multiple budgets, pension and profit-sharing trusts

> supervised clerical and part-time employees

> maintained efficient information retrieval systems

> communicated with and/or directed personnel at all levels.

I have a strong administrative foundation in the fields of accounting, education, manufacturing, and architecture. I am presently the Executive Secretary to the Vice Chairman of the Board at Orway, a progressive manufacturing/direct selling firm.

Your advertisement offers the challenge and opportunity I relish, and I wanted to respond promptly. I will be happy to provide a more detailed resume and further references when we have the opportunity to discuss the capabilities I can provide for the assistance you need.

Jackie's letter of application is a masterpiece in positive self-presentation. Notice that she gives a functional description of her position, rather than relying on her title. In other words, she does not stop by saying she is an executive secretary. She goes on to specify the functions of that position. This functional description is especially important for a woman who finds that she does not have an impressive job title. For example, a woman may have served as a volunteer in several organizations while raising a family. The description *volunteer* gives little indication of her skills in organization, accounting, public relations, or the like. A functional description of capacities would reveal more positive information.

In her letter of application, Jackie also gave specific details about herself. She noted that she developed the position of conference coordinator for a large university. (Jackie specified the name, which I omitted to preserve her confidentiality.) She described the results of her fund-raising efforts in terms of a thirty percent increase in revenue.

Finally, Jackie was not reluctant to describe personal qualities that related to the job. She described herself as assertive, self-motivated, and as having analytical strengths. (Note that Jackie was not confining her self-description to the stereotypic feminine role.) The end result was the presentation of herself as a competent professional woman. Would you be able to write such a letter yourself?

PUTTING IT ALL TOGETHER—YOU'RE A WINNER

One evening I was talking with a group of professional women about fear of success, positive self-presentation, and the exercise of authority. Althea Ball, one of the participants, described her recent experiences relative to the topic. Althea had become familiar with the principles presented in this chapter through my assertive training course, which she had taken several months earlier. Althea credited the course with some of the recent success she had experienced. Althea had just gone through an interview procedure by which her firm, AT&T, screened applicants for the sales department. There was intense competition for positions in the sales division because these positions led to the most rapid advancement. Althea told us, "Just before the inteview began, I went into the bathroom, looked into the mirror, and told myself, 'I am a fantastic speaker.' I repeated the phrase over and over to myself until I began to feel confident. Then I began the interview.

"I found myself confronting what is typically known as a stress interview. It started out low, but as we went along, the questions became more difficult, and I was subjected to a great deal of pressure. I think these interviews provide a means of assessing how much you can take and how you handle yourself under difficult circumstances."

Althea described to us how she had *not* been manipulated to go off her agenda. Neither did she answer a second question before she had satisfactorily responded to the first. "When I was pressured to move too quickly, I simply told the interviewer, 'I'll get to that in a moment.' Then I went on to make my point. Once I was asked to pretend that I was the firm's promotion director and that I had to make a personnel decision. When I had made my decision, the interviewers started pushing me to back down or change my mind. They asked me why I had made the decision that I made, and after I responded, they came on very strongly with, 'You made the wrong decision.' Without getting defensive and without counterattacking, I was able to assert 'You may feel that way, but I am the promotions director, and the decision stands.'

"The entire time I was interviewing, there were no butterflies in my stomach. I felt that I had all the skills needed to handle whatever came up. After the interview was completed, I was told that I was the eighth person out of 200 to get a top rating. What really pleased me, however, was the comment that one of the men made to me when I finished. He ended his congratulations with the statement, 'You're a winner.'"

female-male relationships: forming a new connection

11

Today woman-man relationships are in a state of flux as the roles through which the sexes interact become blurred and indistinct. Until a few decades ago, most women devoted themselves almost totally to the role of wife and mother. The burden of "making a marriage work" was carried by women. A woman's role was that of pleasing a man. So entrenched was this view that George Lawton could write without ridicule in a 1956 article "Emotional Maturity in Wives" that, "a wife who is emotionally mature, in order to make her marriage a success, must become an actress in a repertory theatre and be able to play perhaps twenty-five roles." The roles of seductress, housekeeper, gourmet cook, master diplomat, grand-mistress of the art of canapé making, among others, left little room for a woman to express herself assertively.

More recently, however, the life cycle of women, described by Roxann Van Dusen and Eleanor Sheldon as "the sequence of statuses and roles, expectations and relationships constituting, in the broadest meaning of the word, an individual's 'career'," has been in the process of change. The female life cycle has been moving from a total preoccupation with the family to an orientation toward a lifelong career. As Van Dusen and Sheldon note, "Women are postponing marriage, postponing childbearing within marriage, and reducing their family size expectations." No longer are capable women terminating their educations to get married. The U.S. Department of Labor Statistics show that between 1970 and 1974, the number of women in college increased more than twice as fast as the number of men.

In terms of work, the distinction between married and never-married women is quickly disappearing. The labor force of women, married and living with their husbands, rose over eighty percent between 1950 and 1974 (from 23.8 percent to 43.0 percent). In contrast, there was only a thirteen percent rise for never-married women (50.5 percent to 57.2 percent). Furthermore, as Van Dusen and Sheldon note,

> Because young women have been postponing marriage, and postponing childbearing within marriage, they experience a relatively long period of time after completing high school or college during which they may advance in their careers. And increasingly, women are finding it difficult to give up the economic independence, as well as the challenge, recognition, and satisfaction that they derive from their jobs.

Within this major shift in the focus of a woman's lifetime activities rests the woman-man relationship. The maintenance of both an intimate woman-man connection and a sense of individual identity is the focus of the next two chapters. In this chapter we will look at assertive communication between women and men, at all levels of intimacy. In the next chapter we will examine limit-setting and self-initiation within the female-male connection.

INTIMATE COMMUNICATION

Many women find that asserting themselves in intimate relationships, particularly female-male relationships, involves more risks and therefore more anxiety than self-assertion with strangers, acquaintances, or friends. The woman who has a tendency to catastrophize can find numerous "and that would be awful" possibilities that could occur within an intimate relationship if she were legitimately assertive. A few examples? "I might be rejected"; "He would never want to see me again"; "He might become angry."

But in spite of the anxiety associated with self-assertion in this area, most women see direct, honest, and spontaneous communication in intimate relationships as being most important. After all, intimate contact can provide both intense pleasure and intense pain. Learning how to express our feelings assertively with those people whom we are close to is therefore a valuable skill.

Assertive communication involves both sending messages to and receiving messages from another person. Any such message, as you may recall, consists of at least three parts: (1) the intention of the message, (2) the sending or relaying of the message, and (3) the receiving of the message. Miscommunication can occur between any of these three points.

The way a message is sent (both verbally and nonverbally), for example, may not match the sender's intention. A man may tell a woman with a sound of irritation in his voice, "Yes, I love you" when she asks for an expression of his affection. He may indeed mean what he says, but the message he sends is not congruent with a loving feeling. Also, a message that is transmitted clearly may be distorted at the receiving end. For example, a wife may say to her husband who is cooking, "I think the eggs are burning" with the intention of being helpful. She may make the statement at a low muscle level, in a gentle, nonscolding way. However, her husband may receive the message as a criticism ·of his competence and feel resentful about what he views as being bossed around. In learning how to assertively negotiate intimate encounters, we will focus on all three parts: (1) the intent behind the message, (2) the transmission of the message, and (3) the receiving of the message.

The intention of a message

The intent behind a message has a lot to do with a woman's or a man's basic attitude toward her or his partner and toward herself or himself. Just as some individuals frequently operate through an external "should" system, so do some couples see each other's behavior from the position of a judge with numerous should and should not evaluations. Is he conforming to my expectations of what a husband should do? Is she upholding my standards of what a wife should be? A woman or a man can become so tied up in a judgmental structure that there is little room for the exploration and sharing of individual feelings.

The judgmental structure: The emphasis on shoulds and should nots in an intimate relationship frequently interferes with the ability of each person to be herself or himself. Not only are women and men faced with the dictates of their respective sex roles, but a new set of shoulds and should nots is typically added with the decision to form an intimate connection. In one assertive workshop for women, we were going around the circle of participants, introducing ourselves and getting acquainted. "I'm Jenny Smith. No, I mean I'm Jenny Mathews," one member stated. Then to explain she said, "I've recently gotten married to the man I have been living with, and I still am not used to my new name." As Jenny described her present living situation, it became apparent that her name confusion was only a small part of the confusion within her new marriage. "Before we were married," she explained, "we were really good friends. We enjoyed being together; we related as two people; we liked each other. Now, I don't feel that we even know one another." Jenny was about to cry. It seemed that marriage had changed what had been a good relationship by adding a number of demands and prohibitions. She did not know what to do.

Nena and George O'Neill, in their book *Open Marriage,* outline some of the clauses of the traditional closed marriage contract. These clauses constitute some of the shoulds and should nots through which partners in a marriage come to judge each other's behavior. The clauses can apply equally to unmarried couples who have an intimate connection. With minor alterations, these clauses are

Clause 1: Possession or ownership of the mate. (We belong *to* each other, as opposed to we belong *with* each other.)

Clause 2: Denial of self. (We should sacrifice ourselves and our individual identities to the marriage contract.)

Clause 3: Maintenance of the couple front. Like Siamese twins, we should always appear as a couple.)

Clause 4: Rigid role behavior. (Tasks, behavior, and attitudes should be strictly separated along predetermined lines, according to our concepts of "male" and "female.")

Clause 5: Absolute fidelity. (We *should* be faithful to each other, through coercion rather than by choice.)

Clause 6: Total exclusivity. (We should always be together.)*

The problem with these shoulds is that they give no room for the exploitation and expression of *individual* feelings. And as we have seen, the trust in and reliance on one's own feelings is the basis of self-assertion.

Many couples who come to me for counseling have totally abandoned any attempt to express their feelings to each other. Instead, they attack each other through aggressive "you" messages. "You don't keep the house clean." "Well, why should I? You don't ever come home." "You don't seem to mind when I bring home the paycheck," and on and on. I am supposed to sit in judgment and determine who is right and who is wrong. This is frequently the main agenda— each person wants to justify that she or he is *right*, that she or he has kept to the should structure.

Even in communication so bound by do's and don'ts, shoulds and should nots, however, there is often the intention to establish a mutually nourishing and rewarding interaction. This intention may be totally obscured by harsh, judgmental words, but it is frequently there. Family therapists Shirley Luthman and Martin Kirshenbaum, authors of *The Dynamic Family,* operate according to a "theory of positive intent," which assumes that "in every piece of behavior, no matter how destructive that behavior appears, there is some kernel of an intent to grow." Even in the punishing

*From *Open Marriage: A New Life Style for Couples,* by Nena O'Neill and George O'Neill. Copyright © 1972 by Nena O'Neill and George O'Neill. Reprinted by permission of the publisher, M. Evans and Co. Inc., New York, New York 10017.

"you" messages and the critical attacks between partners, there is often the positive intention of making contact.

The first lesson in self-assertion comes in helping a couple make contact with each other in a way which is not destructive. This involves helping them move from a judgmental framework to a reliance and trust in their own feelings. This shift often allows the couple to communicate the positive intent of their feelings for the first time. The change from accusations to feelings is difficult to achieve because many people equate the expression of feelings with vulnerability. A woman may object, "If I tell my husband (or male partner) where I hurt, he will use it against me," again fearing that his intentions are bad. A man may think "If I let my wife (or female partner) know that I need contact and nurturing, she will think I'm weak, that I am not a man." A couple takes the difficult step of moving from an external to an internal system when they shift from the aggressive attack "you did" to the assertive statement "I want."

Sending the message

I want versus you did: Sara has been married for two years. She and her husband Charles have no children. They both work for the telephone company, Sara as an operator, Charles as a lineperson. The assertive training group Sara attended met in November, right in the middle of football season. When asked who wanted to rehearse a problem situation, Sara immediately chose to deal with her football problem. Sara complained that Charles watched football constantly. He watched college football, professional football, and football previews. Football, Sara felt, was a constant intruder in her home. Sara wanted to share her negative feelings about football with Charles. She began:

SARA (whining tone):   Are you going to watch football again today?

CHARLES (defensively):   Yes. There's a good game on, and I want to see it.

243

SARA: But all you do is watch football.

CHARLES: So what? I work hard. I have a right to relax.

SARA: Well, what about me? You don't care that I never get to do anything I want.

CHARLES (angrily): Go do what you want. I'm not stopping you. Get off my back.

Sara congratulated her antagonist in the rehearsal for playing Charles' part to perfection. "That's just about how our discussions turn out," Sara admitted.

I suggested to Sara that she assert what she wanted from Charles rather than attack what she did not like. I asked her to emphasize the "I want" rather than the "you did." Sara was able to incorporate these suggestions into her next attempt.

SARA: Charles, I want to talk with you about something that's been bothering me.

CHARLES: Sure. Go ahead.

SARA: You (then stopping herself): I want to spend more time with you. I feel that I don't have the chance to be as close to you as I would like.

CHARLES: What would you like to do?

SARA: Oh, take walks together. Just sit around and talk.

CHARLES: I know I've been spending a lot of time on football, but it really helps me unwind. Why don't we do something together after the game—just you and me?

Sara stopped, "You know, the funny thing about this whole mess is that *I* really like to watch football. I guess I have been so angry at Charles that I have lost touch with the real issue."

Unless you are constantly examining and expressing your feelings, it is easy to forget what you really want from an assertive interchange. Also, even when you know what you want from your partner, it is not always easy to express this need in an assertive manner. Most of the couples I have seen in counseling have difficulty honestly and directly stating to each other what they want. It is actually easier to accuse their partners than to bare a part of themselves that feels hurt, needy, or vulnerable. It is easier to attack "you did" than to state "I want" or "I need." However, in terms of its effect on the other person, there is no doubt that an "I" message has a much better chance of being received positively than a "you" message. Most wives want to give to their husbands and *vice versa* when there is no manipulation or guilt inducement involved in the request. Table 11.1 contrasts several "I want-you did" statements.

Conveying the intensity of your needs: Another important aspect of asserting "I want" is that a woman is able to convey clearly the intensity of her need. Many women fail in this regard. Asserting a need or want even once is difficult for the woman who accepts traditional femininity's dictate that she *should* always be other oriented. To go one step further and assert the *importance* of her need is all but impossible. Marianne, for example, revealed, "I will say once in a very soft voice to my ex-husband 'It might be nice if you took the kids this weekend' and if he doesn't respond, I never say it again. The negative self-label *nag* comes in to stop me."

David Knox, in his book *Marriage Happiness: A Behavioral Approach to Counseling,* suggests an exercise for people who have difficulty conveying the importance of their needs to each other. Knox asks each person to put a numerical value on her or his request to indicate its importance. The scale extends from one to ten. Thus the statement, "This is of level-ten importance to me" gives the message that one's partner had better sit up and take notice. A request, "I'd like to go out for a walk. This is level-one" gives the message, "I would like to do this, but if you have something of more importance, that's fine."

This one to ten scale can also be used to help couples make decisions about which they are in conflict. If Karen

TABLE 11.1

You don't love me.	When you come home from work, I would like you to kiss me.
You never think about anyone but yourself.	If you're going to be late, I want you to call me. I worry about you.
All you ever do is work.	I would like to take some time next weekend to go to the beach.
You're a male chauvinist pig.	I want you to listen to me while I'm stating my opinions, even if you don't agree.
You never talk to me anymore.	I'd like to sit down together—with no television—and talk for a few minutes each night.
You just make love when you want to make love.	I want you to respond to me when I'm feeling sexy. We don't have to have intercourse, but I'd like you to satisfy me.
You're cold and selfish.	When I'm excited about something, I want you to tell me that you're happy I've found a new interest.
Why does everything have to go your way?	I want you to go places that I choose more often. I'm beginning to feel resentful.
Why do you drink so much?	I would like you to drink less when we go to parties together.

says that she wants to spend Saturday finishing a report, and Jack wants to spend the day together at the beach, there is a conflict. Here the importance of each person's desires must be taken into consideration. If Karen's report is due on Monday and her standing in her firm is resting heavily upon her report's caliber, then her need to work may be at an extremely high level. If she ignores the intensity of her feelings, she may go to the beach with Jack, but it is likely that neither of them will have a good time. On the other hand, Karen's report may only be of level-three importance—she wants to do it today so she can take off next week—and Jack's need for a day of leisurely contact may be at level eight. The decisions the couple arrives at in each of the two examples would be very different.

Asserting one's needs in terms of degree of importance is simply a tool for developing more effective communication. If either partner is dishonest and picks a high number simply to get what she or he wants, then the purpose of this approach will be defeated. On the other hand, if you do not want to risk letting your partner know your honest feelings, you may give too low a number. This exercise demands not only self-knowledge but also the acceptance of your own needs and of your right to have needs. It demands that you depart at least briefly from the other orientation of the feminine role and risk stating honestly what your true feelings are.

Connie did not exactly define the importance of her wants on a scale from one to ten in asserting herself with her husband Brian. What she did do was try to honestly state what she wanted and its importance to her. "I usually nag-nag-nag or bitch-bitch-bitch to get what I want," Connie offered. "Of course, I'm usually ignored. This time, I decided to let Brian know what I wanted and its importance to me. I found four antique chairs several weeks ago. They were a good price. I know, because I had shopped around. Anyway, I asserted to Brian, 'I would really like to have these four antique chairs that I mentioned to you. I don't think you know how much they mean to me. Having the chairs would really make me happy.' The four dining room chairs were there the next day." Connie's direct, honest assertion of her needs was responded to in a way that her coercive "you" messages had never been.

Directness, honesty, spontaneity: Once two people are expressing their feelings instead of making judgments, that is, communicating through "I" messages as opposed to "you" messages, they can begin to refine their assertive skills. They can ask themselves: Am I communicating directly, honestly, and spontaneously?

247

"Do you want to go to bed?", Gayle asks Steve. "No, thanks. I think I'll stay up and watch the news," Steve replies. The results of this seemingly innocuous interchange depend upon whether Gayle's question is both direct *and* honest. According to C. H. Madsen, a researcher to whom Knox refers, a direct question is one that asks for the specific information desired; an indirect question asks for information in a subtle manner when such information could be obtained directly. Thus if Gayle is actually trying to ascertain from her question, "Do you feel sexy? Do you want to make love tonight?", her question is indirect. Again, according to Madsen, an honest question is one to which the responder can answer no without penalty. If Gayle's question is her way of stating "I want you to go to bed with me, and I will be hurt if you don't," then she has asked a dishonest question. Other questions such as "Do you want to go out after dinner?", "Do you care if I get home late?", or "Do you like what I am wearing?" are dishonest if the responder can only answer in one way without invoking the questioner's negative feelings. Some questions can be both dishonest and indirect. For example, "Are you tired tonight?" may be an indirect way of stating "Would you like to go out tonight?" It might also be dishonest if there is a severe penalty for an answer, "Yes, I'm tired." This indirect and dishonest question may actually be a substitute for the statement, "I need to go out tonight, and it is of level-nine importance to me that you go with me."

Why do people resort to dishonest and indirect questions? Quite simply, in most instances such questions reduce anxiety. For example, to ask directly and honestly, "Do you want to have sex tonight?" is difficult for a woman who has learned that being feminine means being passive. To hear a man say "No, I don't feel like having sex tonight" is shattering to a woman who believes the tenet of stereotypic masculinity that says a man *should* always be ready to perform sexually, regardless of his feelings, regardless of the circumstances, and regardless of external pressures. A woman having such a belief will probably assume that the answer "No, I'm not in the mood for sex tonight" means "You're not attractive. I don't like you. I don't love you. You're worthless." Having these assumptions, it naturally is much easier for her to ask, "Are you tired tonight?"

Furthermore, a question such as "Would you like to go out tonight" produces less anxiety than the statement "I need to go out tonight." Regardless of the intent behind it, a question is automatically framed in the concerned, caring other orientation demanded by the feminine role. The woman who says *I need* is going against traditional femininity by taking care of herself. Moreover, in expressing *I need,* a woman is likely to encounter her own self-labels: selfish, demanding, inconsiderate. She may even face similar labels from other people. To ask "Would *you* like to go out tonight" saves her from acknowledging the discrepancies between her actual feelings and what she has been taught that she should feel.

Directness and honesty force a woman to face herself. By being direct and honest, she shares with another person "This is who I am." As I tell members of the assertive workshops I conduct, "If I am clear about who I am, I can be certain that I won't fit with everyone. And I can be sure that I will find this out pretty quickly. However, there will be some people with whom I can connect in a strong, positive way. Being assertive, I allow myself to find these people, and I do not waste my time on someone who doesn't fit with me. By being assertive, I lessen the chance that I will find myself intimately involved with someone who does not even like the person who I am."

Using appropriate muscle: A second refinement of the assertive skills involved in intimate communication comes in learning to use appropriate muscle. It is something of a joke to talk about the person who is obsequious and sycophantic all day with her or his boss only to come home and take it all out on her or his partner. Yet there is a grain of truth in the observation that although the most important individuals in our lives are those people close to us, they are not always treated with as much consideration as the strangers we encounter. For example, not a few fights between intimates result from the sending of a message, from how it is delivered. "I don't like your tone of voice"; "Don't talk to me like that"; "It isn't so much what you say, as how you say it" are all indicators that we need to reconsider the muscle level with which we interact with our partners.

I find that in intimate communication, just as in all assertive interaction, a low level of muscle generally works best. One assertive group assisted me in drawing up a brief hierarchy of phrases conveying different muscle levels. Table 11.2 presents this hierarchy. You might want to try out each of these phrases by adding an ending portion such as "about your inviting Peter to dinner" or "about what you just said." You can see the different muscle level conveyed by each sentence.

Receiving the message

Acknowledgment: Once two people have learned to state their feelings and their needs directly, honestly, and spontaneously within a relationship, they are ready for the second step in assertive communcation: learning to use acknowledgment. To acknowledge is simply to let another person know that a message has been clearly received and understood. By acknowledging, a person does not agree or disagree. She or he simply notes reception of the communication. The amount of acknowledgment required by a message varies from situation to situation. Sometimes, the simple acknowledgment "Mm hmmm" is sufficient to convey that a message has been received. At other times, when the feelings involved are more intense, a statement that actually goes so far as to restate a person's feelings

---

TABLE 11.2   Moving from Low- to High-Level Muscle

Low level

I feel uneasy
I feel uncomfortable
I don't feel enthusiastic about
I'd rather not
I don't like
I feel upset
I feel annoyed
I feel irritated
I resent
I am angry
I am furious

High level

---

may be necessary to give the other person a sense of having been fully understood. Thus, if a woman says "I have been feeling uptight about your working late so often" to her husband and he fails to respond at all or replies with a perfunctory "Mm hmmm," we can say that satisfactory acknowledgment has not taken place.

Acknowledgment involves *active listening.* Thomas Gordon, author of *Parent Effectiveness Training,* explains that in active listening "the receiver tries to understand what it is the sender is feeling or what his message means. Then he puts his understanding into his own words and feeds it back for the sender's verification. The receiver *does not* send a message of his own—such as an evaluation, opinion, advice, logic, analysis, or question. He feeds back *only what he feels the sender's message meant*—nothing more." This is the technique Carl Rogers developed in his Client-Centered Therapy as a way of responding in a non-judgmental manner to another person.

Acknowledgment is the salve that heals wounded feelings. In conveying my own sense of the healing and soothing properties of acknowledgment, I can think of no better way to put it. So often, all another person needs to hear is an acknowledgment of what she or he is feeling. Unfortunately, both the female and the male sex roles work against simple acknowledgment. The stereotypic feminine role actually interferes only through the "rescue operation." The inordinate responsibility women feel for "making things right" pushes a woman to *do* something. And in acknowledgment, *doing* interferes with *hearing*.

The stereotypic masculine role interferes with acknowledgment to a much greater extent. With most of the couples I see in counseling, the major acknowledgment deficit occurs with the male partner. This is not difficult to explain if we recall that the masculine role deemphasizes feelings. Instead, men are supposed to perform. "Do something" is a major should of stereotyped masculinity. When a man who has grown up with this problem-solving orientation is faced with a strong expression of negative feelings, he feels pressured to perform—to stop the feeling by solving the problem behind it. Many men I see tell me that the situation they hate most is one in which a woman is crying. These men often feel helpless because they do not know how to deal with feelings.

In one workshop for women, we had almost completed our initial introductions when Gloria spoke up. "I'd like to say something else. When I talked before, I really didn't say what was bothering me." With that statement, Gloria burst into tears. "It's really my fellow I'm most concerned about. He likes me fine when I'm positive, when I'm happy. But he can't tolerate my negative feelings. He doesn't want to be around me if I cry or get angry or make demands. I go around trying to pretend I'm happy all of the time. Only I'm not."

I wondered aloud with Gloria if perhaps her fellow felt that he had to do something when she was sad or angry and yet did not know what to do except withdraw. Gloria thought that such might be the case. I suggested to her,

"If a woman is connected to a man with this type of problem, she can, through her assertion, often teach him what she wants. She can help him remove some of his self-imposed pressure to perform which prevents him from giving her what she needs most at the moment: intimate contact." How can she do this? By simply asserting her desires. Gloria might say to her fellow, "I want you to listen to my feelings and just stay with me. I don't expect you to do anything. I don't want you to solve the problem. It just helps when you let me know that you hear my feelings." Table 11.3 presents several additional statements that help teach people what you need from them when you are upset.

The acknowledgment vacuum: When a person does not receive any acknowledgment, her or his feelings tend to increase in intensity, so that the next expression usually comes on at a higher muscle level. I often see couples caught in what I refer to as an acknowledgment vacuum. One member (let us say the female partner) makes a statement that the other member ignores or brushes aside. Having no firm acknowledgment, she makes the statement again, this time at a higher level. She may at this point get a short reply "Is that so?" or "Um hmmm," that does not begin to match her feelings. Her statement continues to intensify. The male partner is finally forced to respond. He responds, but he also calls her a nag and wonders to himself what he did to deserve such a bitchy, complaining woman. What he does not realize is that because he failed to acknowledge his partner when she was expressing herself at a low level, he is equally responsible for the interchange. An acknowledgment vacuum has been created. Figure 11.1 illustrates the operation of this process.

Of course, when there is an habitual lack of acknowledgment, the assertion of intimate feelings will tend to withdraw. Acknowledgment and the increased closeness and understanding that it brings is one of the main rewards for

---

TABLE 11.3 Telling Other People What You Want

I just want you to say you understand that I feel sad.

I want you to tell me that you can appreciate how going to a party where I don't know anyone isn't enjoyable to me. I don't want you to scold me for not socializing more.

I want you to hold me until I feel better.

Even if you disagree, I want you to let me know that you can understand my position.

---

intimate communication. Without this reward, the communication ultimately stops.

Again, it is important to remember that acknowledgment simply involves a restating of a person's feelings in words which convey that a communication has been received and understood. As couples learn how to use acknowledgment, they often see a major change in the quality of their relationship. For example, Donna relayed to me a major change in her interaction with her husband Tim.

> I was at my drawing board working up a layout for a client, and my pen wouldn't work properly. I began to get upset, and I started grumbling about the pen's inefficiency. Then I began to catastrophize out loud about never getting the job done if the pen wouldn't work. All of this time, I was aware that Tim was listening, and I began feeling angry that he wasn't acknowledging me. So I said, "Tim, I'm talking about this pen not working and I'm not being heard." And Tim replied simply, "No. I'm listening. I really know how it feels to have a pen that doesn't work when you want it to." Then he went back to work. That was actually all that I needed to hear. In the past, I would have had to have been hysterical before I was acknowledged. Then Tim's response would have naturally been negative, and we would have been off and running.

This time Donna made a statement to Tim expressing her awareness that he had not acknowledged her while her feelings were still at a low level. Tim, for his part, then immediately acknowledged her feelings, a simple enough interchange once it is learned.

254

FIGURE 11.1 When a person is not acknowledged, the intensity of the feeling increases. Assertive communication involves being a good receiver. Do you acknowledge other people? Do you show them how to acknowledge you?

Checking out your perceptions. Are you receiving what is being sent?:   Acknowledgment provides a very good way of checking if you have received the message that was sent. If Nancy, for example, says, "I never want to do this again" after driving through Friday night traffic to the mountains, Arthur needs to know what *this* means. By providing acknowledgment in the form of statements such as "You feel that going skiing just isn't worth the effort," "You really dislike driving at night," or "You want to leave next time on Saturday morning," Arthur will be able to discover an accurate meaning of Nancy's message. Of course, Arthur could also say "I hear you're upset. Tell me more about it." What is important is that Arthur receives the correct message and then acknowledges it.

I once worked with a couple who rarely checked out their perceptions. In one of our counseling sessions, the wife found out that for fifteen years she had erroneously assumed that her husband disliked the theater. He had once been upset when they were at the theater, so she concluded that he did not enjoy going. Actually, he had been annoyed about sitting in the balcony. It is easy to see from the preceding example how such a misunderstanding could develop.

Checking out the accuracy of one's perceptions is extremely important in any intimate relationship. We have talked about how to send a clear, direct message. A person also has some control over the message that she or he receives. This control comes from our ability to always check out the intention of a message before we react to how it was conveyed. An exercise that helps two people determine if the communication intended is actually the communication being received involves having each member of a pair repeat fully what the other person has said before going on to make any statement of their own. Thus, before Irene responds to Doug's statement with her own comment, she must first repeat what she has just heard

Doug say. When a person repeats what she or he has just heard, there is often a substantial distortion of the message. With troubled marriages, this distortion tends to be toward the assumption of negative intent.

Doreen and Jim clearly illustrated this tendency. Doreen and Jim were discussing their sexual relationship and how their lack of time alone, away from children, friends, and relatives, was interfering with their contact with each other. Jim offered the suggestion, "We should plan to have the kids spend one of the weekend nights with either your parents or mine." Doreen countered, "I would have done that long ago if I didn't think you would object. You always seem more interested in spending your time fishing all weekend, so that you're tired by the time Saturday night comes. I thought you would just as soon have the kids with you, since you never see them on the weekend anyway."

When I asked Doreen what she had heard Jim say, she replied, "He criticized me for not sending the kids away on the weekend." Because Doreen received Jim's message as a criticism, she responded by sending him a countermessage in which she defended herself and counterattacked. By having Doreen restate what she heard *before* she replied, and by checking out if the message she received matched the message Jim had intended to send, the number of critical statements in Doreen and Jim's interaction was drastically reduced.

The skills we have discussed—sending an assertive mesage, assuming positive intent, acknowledging another person—are vital to an important aspect of the intimate connection that we will now examine.

SEXUAL INTIMACY

In our society today it is relatively easy for a woman to become sexually intimate. The prohibitions of the Victorian society against women enjoying sex are all but past, and women are finding new freedom to explore their sexual feelings. However, the ease in developing sexual intimacy has not necessarily led to a corresponding ease in developing emotional intimacy. Not infrequently a woman spends the night with a man, has sexual intercourse with him, and then discovers that she feels uncomfortable calling him on the telephone the next day. In such situations the woman's level of sexual intimacy is far greater than her level of emotional intimacy.

Lazarus, in his book *Behavior Therapy and Beyond,* developed a diagram (Figure 11.2) that demonstrates different levels of intimacy. (From *Behavior Therapy and Beyond* by Arnold Lazarus. Copyright 1971 by McGraw-Hill Book Company. Used with permission of McGraw-Hill Book Company.)

The A level, or the outer rung, describes a relatively superficial interaction that occurs between two people. At the A level, an individual offers information that could be comfortably shared with a stranger. The B level involves the kind of small talk that goes on between acquaintances. Political views, talk about one's job, what one likes to do in one's spare time all fall within this category. At level C we begin to provide more intimate disclosures of who we are. Discussions of our needs, our limits, what we want from a relationship, how we feel about the person whom we are with, how they feel about us—these are C-level concerns. At level D, as in the previous level, we talk about who we are as unique individuals. At this level we reveal our fears, our needs, our hopes. In level-E disclosure we present ourselves without disguise. Here a woman feels free to talk about anything. Nothing is censured or omitted. The diagram in Figure 11.2 can also be viewed from a sexual orientation. The A level involves little or no physical contact. The B level involves friendly touch. The E level involves full sexual expression.

A woman may find herself at level E sexually, without having progressed past level B emotionally. On occasion

258

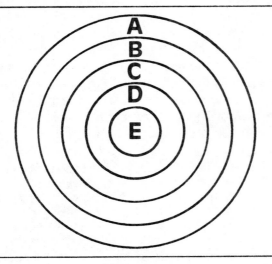

LEVELS OF INTIMACY

EMOTIONAL

A SUPERFICIAL INTERACTION
B SMALL TALK
C WHO WE ARE - IDEAS, OPINIONS
D WHO WE ARE - NEEDS, FEARS, HOPES
E FULL INTIMATE DISCLOSURE

SEXUAL

A LITTLE OR NO PHYSICAL CONTACT
B FRIENDLY CONTACT
C AFFECTIONATE CONTACT
D PASSIONATE CONTACT
E FULL SEXUAL EXPRESSION

FIGURE 11.2 The concentric circles represent different levels of sexual and emotional intimacy. Do you find yourself at one level sexually and another level emotionally because you are afraid to assert yourself?

this may be exactly what she desires. I am not saying that a woman cannot want or enjoy a sexual relationship under these circumstances. What I am saying is that in our present society, sexual barriers are often broken more easily than emotional barriers. For many people, there is less risk in becoming sexually involved than there is in developing emotional intimacy.

In one assertive training booster session, we devoted an entire meeting to female-male relationships. (The booster session is made up of a group of graduates from the assertive training workshop who meet monthly to reinforce the progress that they have made in self-assertion.) During the first half of the meeting, we discussed problems women have in asserting themselves with men. At least five of the ten women in the group were finding it difficult to assert themselves emotionally on an intimate level.

Betsy summed it up first.

> You know how it is. Around the third or fourth date, there is a decision either to get more involved or to back up, to go to bed or to become friends. The first date you go to the movies or out to dinner. The second date you have dinner at his house with another couple. The third date you invite him over. Then you either sit there watching television or talking small talk, or you go to bed. What I don't like is not having any idea about where I stand in the relationship.

> I had a situation just the other night, which is rather typical. I've dated Bob four or five times—with the dates spread out over a two-month period. He asked me to have dinner, and after we had finished, he made a move to get me to go to bed with him. I like him, I think, but there hasn't been much intimate contact between us. I had no idea at that point what to say.

Since Betsy's difficulty in moving to a more intimate level was a concern of other women in the group, we decided to have her role play how she would like to assert her feelings with Bob. The rehearsal began:

BOB: Why don't you spend the night here tonight?

BETSY: Bob, I'd like to talk with you about my feelings about that. I feel that we are at a point in our relationship where we could go to bed together, or we could just become friends. And I don't know what I want to do. I do know that I don't want a sexual relationship with a man until I feel close to him emotionally.

BOB: You're not one of those people who has to be in love, are you?

BETSY: I guess that I want to be committed to someone. Good sex to me involves some commitment.

BOB: I'm really feeling pressured from you. Why can't we just see what develops?

BETSY: My intention isn't to pressure you, but to tell you what I feel. Your feelings may be completely different. I guess I just want to talk with you about us, and to tell you what I want from a sexual relationship. It's also fine with me if we don't get involved—or if we take more time to get to know each other better.

In this rehearsal, Betsy voiced her feelings without intruding on Bob. She simply told him her present position. The interchange, depending on Bob's next response, may or may not lead to greater intimacy. The point is that through her assertion Betsy finds out what she needs to know to determine her own actions. If Bob does not "want to get involved," Betsy can make her decision about sexual intimacy knowing that Bob wants something different from what she wants at this point. He is free to change his mind— as she is.

The reluctance to speak directly and honestly, to keep a relationship on the same emotional and sexual level, can lead to a woman or a man being hurt in the interchange. For example, Susan expected that her sexual involvement with Roy meant the same thing to him that it meant to her. For Susan, level-E sexual intimacy involved a deep personal commitment to one other person. When she found that Roy did not want to commit himself to her (or to any one person for that matter), she felt betrayed. She had based her sexual intimacy on false assumptions that she had never checked out with Roy.

The issue of matching emotional to sexual intimacy is not a female problem alone. As women become freer to initiate contact with men, including sexual contact, men are finding themselves facing the same difficulties. I was conducting a fairly large class in assertive training for women and men one summer. Because of the size of the class, I was both pleased and slightly surprised when Paul brought up the problem of how to say no to a woman who initiates sexual contact when he himself does not want to become sexually involved. "I never thought that I would be bringing this up," Paul said, "but just within the last year I've been with some women who are sexually quite assertive. I had one experience where I found myself unable to let the woman know my feelings, and it was very unpleasant. I ended up by walking out on her in the middle of the night, and I don't want to treat another person like that." The assertion that Paul practiced was a direct and honest statement of his feelings. "I like you, but I really don't want to get sexually involved right now." This is an assertive statement that few men feel free to make. To do so requires departing from the demand of the stereotypic masculine role that men always be willing to perform sexually. This is also a statement that several years previously, because of the lack of female assertion, few men would have needed to make.

ASSERTIVE SEXUAL COMMUNICATION

Today both women and men are gaining permission to express who they are as sexual beings. As William Masters and Virginia Johnson note in *The Pleasure Bond,* "No longer is sex looked upon as something that a man does *to* a woman or even *for* a woman, but something that a woman and a man do *with* each other." This view of sexual contact assumes that neither partner is *responsible* for the other's enjoyment or satisfaction. But both partners can enhance their relationship by freely asserting their sexual needs and desires to each other. In perhaps no area is assertive communication more difficult than in the sexual area. The traditional sex roles of women and men have much to say about what a person *should* or *should not* do sexually.

Sexual communication is hindered first of all by the anxiety many people feel when they use sexual language. For the most part, sexual language consists of either scientific terminology or street talk. A couple may speak of coitus or sexual intercourse, or of fucking, screwing, or balling. Making love is a vague alternative. Sexual words in and of themselves often cause anxiety. Without both partners feeling free to say exactly what they mean, however, distortions can occur.

An exercise in overcoming this initial hinderance to effective assertion in the sexual area was suggested by Knox in *Marriage Happiness*. Knox instructs couples to write down independently all the sexual words they know, and then to say each of these words one after another together, until the verbalization of these previously forbidden words elicits no negative reaction.

Beyond developing an ease with sexual language, women and men must learn to be direct, honest, and spontaneous in conveying what they like and do not like about their sexual relationship. Here again, the traditional feminine and the traditional masculine roles can interfere with free self-expression. For example, if a couple accepts the notion that a man should automatically know how to please his partner, the couple will assume that little or no communication is necessary for mutual sexual pleasure. If a woman accepts the view that a woman should not know much about her own sexuality, that she should be taught by, rather than teach, her partner, and that she should be passive in her sexual interaction, she is unlikely to give her partner the information about her own likes and dislikes that he must know to please and satisfy her.

Because traditionally women have been taught that it is their obligation to please their partners, the honest expression of negative feelings within a sexual relationship can be extremely difficult. Because of a desire not to hurt their partners' feelings, many women pretend to be aroused when they are not, or pretend to have an orgasm when they do not. The cost of this deception, although often good intentioned, is high. Without accurate feedback, a woman's partner cannot be aware that her sexual needs are not being met.

Paula found that her sexual relationship with Peter was not as satisfactory as her previous sexual relationships had been. Peter was almost always ready for sexual intercourse before she was. Paula wanted more foreplay—more kissing and mutual caressing. She had tried unsuccessfully to convey this message to Peter through her nonverbal behavior. Although this had not been sufficient, Paula felt uncomfortable about telling him directly that she felt unsatisfied. What if she hurt Peter's feelings? What if he became angry that she was sexually experienced? What if he felt that she was too aggressive? But in spite of her fears, Paula basically trusted that Peter was secure enough in his own sexuality not to be crushed by her assertion. She therefore leveled with him about her needs, and he readily changed his behavior in a way that was mutually acceptable.

As with all assertion, Paula's *immediate* expression of concern allowed the problem to be settled while still at a low level, before she became resentful and before Peter had been misled. Dissatisfactions that have been ignored for a long period of time are more difficult to resolve. Masters and Johnson caution that when a woman admits that she has faked orgasm, "there is undeniably a risk of injuring the marriage itself, particularly if the revealing of the deception is not handled expertly." Sometimes professional assistance is required to remedy a situation in which a woman has not been honest with her feelings.

The importance of direct and honest communication between partners becomes even more understandable when we consider that two of the most basic procedures in sexual therapy focus on sexual communication. The first, sensate focusing, is a procedure Masters and Johnson use in their treatment of both female and male sexual problems. A couple experiencing any anxiety-related dysfunction (such as painful intercourse, difficulty in achieving arousal, erection, or orgasm) is typically instructed to touch, caress, and pleasure each other in whatever manner is most pleasing. During the first several sessions, breast and genital contact is prohibited, so that the emphasis remains on pleasuring rather than on sexual performance. Jack Annon, sexual therapist and author of *The Behavioral Treatment of Sexual Problems,* instructs couples during sensate focusing to "communicate as much as possible with each other, both verbally and nonverbally, as to what (is) found pleasing." Sensate focusing is a way of finding out the individual sexual preferences of each person, without being hindered by the assumption that either partner *should* know the other person's needs or desires in advance.

The second procedure, which involves assertive communication, is the checking out of one's perceptions. We already talked about how the intended message is not always the message received. Since the assertion of sexual feelings is so frequently associated with anxiety, it is not surprising that in this area miscommunication is often the rule instead of the exception. Annon gives several examples of the detrimental effects of the failure to communicate in his description of the therapy of Mr. Inn and Ms. Ivy, a couple who were having sexual difficulties (failure to achieve erection for him; failure to achieve orgasm for her).

One important aspect of their therapy was the development of more effective communication. They were taught both to send clear messages and to check out their perceptions. Annon gives two specific examples of how the lack of communication can lead to unnecessary anxiety.

Ms. Ivy felt very uncomfortable about having intercourse during her menstrual period since she did not know Mr. Inn's feelings. Once she asked, she was surprised to learn that Mr. Inn did not mind her menstrual period at all. "Conversely," as Annon explains, "Mr. Inn was relieved to discover that Ms. Ivy did not mind his ejaculation, and in fact, wished he would not always jump up to take a shower immediately after (intercourse) but stay and hold her awhile."

Becoming more assertive in the female-male relationship raises genuine fears for many women. It is entirely natural that this would be the case. The stereotypic feminine role has been most stringent in the area of the woman-man connection, and a woman who decides to express herself as a unique person without bowing to sex role demands is without doubt entering unexplored territory. In this respect, however, I agree with Masters and Johnson, who state

> Any woman who has the will and the courage to break out of the cell that historically has been considered appropriate for females, a cell comfortably padded with privileges, has something of tremendous value to offer a man—the key to his own prison door.

the female-male connection: maintaining closeness and space

12

The female-male connection *is* changing. Even though the basic tenets of stereotypic femininity (that a woman live for and through others, that she rely on a male provider for support, that she emphasize beauty and self-adornment, and that she operate from a nonassertive position) still have great power to control, many women are altering the ways in which they relate to men. The change is most evident in two major areas of self-assertion: setting limits and self-initiation.

SETTING LIMITS: THIS IS ME. I'M SEPARATE

The general difficulty women have in setting limits is not mitigated by an intimate relationship. In fact, in an intimate female-male interaction, the clauses and tenets of the closed marriage contract work with those of stereotypic femininity to interfere with the appropriate assertion of boundaries. You may recall that one clause of the closed marriage contract is the denial of self. The sacrifice of one's own identity to a relationship has typically had a greater impact on women than men. Desiring to please, to fulfill the needs of another person, many women gradually give up who they are as unique individuals and become carbon copies of their husbands.

The female-male relationship is actually a crucial test for many women. To assert and cultivate one's own identity and at the same time maintain contact and intimacy with another person is a difficult task. Not infrequently a woman will simply step out of this conflict by totally ignoring how she differs from the man in her life. Wanda, for example, did not pursue her interest in music after she married Bill. Before her marriage, Wanda played in a semiprofessional quartet and went to weekly concerts. But because Bill did not enjoy music, she gradually gave up her own musical involvement. Wanda's view of herself as a good wife did not allow any development of herself as a person separate from her husband.

In contrast, the woman who does honor her own need for personal space and autonomy will find that she must assert her limits with her partner. Fran wrote to me describing such a limit-setting situation. She titled her account "Big Brother Is Watching You."

I was talking with a friend on the telephone when the operator cut in with (my husband) . . . "has an emergency call he wants to make to (my number). Will you take this call? I said I would and told the friend I would call him back. Then my husband called and asked if I wanted him to pick up anything from the store. I said no, and asked what the emergency was. He said he just wanted to know before he went out to lunch, and that I had been talking for a hell of a long time. I told him the friend was giving me useful information important to both of us for a new project we were working on, and I did not think it had been long. He said he had timed it on his stopwatch, and that it had been all of *fifteen minutes*!

I felt angry, put down, and determined to straighten it out. When my husband came home I said there was something I had to speak to him about before dinner. I told him I did not regard his call as a true emergency and if he did that again I would be inclined not to honor it. If it was a real emergency it would be like crying wolf once too often. Again he brought up the business of timing my conversation. I said that was what I felt most uncomfortable about, as it made me feel as if "big brother is watching you." I said that I thought whom I talked to, and for how long, was *my* choice, and as long as it was not a toll call, I saw no reason for limiting it. He said I had often complained about other women gabbing too long, and now the shoe was on the other foot. I said that had nothing to do with the present situation. I said that this involved my private civil liberties and that I would not accept such strictures. I added that I wanted him to understand why I felt uncomfortable about this, so that it wouldn't come up again. Beginning to leave the room, he said that I gave him the feeling "You're a naughty boy, and mustn't ever do that again." I followed him and said I didn't want him to feel defensive about it, that I just wanted to make *my* uncomfortable feelings clear.

I felt wonderfully light and relaxed afterward . . . to think of being free of the usual resentment, anger, and hurt, or from being argued into a corner! I felt much more in control of my life, with less need to control my feelings. We both felt more relaxed and stayed up later than usual working on the above-mentioned project together.

Teaching your partner how to treat you

By her assertion, Fran clearly defined her limits to her husband. She made clear her need for separateness and space. Unfortunately, if a woman has not been direct, honest, and spontaneous in the past, the assertion of who she is as a distinct person may come as a surprise to her partner. For example, after completing an assertion workshop, Amy began almost immediately to come out with her limits to her husband Jerome. She did this in an assertive, not aggressive, manner. But her changed behavior was met with Jerome's criticism, "I don't like your act." He was totally out of touch with Amy's real likes and dislikes. Although she was able to reply, "This is not an act. This is actually who I am," her assertion was made more difficult by her former pretense.

It is in a beginning relationship with a man that a woman has the best opportunity to start out on an equal basis. This means that she can from the start teach her partner how she wants to be treated. She can set her limits before a negative pattern is firmly set.

This is what Carla did with Mike, a man she had been dating for a short period of time. Carla and Mike had planned for several weeks to go to the symphony. Carla had made reservations for them and was looking forward to a special evening. But on the day of the symphony, Mike called Carla to tell her that he had decided not to go. He was angry because when he telephoned the night before, Carla had not been at home. He had assumed (accurately) that Carla was out with another man. In talking to Mike, Carla was very clear about her feelings. "Mike, I never led you to believe that you are the only man I am dating. I don't think our relationship has moved to that point yet. But I want you to know that I really resent your canceling out on our arrangements at the last minute. That is something I don't like and that I do not plan to accept."

After Mike hung up, Carla was upset. However, rather than brood, she worked on a report she had to write and called to ask a friend if he would like to accompany her to the symphony. About five o'clock, Mike called back and told Carla that he had changed his mind. "Mike," Carla replied. "I don't operate that way. I considered what you said when you called and, although I disagreed with you, I assumed that you were being honest with your feelings. I made my own plans accordingly. I would like to see you again, though. Maybe we can get together this weekend to talk things out."

By her assertion, Carla is letting Mike know first that she does not appreciate plans being changed as a form of punishment or control. Second, she is teaching him that she takes care of her own needs, and third, she is making it clear that she deals with problems and misunderstandings through discussion, not through action. Because Carla asserts herself from the beginning, she will have enough knowledge of Mike's responses to decide if she and Mike fit as a couple. Only because Carla is direct with who she is and how she expects to be treated can this determination be made *before* she has totally committed herself to him.

When a woman by her lack of assertion has allowed a relationship to develop in a way she does not like, shifting the pattern becomes more difficult. This does not mean that a shift cannot be accomplished, but it may involve a more precise, systematic approach.

This proved to be the case with Rosemary and Earl, a young couple I saw in counseling. Rosemary felt that her relationship with her husband Earl was very unequal, especially in terms of outside activities. Earl was an attorney whose practice depended to a major extent upon his having prominent social contacts. These contacts provided a major referral source for him. Earl expected Rosemary to accompany him to various social functions, an expectation she was enjoying less and less as she grew more resentful. On the other hand, Earl rarely accompanied Rosemary anywhere, making the excuse of having too much work or of being too tired.

Rosemary was beginning to withdraw from Earl, and it was clear that a major source of her resentment involved their division of outside activities. Rosemary's own method of changing Earl's behavior—crying, getting angry—had not worked at all or had only worked temporarily. Occasionally Earl had gone somewhere with her to stop her from complaining, but neither of them enjoyed these coerced activities.

I set up with Rosemary and Earl an exchange contract (a behavioral procedure developed by Richard Stuart) that would allow each person an equal part in determining outside activities. To make the exchange absolutely clear to both Earl and Rosemary, I gave them a set of tokens. Whenever Earl went somewhere that Rosemary requested, that is, to a movie, for a walk, to a concert—and Earl went without resentment—Rosemary gave him a token. A token is simply a concrete symbol which denotes that an exchange has taken place. Rosemary and Earl exchanged red and blue poker chips. Some activities, those which took more time, earned Earl two tokens. The same system operated in regard to the social gatherings Earl wanted to attend. Rosemary earned one token each time she went to a party or a dinner, again without complaint. Both Rosemary and Earl began with three tokens each. If Rosemary went with Earl three times, she would earn all three of his tokens. At that point, until Earl earned a token by going somewhere with Rosemary, he could not ask her to go anywhere else. After he went out with Rosemary again, however, and he earned another token, Earl could request another date. Rosemary and Earl kept the tokens on the dresser, so that each was well aware of how their relationship balanced in this area.

In the process of exchanging tokens, Rosemary discovered that she had in the past underestimated what Earl actually did with her. Earl realized that he had tended to see Rosemary's needs as unimportant. Gaining a clear picture of their activities allowed them to regain a sense of equality in this area. As Rosemary felt the balance shift to a more equal arrangement, her hostility toward Earl lessened. Fortunately, both Rosemary and Earl were able to reexamine all their interactions within this framework and in general were able to work out a more equitable relationship. By this time, the exchange contract used by Rosemary and Earl was no longer needed. The natural give and take of a good relationship had reestablished itself.

It should be noted that there are some occasions where a relationship is actually built on a contract of inequality. One partner may simply have no desire for a different kind of interaction. Brenda, for example, told one group that her boyfriend Tom, a man she had been dating exclusively for ten months, clearly indicated to her that he did not want her to telephone him. Although she objected, Tom was adamant that he would determine when and under what conditions they saw each other. A woman in another group revealed that her husband of twenty-five years refused to have any sexual contact with her. Moreover, he refused to seek professional help. A third woman described a situation where she was constantly criticized by the man she was living with. He ignored her when she was ill; he was rarely affectionate toward her; he did not want to hear her feelings.

These women are involved in relationships where there is a distinct possibility that their partners will not be willing to shift their behaviors. Even if these women assert themselves, they may find that their partners just do not care what they want. They may find that their partners are unwilling even to negotiate an exchange contract. In such situations a woman may need to ask herself the question; "Is the price of this relationship in terms of my comfort and self-esteem too high?" She may also want to determine "Am I willing to raise my muscle and set a consequence if my partner is unwilling to change?"

In one group, Patricia was reviewing past relationships in the context of self-assertion when she made what I considered to be a very important statement. She said, "If I am constantly forced to assert myself in a relationship, if I have to be vigilant in order to protect my space, if I have to reassert my needs again and again, then I have to ask myself if I really fit with the person with whom I have to be so assertive."

Terminating a relationship

One of the most difficult limit setting situations women face involves terminating a relationship that does not fit. At a number of points in a female-male interaction a woman may find that the connection is not right for her. The decision to limit a relationship may be made when a man she has been talking to asks her for her phone number, or it may be made after years of marriage.

Laura had been dating Jeff for about a month. She liked him and thought that he was a nice person, but she was not interested in developing an intimate relationship with him. In fact, as Laura revealed, "I'm at the point where I would genuinely rather have a good book to read than spend my time going out with Jeff." Laura had tried to tell Jeff that she did not want to continue dating him, but because of her own anxiety and guilt, she had not been successful in giving him a clear message. Laura explained, "My next date with Jeff is coming up in a few days, and I want to settle the issue once and for all. That's why I'm volunteering to role play this situation in front of this group when I'm feeling scared to death."

When I talked directly with Laura prior to her rehearsal, it became clear that she felt that telling Jeff she was not

274

interested in a relationship with him was putting him down. "It's like I'm saying he's undesirable," Laura lamented. I suggested to Laura that her not wanting a relationship with Jeff said nothing at all about his value or worth as a human being. It said nothing about his desirability. "Every other woman in this room might want a relationship with Jeff, but that does not mean that he fits with you. Whether or not you fit with Jeff says nothing about his "okayness," I told Laura.

From this perspective, Laura began her rehearsal.

LAURA: Jeff, I want to talk to you about something.

JEFF: Okay. Go ahead. We don't have much time though, if we're going to make the movie.

LAURA: Well, Jeff, I want to talk with you before the movie for a specific reason. I've tried to tell you this before, but I haven't been very clear. I am uncomfortable with continuing to see you in a dating relationship. I like you, but I don't feel that we really fit as a couple.

JEFF: What don't you like about me? Maybe I can change it.

Here Laura interjected to her role-playing partner, "That's Jeff all right. That's just what he would say. If I were to tell him, 'I don't like blue eyes,' he would reply 'I'll change them.' Then continuing, Laura replied:

LAURA: Jeff, I don't want you to change. There isn't anything wrong with you. I just don't want to continue our relationship.

JEFF: That really leaves me hanging.

LAURA: I'm sorry about that. I'm making this decision based on my feelings. I'm not angry at you or withdrawing from you because of something you have done. It just isn't right for me to invest any more time in developing a relationship with you.

Believe it or not, Laura is doing Jeff a favor by telling him her feelings. If there were any specific reasons for Laura not wanting to continue their relationship, she would be doing him a favor to be specific. Jeff has a right to know what Laura's reality is. Otherwise, Laura would be at least partially responsible for allowing him to form a set of assumptions not based on fact.

Allowing a fantasy relationship to develop—a relationship that is not based on each person's honest feeling—all too often leads to an abrupt realization, "I don't really even know you." Any pain that Jeff may now feel would not be diminished by putting off this assertion. In fact, in an intimate relationship, immediate self-expression actually minimizes the chance of hurting another person. That is not to say a woman should know before going out with a man that they will live happily ever after so that she runs no risk of hurting him. It does mean that she needs to keep him up to date on her honest feelings.

Teaching your partner to be more assertive

Many women have told me that the change they most want to make in an intimate relationship involves teaching their partners to be more assertive. As we have seen, many men find it difficult to express their feelings, especially their intimate feelings.

As I was writing this section, I received a letter from Jean Martin, a woman who had just completed my assertive training class. Since her letter fits so well with what I am trying to convey, I would like to share it with you.

> Using the definition of assertiveness as "making my needs known without infringing on another person's territory," I opened an area in my marriage that is often closed. In my marriage I feel that I can express my ideas, release my emotions, and make my needs known but I don't often get a verbal response. This makes me want to climb inside my husband's head to find out what he is feeling and thinking about me.
>
> After two full days of thinking assertively at our workshop, I wanted to share my thoughts with my husband, Mike. We went into a room where we could speak uninterrupted by people, television, or radio. I talked about the class for several minutes and then discussed some of the things that are very important to me in our relationship. I said that it was important to me to know how he felt about these

things. We usually have these chats in bed, and I can't see his face so this was really neat. He talked, and I asked him if this type of conversation made him feel uncomfortable. He said that it did, and again I said it was very important for me to know how he felt. He continued.

After an hour of discussion, I had expressed my anxiety about quitting work, raising a child, and my role as maid and cook. I also talked about the good feelings I presently have about our relationship. Mike responded with his inside feelings (not that it was a "nice dinner" feeling) and expressed some good feelings he had about me.

When we had finished, I felt I really knew how Mike was looking at our life together. I needed his verbal expression and I got it. I hope we can continue to keep this two-way communication actively open.

In the preceding example, Jean was able to alter the pattern of her interaction with Mike simply by letting him know what she wanted. I would like to comment briefly on two additional ways of teaching your partner how you want to be treated. The first involves demonstrating by your own behavior what you want. Rhoda McFarland described this process when she wrote:

I have found in my personal relationship with a man who is becoming important to me that when I began to make positive statements to him—I like you, I feel comfortable with you, I like being with you—he began to make positive statements to me. Also, he has contacted me more frequently than he did before, and I can sense a more open attitude on his part. I feel that he trusts me more than he did. I do like the results of making positive assertion!

Behavioral scientists have documented that the behavior of one person has a tremendous influence on the behavior of another person. Milgram found that subjects were much less prone to deliver high levels of shock to another supposed subject, if they saw someone else refuse to do so. Experiments on self-disclosure reveal that a person tends to disclose more about herself or himself if another person has already revealed something intimate. We know that an aggressive response will lead to an aggressive response. "You" messages provoke "you" responses. Alternatively, a woman's freedom to express her positive feelings allows her partner to express his positive feelings.

In the previous example, Rhoda was able to express her positive feelings to her male friend because she was not tying herself to the traditional feminine role. Initiating the expression of positive feeling is difficult for most women in a beginning female-male relationship. The traditional pattern has been for a woman to yoke her expression to that of a man. If he says "I like you," then she is permitted to say "I like you." Since many men are not assertive in expressing their positive feelings, this has frequently meant a lack of positive interaction within a relationship.

A second way of teaching your partner how to treat you is by reinforcing the actions that you like when they occur. Again, psychologists have noted that reinforcing (praising, complimenting, acknowledging) behavior leads to that behavior occurring more frequently. Unfortunately, many women try to get more positive contact by coercive means—by complaining, accusing, and attacking. Such tactics usually lead to their partners escaping and withdrawing rather than to their coming closer. If, on the other hand, positive expression is followed by a positive response, "I like it when you say that to me," "That really feels good," "I like it when you hold me," this expression will tend to occur more frequently.

I was once working with a couple who had developed a "you did"—"no, you did," complain-countercomplain pattern of interaction. To try to interfere with this habit, I asked each of them to alternate, telling each other *not* what they disliked but what they liked. The husband, whom the wife had bitterly complained never gave her any positive feedback, offered the first compliment. "Elizabeth, I like how you are concerned about the underdog and how you always help people who are in trouble." Although uncomfortable with his expression of positive feelings, Frank seemed to genuinely see Elizabeth's behavior in this area as something that he admired. Unfortunately, Elizabeth was not able to reinforce this positive expression. Instead, she accused, "Well, I guess I can sympathize with other people, because I know so well how it feels to be stepped on," an attack directed pointedly at her husband. Elizabeth's habit of attacking and her built up hostility prevented her from encouraging Frank's positive response.

In many instances it is difficult for a woman to reinforce her partner's initial attempts at positive assertion. She may see her partner's lack of positive expression as a reflection of his feelings toward her, rather than as a consequence of what he has learned. Bem has shown in her experiments that "masculine" men, men who conform to the traditional masculine role on the Bem-Sex Role Inventory, are less assertive than any other group in expressing positive feelings. These men demonstrate fewer affectionate, caring responses in playing with a tiny kitten, in interacting with a baby, and in responding to an emotionally disturbed person. If a woman can realize that the assertion of positive feelings is as difficult for many men as limit setting is for many women, she can begin to reinforce, not punish, such expression when it occurs.

SELF-INITIATION

As the traditional feminine role begins to crumble, more and more women are now finding themselves initiating contact with the opposite sex. No longer satisfied with passively waiting for someone to approach them, women are taking the initiative. This is a new role for women. As a divorced friend of mine commented, "For the first time in my life, I'm asking men out and not just waiting to be asked." Women are also for the first time encountering *direct* rejection. My friend, who is a very well-adjusted woman, added, "What almost threw me at first was that some men say no. It's a totally new experience for me." Rejection, and the fear of it, is something that any woman who wants to reown her own power to choose a partner for herself must challenge. She must overcome the catastrophic attitude, "It would be awful if I were rejected."

In my initial lecture to assertive training classes, I usually give a specific example of how catastrophizing can interfere with self-initiation. The example sets forth the typical "and that would be awful" self-dialogue. Let us say that I am at a party. I see a man across the room who I would like to meet. If I am assertive, I will immediately walk over to him and say "Hi. Are you enjoying the party?" If I am catastrophizing, however, before I take one step I will begin thinking to myself 'Okay. I want to meet him, but does he want to meet me? If he doesn't, that would be awful. If I start walking in his direction, he might see me coming, turn around and go the opposite way. How humiliating! Everyone would see me. No. I'll just sit here and see if he notices me.'" To avoid rejection from someone else, I reject myself. Rejection, however, is not awful if a woman's positive feelings about herself as a person are not hinged on the response of someone else. If a woman has fully accepted the concept of "fit," she knows that a multitude of factors— many of them uncontrollable—determine whether or not two people want to connect as a couple.

How does a woman initiate contact with a man? She can start by clearing away her own internal interferences. In other words, she can critically examine her own rigid requirements, catastrophies, and negative self-labels about taking the first step in a female-male relationship. You may want to think for a moment and write down any of your own obstacles to assertion in this area.

Negative self-labels
   I would be   pushy _____
                    overanxious _____
                    _____

Requirements
 I'll assert myself if he looks interested
           he doesn't talk to anyone else

Catastrophies
 It will be awful if he doesn't like me

Second, a woman can practice "active looking," the exercise mentioned in our chapter on nonverbal behavior. She can give herself space to actually see who is at a party or who is attending a meeting. Active looking is in itself an assertive action that allows a woman to send the nonverbal message "I'm interested." A woman who is in this active position is likely to encounter someone's eyes, at which time she can smile, nod, and say "hello." She can also walk over and introduce herself, "Hi, I'm Marcie Watkins."

This third step—introducing oneself—provokes a great deal of anxiety in many women. In one group, Grace wanted to practice just this one aspect of self-initiation. For her rehearsal, Grace decided that she wanted simply to walk over to a man, introduce herself, and ask, "Do you mind if I join you?" Not, by the way, a simple task. Grace went through this brief rehearsal four times. Twice she stopped to turn around and walk back to where she came from before she had made the initial contact. During her third attempt, she knocked over a cup of coffee sitting on a nearby table. On the fourth occasion, Grace successfully completed her self-introduction. Each assertive attempt had slightly reduced her anxiety. I heard later, through another person, that Grace had never had the opportunity to introduce herself to the particular man she had had in mind during her rehearsal. He had moved to another city before she had made contact with him. What she had done was to introduce herself to two other men, and I heard that she had been very pleased with the results.

After an introduction, the fourth step of self-initiation is beginning a conversation. This can be especially difficult for a woman who has rigid requirements for herself; that is, my conversation *must* be witty, eloquent, and brilliant. If someone waits for this requirement to be met, she may never say a word. Usually the most effective opening remark is a simple comment about the situation. "How do you like this party?" fits if you are at a party. "Are you getting a lot of skiing in?" is an appropriate comment to a man you meet at a ski club. "Do you come here often?" can be made to a man sitting next to you at the symphony.

This kind of active self-initiation typically has positive consequences. As I was completing this chapter, I got a phone call from a woman who had taken my course about a year ago. She reminded me of how I had encouraged women not to operate from the passive position of stereotypic femininity. She mentioned that I had spoken about women feeling free to take the first step in a female-male interchange. She said she had taken this message seriously and thought I would like to know that she is now living with a man who she herself asked out on a first date!

In my own view, the woman who sees herself as a full person will reown her own power to judge the kind of man she wants to meet. Through active self-initiation, she will remove the final barrier to expressing her unique individuality. Such a woman forms the most powerful female-male connection possible: that of two whole, complete human beings.

power

13

Power, defined by J. French and B. Raven as "the ability to influence another person or to get another person to think, feel, or do something" is an important concept for women to consider. We have already noted that a major tenet of the stereotypic feminine role has been the requirement that women dispense with any forcefulness, assertiveness, or power strivings. We have seen that women often experience themselves as powerless and helpless to control their own lives. We have described how an external "should" system saps a woman of the power of her feelings and how our culture denies a woman the power of her anger. We have also seen how self-assertion can help a woman regain control over her own life—to be who she is and to do what she is capable of doing. Our discussion falls short, however, until we look directly at power: what it is, what it means, and how it is related to self-assertion.

To understand power, we must first be aware that power has more than one source. In their article "The Basis of Social Power," French and Raven define five sources of power:

1. Reward power—the power to give or withhold something that is perceived as being valuable by another person.
2. Coercive power—the power to inflict some kind of punishment that the other person wants to avoid.
3. Legitimate power—the power to exert authority legitimately, to use the influence of one's title or of one's position.
4. Referent power—the power that other people give us because they respect us, like us, approve of us, or are attracted to us.
5. Expertise power—the power that other people give us because of our special knowledge and competence.

Almost all people draw from one or more of these power sources in their attempts to influence others. For example, an employer has reward power—the ability to give a raise or a promotion—and coercive power—the power to fire. An employer also has legitimate power—the power of her or his position. She or he is the boss. Whether an employer has referent or expertise power depends upon her or his personality, knowledge, skill, and attractiveness. Many an employer has less referent power and/or less expertise power than the person who works under her or him. Many women, having not been allowed to move up the company ladder, function as executive secretaries, positions with little legitimate power but with great expertise power.

The number of power sources an individual draws upon has a cumulative effect on that person's actual ability to influence others. Thus a person who has legitimate and referent power has more total influence or control than does the person who has only legitimate power. We have all known business situations where the real person of influence is not the one who holds the powerful title.

In the past, power has been seen to a large extent in terms of coercion—the power to inflict some kind of punishment on another person. This kind of power is still a major factor in many female-male relationships. Susan Brownmiller, the author of *Against Our Will,* describes in her book how rape, a traditional male coercive tactic, has made it very difficult for women to enjoy the same freedom and independence as men do. And wife beating is a surprisingly common social phenomenon used as a coercive method of control in many families. Because of discrepancies in strength and internal prohibitions against aggression, women have used coercive power much less than men. When women have used coercion, it has typically been verbal coercion. Women have been comically portrayed as "nags" throughout the centuries.

Coercive power is, in my opinion, most often a destructive power source. Although punishment may change someone's behavior, it does so only temporarily and with the probability of undesirable side effects. For the most part, except when used protectively, the use of coercive power is very much an aggressive response and is not at all compatible with the concepts of self-assertion.

On the other hand, reward power is a power source women have frequently used. Samuel Johnson's remark that "Nature has given women so much power that the law has wisely given them very little" hints at the use of reward power by women. At a time when there were almost no direct avenues to power for women, the ability to grant or withhold sexual contact was a potent source of reward power. Even today, books that urge women to stay within the outline of the traditional feminine role encourage the use of reward power. Morgan's *The Total Woman* urges women to reward (although Morgan does not see her advice in terms of reward power) their husbands by accepting them, appreciating them, admiring them, and adapting to them. In return, a woman's life is supposed to change. Her husband will bring her gifts and will express affection to her. Hostilities will melt away. Morgan devotes several chapters to what she terms "sizzling sex." According to Morgan, a woman can gain control over her life and her happiness through her reward power.

Certainly nothing is wrong with reward power when it is used in a nonmanipulative manner. As we have seen, the use of rewards in a marriage can allow two people to get what they want in a mutually satisfying and creative way. Unfortunately, the stereotypically feminine woman has learned to use reward power in a manipulative manner.

Once when I was speaking to a large convention audience, a woman gave the following example of this kind of manipulation: "I have a sister-in-law who will say to my brother in a soft, seductive tone, 'Darling, would you tuck the kids into bed? You do it so much better than I do,' and he will gladly comply with a smile on his face. What do you think of that?" My answer, "If I am using *dishonest* flattery to get someone to do something I want them to do, I am manipulating them and my own manipulation of someone else always results in a loss—a loss of my personal integrity and self-respect or a loss of my respect for the other person. To be forced to manipulate another person in order to influence them shows simply that I have little direct power or control over my own life."

WOMEN AND POWER

"Most of the women I know," claims Michael Korda, author of *Power!,* "either try to charm or nag because they have not found the authentic voice of power." Korda's statement shifted into the framework of French and Raven says that women use reward power or coercive power—little else. Because direct power strivings have been prohibited by the stereotypic feminine role, women have had little taste of legitimate or expertise power. Women have been forced to dilute their own ambition and competitive strivings and be satisfied with being "the woman behind the man," achieving their power and recognition indirectly through someone else.

The inhibition of direct power strivings has had an effect on the lives of many women. It has forced women to gain their status and recognition almost exclusively through an external source. As a close friend of mine said, "In my own experience, most women get their status in one of three ways: through their husbands, through their children, or through their houses. Their husbands usually come first. A woman's status is defined by her husband's profession and his status within his profession. If her husband isn't a doctor or an attorney or a big moneymaker, she feels apologetic, even inferior. Women push like mad to keep their husbands going up the career ladder—whether the man wants to go or not. Then there are their children. Mothers start preparing their sons in kindergarten for Harvard or Stanford. Their whole life is built upon what little Johnny does or does not do. If Johnny is bright, a great deal of recognition comes the mother's way. She is chosen to be on committees; other mothers stop to speak to her. On the other hand, if her child isn't doing so well—and I had sons who fell into both categories—all kinds of backs turn on her. Look at the neighborhood swim-meet or the Little League game—who do you really think is getting the most recognition?

"Another source of power, at least with middle class and upper class suburban women, is their house. Do they have a good address? A woman's entire identity—her total feelings about herself—can rest on the neighborhood she lives in. And the decorations. I know a woman who calls her decorator before moving any object in her home. She may not like what he does with it, but her status is so tied up in her house and how it's decorated that she is scared to do anything by herself."

It is indeed unfortunate that rather than acquiring the ability to control and influence their own lives directly, women have all too often accepted frivolous symbols of status: decorator houses in good neighborhoods, jewels, furs. Look at any society page. Women, who themselves are frequently ornaments of male power, are defined by the decorations they wear. As one society column notes, "It was old-home-week at Michael's where the Southampton crowd descended en masse for new furs. Joy took a floor length sable, Sue a Sabra Dusk mink, Ellen bought a floor length Alaska lynx cape, and Sara and sister-in-law Adrian, a pair of lynx jackets." Acceptance of personal adornment as their only avenue to power causes women to totally ignore any humanitarian considerations, such as that beautiful wild animals are trapped and killed solely for the purpose of female vanity.

Women's lack of direct power permeates all society. Social custom alone puts men in a power position; he drives the car, opens the door, handles the money. The effect of social custom is in fact so strong that many women who find themselves in a position of direct power for the first time go to some extremely awkward means to keep this power hidden, to keep themselves from being seen in a position so contrary to the feminine role. For example, a woman taking a male client out to lunch may feel uncomfortable or feel that her client will be uncomfortable if she pays the bill. However, that is an important aspect of the business relationship. To solve her power-custom dilemma, she may hand the man the money under the table or arrange to pay the bill by credit card on her way to the rest room. Women and power have just begun to get acquainted, and society is having an awkward time negotiating their introduction.

LEGITIMATE POWER

Women have had and continue to have less legitimate power than men. The United States Senate, our country's most influential legislative body, claims no women members. Of the 435 members of the House of Representatives, in 1976 only 18 were women. The President has always been a man. Only three women have ever been named to the Cabinet. The Supreme Court traditionally has been all male. Korda notes that "from childhood on, at every level, the symbol of ultimate authority tends to be a man."

In 1971, Caroline Bird wrote in *Born Female: The High Cost of Keeping Women Down* that fewer than ten percent of persons in the prestige professions were women. Only nine percent of all full professors, nine percent of scientists, seven percent of all physicians, three percent of lawyers, and one percent of engineers were women. Women clearly were behind in legitimate power based on position and title. Power discrepancies based on money were also the rule, not the exception. In 1969, according to John Kenneth Galbraith, more than ninety-five percent of all jobs paying more than $15,000 per year were held by men.

Since 1971, women's legitimate power has significantly increased. Affirmative action hiring and promotion practices have resulted in women holding more positions of authority. A recent *Time* magazine article noted that the total number of women in elected office (7,000 women) is double what it was five years ago. Today, seven percent of lawyers and nine percent of physicians are women. Women have also moved into blue collar occupations where salaries are much higher. For example, 3,000 women now work on the Alaskan pipeline.

The increase in legitimate power, where it has occurred, has not come about by chance. In most instances the gain in legitimate power has been made because women are (1) refusing to accept their traditional place in society and (2) asserting themselves by initiating opportunities and by setting limits when they have been unfairly treated. For example, changes in female hiring and promotion practices have come about largely because women are becoming more willing to assert themselves with the muscle of a law suit or a sex discrimination complaint. *Business Week* noted that sex bias complaints filed with the Equal Employment Opportunities Commission increased from 3,497 in all of 1970 to 22,110 during the first *six months* of 1975. Women are beginning to use their legitimate muscle to increase their legitimate power.

Still, more than forty percent of women workers remain clustered in what *Time* terms "female ghettos," working as salesclerks, secretaries, bookkeepers, receptionists, and telephone operators. These "women's jobs" depend upon persons willing (or forced) to accept pay not commensurate with their skills or training, jobs considered appropriate only for the "secondary wage earners." Women have rarely challenged the low status and low pay of their positions. Perhaps because of the feminine role's injunctions against forcefulness, aggression, and power strivings, women have been reluctant to exercise the power of the strike in the manner in which men in blue collar positions have frequently done. "Alice Doesn't Day," a woman's no-work strike set on October 29, 1975 by the National Organization for Women, was an acknowledged failure in this regard.

In our culture, women who chose not to work in paying positions but instead choose to devote themselves to being a mother and to raising their children are in a particular bind. Our society sees little legitimate power connected to the position of homemaker. "I'm *just* a *housewife*," many women say. Other women are rightfully incensed that home-making and child rearing are devalued in our society where worth is often equated with earning capacity, and mother-ing and homemaking earn no money.

Because of the lack of legitimate power connected to homemaking, a woman is often treated unfairly. Linda, a young mother with a one-year-old daughter and a three-year-old son, gave the following example of this problem. "I asked my husband to babysit tonight (from 7:30 until 8:30, the children's bedtime). He replied, 'I'd like a free evening too. I bought it.' I thought 'I'm sorry' and accused myself 'You worthless person, infringing on his precious time. How can you want to play bridge when you should take care of the children? You don't work outside the home. How could your free time be that important?' I'm sure you have the picture. I might add that my husband is an attor-ney and because of his involvement with his practice and his clients, his time is by choice very structured and his needs and wants have always taken priority over family life."

THE POWER OF THE PERSON: REFERENT AND EXPERTISE POWER

In addition to discrepancies in legitimate power, there is typically a vast difference between women and men in referent power and expertise power, the power given to a person because of her or his individual attributes. Hall's study on female-male group interaction clearly illustrates the discrepancy. Although no person in Hall's experiment had any more legitimate power than any other person (all were prospective teachers), in fourteen of the nineteen problem-solving groups a man was chosen as the most influential (powerful) group member. The male members gained their influence solely through their personal interaction within their group.

Hall gives some clear data relative to why women in these groups were not given expertise and referent power by the other group members. In the group, women made fewer overall comments and fewer comments directed toward solving the problem at hand. They did not supply information, analyze the task, or suggest solutions. Instead, they conformed to the prescribed feminine role of giving positive feedback to other people. Further, women failed to support their own ideas with facts, statistics, or argued reason. Since the women gave little indication of their knowledge, the lack of expertise power given to female group members need surprise no one.

In an article "Up The Ladder, Finally," about the corporate woman, *Business Week* interviewed several top level women executives, women who do hold key positions of legitimate power. There are very few such women directing the country's major corporations. According to *Time,* in the 1,300 largest United States companies there are now about 150 women directors. *Business Week* estimated that there are 15 or so women among the 2,500 presidents, key vice-presidents, and chairpersons who control the country's major corporations. Women who comprise that one percent of top management are, according to the *Business Week* article, "very special people. They work, they achieve, they fight for their judgments, they let no one push them around." ("Up the Ladder, Finally," *Business Week,* Nov. 24, 1975)

A very important characteristic of these women seems

to be their ability to be assertive. Kay Mazuy, senior vice-president for Shawmut, is described by a former employer as "quietly aggressive," another word perhaps for assertive. "She would stick by her guns if she saw the figures differently than others," a former employer says. Juliette Moran, executive vice-president for GAF Corporation notes, "We all argue in my department. But it's my responsibility at some point to say yes or no."

The traits attributed to these powerful women—assertiveness, the ability to stand up against group pressure, self-reliance—are clearly not those descriptive of stereotypic femininity. Powerful women seem to freely exercise their authority, to crave rather than fear success, and to have overcome the feminine prohibitions against positive self-presentation. As Diane Levine, vice-president for advertising and promotion at Continental Air Lines freely states, "I've worked for four major companies and none has made less than several million dollars from my efforts." Such positive self-presentation seems to be a basic characteristic of powerful women. Representative Shirley Chisolm, in a speech in San Francisco, showed no reluctance to speak positively about herself. "I am not an ordinary woman," she firmly declared. "I am a versatile woman. I was told not to go to the south. I went to the southland and let them see me in person—a rational, sane human being with intellectual capabilities."

Contrast these powerful women with those women who because of the traditional feminine ban on assertion and power striving learn to hide the power which they actually have. This was clearly brought to my attention in a workshop of professional women, all at the management level in their organizations. These women had all "made it" to some degree. They were influential, well paid, and successful. But only a few of them felt fully comfortable with their power. Most admitted that in introducing themselves they rarely mentioned their positions. They took care not to let anyone know about their authority. In other words, if at a party a woman was asked "What do you do?", she would say, "I work for Jones and Jones advertising agency" rather than assert, "I am head of sale for Jones and Jones advertising." A woman banker would say, "I work for United States Bank," leaving everyone to assume she was a bank teller rather than state, "I am a branch vice-president of United States Bank."

The tendency to play down one's accomplishments was brought out even more vividly by a young accountant who is currently working on her master's degree in business administration. The accountant is one of five women in a class with thirty-seven men. In discussing the reluctance of women to speak positively about themselves or to reveal their positions, she offered, "I see it plainly in my class. We all started with the same amount of legitimate power. We are all students. However, I noticed that the men in the class were not at all reluctant to assert their competence with statements like "I supervise a thirty-person office" or "I plan media on a $9 million account," whereas I and the other women said very little. I may be imagining it, but the professor seems to treat the men in the group with more respect."

Referent and expertise power are not automatically given. Women must be free to present themselves positively before they are responded to in a positive manner.

⌣ ANDROGYNY AS POWER

Phyllis Chesler, author of *Women and Madness,* has commented that the modern female condition is one of powerlessness. You may recall from our earlier discussion Chesler's contention that the woman who is only compassionate, sensitive, and docile without at the same time being assertive, self-reliant, and forceful is likely to be victimized. Judith Bardwick, a prolific writer about women, feels essentially the same way. She writes that the feminine traits of dependency, passivity, and need for approval seriously hinder *most* women. Bardwich even goes so far as to state that nothing less than radical changes in child-rearing practices will allow women to become as productive and as creative as men.

In his book *Power,* Michael Korda acknowledges that the largest visible group of people who do not have power are women. Women find it difficult to acquire power, Korda explains, because "power is essentially male." Power strivings are an accepted, and an acceptable, part of the masculine role, whereas the acquisition and use of power goes against a major tenet of stereotypic femininity. Does this mean that a woman who desires to have influence and control over her own life must take on the yoke of stereotypic masculinity to achieve this end? Does it mean that a woman must become insensitive or give up her ability to be compassionate and concerned about others? Some women seem to think so. Some women pride themselves on "handling a situation just like a man" or on "showing no feminine emotion."

In assertive training groups, I have frequently encountered women who operate from a "masculine" position, women who typically respond aggressively rather than assertively or interact almost always at a high muscle level. Although these women have little problem enforcing their legitimate power and may even be granted expertise power by their associates, they do not usually acquire much referent power. In fact, other people usually do not like them. When a woman's assertion takes place at level-three and level-four muscle ninety percent of the time, she is likely to be resented. People tend to react defensively to her.

Women who are caught in this pattern usually blame their lack of advancement on other people's negative attitudes toward women. This certainly may be part of the problem. However, a major factor in their lack of power comes from their own inability to relate with empathy and warmth to other people. These women are frequently uncomfortable with low level muscle. They eschew their softness as indicating vulnerability. They actually lose power by confining themselves to a narrow, although high, muscle range. When a woman's tone is always firm, when her voice is always loud, she loses the power of contrast. As one woman learning to rely more on level-one muscle commented, "It's frankly exhausting to always be yelling—and a lot of people simply turn you off."

Our brief look at several of the women who have made it to the top confirms that powerful women need not be bound by the dictates of stereotyped femininity *or* stereotyped masculinity. These powerful women *are* assertive, willing to take a stand, ambitious, and competitive. They feel no discomfort exhibiting those traits which have heretofore been considered positive for men alone. But neither are these women merely imitating the behavior of men. "I'm not in any way a traditional, tough-talking managing editor. I don't go around banging shoes on desks or yelling at reporters," states Carol Sutton, managing editor of Louisville's *Courier-Journal* and one of *Time's* Women of the Year. Sutton in no way has to take on the stereotypic masculine role to get the job done. Powerful women instead embody the concept of androgyny. They freely express themselves without regard to whether their behavior is masculine or feminine. When the situation calls for forcefulness, they can be forceful. When the situation calls for softness, they can be soft.

Sandra Bem has found that a rather large percentage of women can be considered androgynous from their response on the Bem-Sex Role Inventory. In fact, thirty-five percent of the Stanford undergraduates Bem tested did not confine themselves to either the traditional feminine or the traditional masculine role. These women admitted to being individualistic and tender, self-reliant and warm, competitive and sensitive to others. These androgynous women differed substantially from their stereotypically "feminine" sisters, women who described themselves as having *only* desirable feminine characteristics. Androgynous women were able to meet the demands of diverse situations, whereas stereotypically feminine women were not.

Bem came to this conclusion after comparing androgynous women and men with their stereotypically feminine or stereotypically masculine counterparts on a number of tasks. The tasks included those traditionally considered feminine, such as playing with a kitten, as well as those usually viewed as masculine, such as standing up against group pressure. In one "masculine" task, which looked at conformity versus independence of judgment, subjects were asked to rate cartoons for their humor. But before doing so, they heard what they assumed were other students giving an erroneous evaluation; that is, they said a cartoon was funny when it was not or *vice versa.* (The subjects were actually hearing a preprogrammed tape.) The stereotypically feminine women were much *less* independent in their judgment than were the androgynous women. Furthermore, in a direct test of self-assertion, the stereotypically feminine women found it much more difficult than the androgynous women to say "no" to an unrealistic demand on their time.

In a third experiment, sex-typed women consistently avoided traditional male acitvities such as oiling a hinge or nailing boards, even though they were paid more for engaging in their activities. When forced to do a cross-sex task, feminine women felt less attractive, less likeable, more nervous, and less feminine than women who were not sex typed. In short, feminine women were much more restricted in their behaviors than were androgynous women.

Interestingly, on tasks that fit with the traditional concept of femininity, androgynous women functioned as well as stereotypically feminine women. In responding to a tiny kitten, in playing with a baby, in reacting to a person with emotional problems, androgynous women were able to freely express warmth, playfulness, and concern. In fact, androgynous women were much more playful with the tiny kitten than were the feminine women. Only in reacting to an emotionally upset person were feminine women more responsive. We might even speculate that this difference reflects some difficulty the stereotypic woman had in setting limits. We know that many women in assertive training express an inability not to get caught up in the personal problems of other people—even when they have no desire to do so.

The power of the androgynous woman comes from her ability to be herself—to express all aspects of who she is. The androgynous woman is free to take hold of her legitimate power. And, as the androgynous woman operates without minimizing her competence, knowledge, or authority, she is given both referent and expertise power.

THE ANDROGYNOUS WOMAN

The assertive woman is an androgynous woman. She is a powerful woman. One of the first things that assertiveness brings to a woman is a new sense of power. She is no longer at the mercy of other people. She takes charge of her actions. She evaluates her environment. She determines what does and does not fit, and she acts upon that personal determination. Operating from what her feelings tell her rather than on the basis of external directives, she does not allow herself to be victimized. She does not expose herself to situations that cause her pain or to interactions that she later regrets. If a party is not to her liking, she feels free to leave it or to entertain herself. If a particular relationship is destructive, she takes care of herself by asserting her limits. If she cannot change her environment, she